新编国际商务英语系列教材

新编金融英语教程
New Financial English

李浚帆　主　编

周丽娜　副主编

清华大学出版社

北京交通大学出版社

·北京·

内 容 简 介

本书分为5篇，共10章。第1篇分为2章，分别介绍有关货币与信用的基本知识；第二篇分为2章，分别介绍银行类金融机构和非银行类金融机构；第3篇分为3章，分别介绍金融市场与金融工具、货币市场和资本市场；第4篇分为2章，分别介绍国际收支和国际金融市场；第5篇共1章，介绍金融调控。

本书既可以作为商务英语、国际金融、金融等专业学生的英语教材和教师进行双语教学的参考书，又可以作为银行、证券、保险等金融行业从业人员的英语工具书，也可以作为准备参加全国金融专业英语证书考试（FECT）的人员的复习参考资料。

图书在版编目（CIP）数据

新编金融英语教程/李浚帆主编. — 北京：清华大学出版社；北京交通大学出版社，2008.12
（新编国际商务英语系列教材）
ISBN 978 – 7 – 81123 – 486 – 2

Ⅰ. 新…　Ⅱ. 李…　Ⅲ. 金融 – 英语 – 高等学校 – 教材　Ⅳ. H31

中国版本图书馆 CIP 数据核字（2008）第 194501 号

责任编辑：张利军
出版发行：清华大学出版社　　邮编：100084　　电话：010 – 62776969　http://www.tup.com.cn
　　　　　北京交通大学出版社　邮编：100044　　电话：010 – 51686414　http://press.bjtu.edu.cn
印　刷　者：北京鑫海金澳胶印有限公司
经　　销：全国新华书店
开　　本：203×280　　印张：16　　字数：486 千字
版　　次：2008 年 12 月第 1 版　　2008 年 12 月第 1 次印刷
书　　号：ISBN 978 – 7 – 81123 – 486 – 2/H・137
印　　数：1 ～ 4 000 册　　定价：28.00 元

本书如有质量问题，请向北京交通大学出版社质监组反映。对您的意见和批评，我们表示欢迎和感谢。

投诉电话：010 – 51686043，51686008；传真：010 – 62225406；E-mail：press@bjtu.edu.cn。

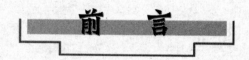

前　言

　　中国加入 WTO 已将近七年，按照中国入世后服务行业开放的时间表，中国金融业已基本实现全面开放。这必然对国内的金融从业者提出了更高的要求。同时，随着金融全球化的日益加深，越来越多的国际金融机构与创新业务进入中国。对于中国高校金融专业的学生来说，也必须尽早顺应全球化的潮流，积极与国际接轨。因此，熟练掌握与金融相关的英语词汇和习惯用法已是迫在眉睫的任务。为了帮助广大学生更好地完成这一任务，特编写这本《新编金融英语教程》，作为商务英语、国际贸易、国际金融、金融等专业学生的核心专业课教材。

　　本书既可以用作商务英语、金融等专业学生的英语教材和教师进行双语教学的参考用书，还可以作为银行、证券、保险等金融行业从业人员的英语工具书，也可以作为全国金融专业英语证书考试（FECT）的复习参考书。

　　与其他同类教材相比，本书具有以下 4 个重要特色。

　　1. 系统性。本书借鉴了金融及货币银行学中文教材的结构体系，涵盖货币、银行、保险、证券、外汇等与金融相关的基础概念和知识，用英语对金融的相关知识进行了全面系统的介绍。

　　2. 丰富性。本书涉及的专业知识非常丰富，形式也多种多样，每章都穿插了一定数量的图表或补充阅读材料，每一篇后面均附有典型案例资料，这样既丰富了内容与形式，有利于读者拓宽知识面，又能够增加可读性及趣味性，有助于提高学生的学习兴趣，培养创新思维能力。

　　3. 时代性。本书基本上采用近两年最新的数据及案例资料，紧紧把握时代脉搏，力图将最新的知识呈现给读者。

　　4. 国际性。本书注重在内容及语言上与国际接轨，尽量采用国际通用的专业术语及表达方式，对中国金融体系与发达国家不同的地方也尽可能进行特别说明。

　　本书共 10 章，由李浚帆担任主编，负责全书的策划及统稿等工作，美国奥古斯坦纳大学助理教授周丽娜担任副主编，为主编提供全面协助。本书的具体编写分工如下：周丽娜负责编写第 1、2 章，梁雁负责编写第 3、4 章，霍晓荣负责编写第 5、6、7 章，李浚帆、孙雪静共同编写第 8 章，李浚帆、梁雁共同编写第 9 章，李浚帆、王墨共同编写第 10 章。

　　本书得以面世，有赖于北京交通大学出版社的热情支持，在此深表谢意。

　　由于作者水平有限，书中难免存在错误与遗漏之处，敬请广大读者批评指正。

编者

2008 年 12 月

Contents
目 录

Part Ⅰ Money and Credit
货币与信用

Part Ⅱ Financial Institutions
金融机构

Part Ⅲ　Financial Market
金融市场

Part Ⅳ   International Finance
国际金融

Part Ⅴ Financial Regulation and Control
金融调控

PART I

Money and Credit

货币与信用

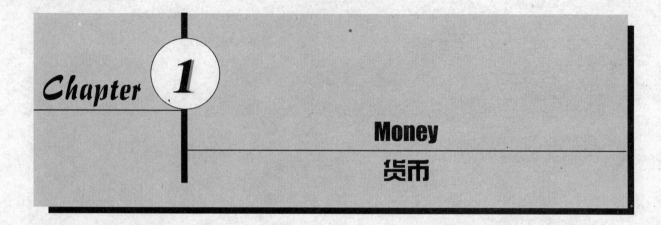

Chapter 1

Money
货币

Learning Objectives

- ☑ To understand the definition of money
- ☑ To learn about the origin and development of money
- ☑ To grasp the functions and characteristics of money
- ☑ To understand the basic concepts about money circulation
- ☑ To learn the important theories of money

 Opening Vignette

History of Money

In the Beginning: Barter

Barter is the exchange of resources or services for mutual advantage, and may date back to the beginning of humankind. Some would even argue that it's not purely a human activity; plants and animals have been bartering — in symbiotic relationships — for millions of years. In any case, barter among humans certainly pre-dates the use of money. Today individuals, organizations, and governments still use, and often prefer, barter as a form of exchange of goods and services.

9000–6000 BC: Cattle

Cattle, which include anything from cows, to sheep, to camels, are the first and oldest form of money. With the advent of agriculture came the use of grain and other vegetable or plant products as a standard form of barter in many cultures.

1200 BC: Cowrie Shells

The first use of cowries, the shell of a mollusc that was widely available in the shallow waters of the Pacific and Indian Oceans, was in China. Historically, many societies have used cowries as money, and even as recently as the middle of last century, cowries have been used in some parts of Africa. The cowrie is the most widely and longest used currency in history.

1000 BC: First Metal Money and Coins

Bronze and Copper cowrie imitations were manufactured by China at the end of the Stone Age and could be considered some of the earliest forms of metal coins. Metal tool money, such as knife and spade monies, was also first used in China. These early metal monies developed into primitive versions of round coins. Chinese coins were made out of base metals, often containing holes so they could be put together like a chain.

500 BC: Modern Coinage

Outside of China, the first coins developed out of lumps of silver. They soon took the familiar round form of today, and were stamped with various gods and emperors to mark their authenticity. These early coins first appeared in Lydia, which is part of present-day Turkey, but the techniques were quickly copied and further refined by the Greek, Persian, Macedonian, and later the Roman empires. Unlike Chinese coins which depended on base metals, these new coins were made from precious metals such as silver, bronze, and gold, which had more inherent value.

118 BC: Leather Money

Leather money was used in China in the form of one-foot-square pieces of white deerskin with colorful borders. This could be considered the first documented type of banknote.

806 AD: Paper Currency

The first paper banknotes appeared in China. In all, China experienced over 500 years of early paper money, spanning from the ninth through the fifteenth century. Over this period, paper notes grew in production to the point that their value rapidly depreciated and inflation soared. Then beginning in 1455, the use of paper money in China disappeared for several hundred years. This was still many years before paper currency would reappear in Europe, and three centuries before it was considered common.

1535: Wampum

The earliest known use of wampum, which are strings of beads made from clam shells, was by North American Indians in 1535. Most likely, this monetary medium existed well before this date. The Indian word "wampum" means white, which was the color of the beads.

1816: The Gold Standard

Gold was officially made the standard of value in England in 1816. At this time, guidelines were made to allow for a non-inflationary production of standard banknotes which represented a certain amount of gold. Banknotes had been used in England and Europe for several hundred years before this time, but their worth had never been tied directly to gold. In the United States, the Gold Standard Act was officially enacted in 1900, which helped lead to the establishment of a central bank.

1930: End of the Gold Standard

The massive Depression of the 1930's, felt worldwide, marked the beginning of the end of the gold standard. In the United States, the gold standard was revised and the price of gold was devalued. This was the first step in ending the relationship altogether. The British and international gold standards soon ended as well, and the complexities of international monetary regulation began.

The Present

Today, currency continues to change and develop.

The Future: Electronic Money

Digital cash in the form of bits and bytes will most likely become an important new currency of the future

Warm-up Questions

1. What do you think the money is?
2. Why did money take these many various forms in history?
3. What form do you think the money will take in the future?

1.1 An Overview of Money
货币概述

1.1.1 The Definition of Money 货币的定义

What is Money? At first sight, the answer to this question seems obvious; every people in the street would agree on coins and paper currencies[1], but would they accept them from any country? What about checks? What about I.O.U.s[2](I owe you), credit cards and gold? Many rich people in different parts of the world would rather keep some of their wealth in the form of gold than in official currencies. The attractiveness of gold, from an aesthetic point of view, and its resistance to corrosion are two of the properties which led to its use for monetary transactions for thousands of years. In contrast, today, a form of money with virtually no tangible properties — electronic money — seems set to gain rapidly in popularity.

So we can only define the term of money literally as — anything that is commonly accepted by a group of people for the exchange of goods, services, or resources. Every country has its own system of coins and paper money which is different to other countries.

1.1.2 The Origin and Development of Money 货币的起源与发展

1. The emergence of money

The use of early money may date back to at least 100,000 BC. Trading in red ochre is attested in

Swaziland, from about that date, and ochre seems to have functioned as money in Aboriginal Australia. Shell in the form of strung beads would have served as good with the basic attributes needed of early money. In cultures where metal working was unknown, shell or ivory were the most divisible, easily storable and transportable, scarce, and hard to counterfeit objects that could be made. Early money would have been useful in reducing the costs of less frequent transactions that were crucial to hunter-gatherer cultures, especially bride purchase, tribute, and intertribal trade in hunting ground rights and implements. Jewellery has often been used for currency and wealth storage in some historical and contemporary societies, especially those in which modern forms of money are scarce, in addition to being used for decoration and display of status and wealth.

In cultures, of any era, that lack money, bartering would be the only ways to exchange goods. Bartering has several problems, most notably the coincidence of wants problem. If one wishes to trade fruit for wheat, it can only be done when the fruit and wheat are both available at the same time and place, which may be for a very brief time, or may be never. With an intermediate commodity (whether it be shells, gold, etc.) fruit can be sold when it is ripe in exchange for the intermediate commodity. This intermediate commodity can then be used to buy wheat when the wheat harvest comes in. Thus the use of money makes all commodities become more liquid.

2. Commodity money

Many early instances of money were objects which were useful for their intrinsic value as well as their monetary properties. This has been called commodity money; historical examples include iron nails, pigs, rare seashells, whale's teeth, cattle and etc. In medieval Iraq, bread was used as an early form of money. The use of shells or ivory was nearly universal before humans discovered how to work with precious metal. In China, Africa, and many other areas, use of cowrie shells was common. In China the use of cowrie shells was superseded by metal representations of the shells, as well as representations of metal tools. These imitations may have been the precursors of coinage.

Salt and spices had also been used as money. From 550 BC, accepting salt from a person was synonymous with receiving a salary, taking pay, or being in that person's service. Definite indications are available that both black and white pepper have been used as commodity money for hundreds of years before Christ, and several centuries thereafter. Being a valuable commodity, pepper has naturally been used as payment. In the Middle Ages, there was a French saying, "As dear as pepper". In England, rent could be paid in pounds of pepper, and so a symbolic minimal amount is known as a "peppercorn rent[3]".

One interesting example of commodity money is the huge limestone coins in the Micronesian island of Yap, quarried with great peril from a source several hundred miles away. The value of the coin was determined by its size — the largest of which could range from nine to twelve feet in diameter and weigh several tons. Displaying a large coin, often outside one's home, of course, was a considerable status symbol and source of prestige in that society.

Precious metals such as copper, silver and gold, have been a common form of money in ancient and modern history. Even in the modern world, in the absence of other types of money, people have occasionally used commodities such as tobacco as money. This happened after World War II when cigarettes became used unofficially in Europe, in parallel with other currencies, for a short time. It also occurs in some remote parts of countries such as Colombia and Bolivia, where cocaine, or its precursor, coca paste, is used as commodity money.

Once a commodity becomes used as money, it takes on a value that is often different from its intrinsic worth or usefulness. Being used as money adds an extra use to the commodity, and so increases its value. This extra use is the convention of society and the scope of its use as money within the society affects the value of the monetary commodity. Fluctuations in the value of commodity money can be strongly influenced by supply and demand, whether current or predicted. For example, if a local gold mine is about to run out of ore, the relative market value of gold may go up in anticipation of a shortage.

3. Standardized coinage

These early metal monies first used in China developed into primitive versions of round coins. Outside of China, the first coins developed out of lumps of silver. They soon took the familiar round form of today, and first appeared in Lydia (in today's Turkey), and were further refined by the Greek, Persian, Macedonian, and later the Roman empires.

A Roman denarius, a standardized silver coin, was the discovery of the touchstone which led the way for metal-based commodity money and coinage. Any soft metal can be tested for purity on a touchstone, allowing one to quickly calculate the total content of a particular metal in a lump. Gold is a soft metal, which is also hard to counterfeit, dense, and storable. As a result, monetary gold coinage spread very quickly from Asia Minor, where it first gained wide usage, to the entire world.

Using such a system still required several steps and mathematical calculation. The touchstone allows one to estimate the amount of gold in an alloy, which is then multiplied by the weight to find the amount of gold alone in a lump. To make this process easier, the concept of standard coinage was introduced. Coins were pre-weighed and pre-alloyed, so as long as the manufacturer was aware of the origin of the coin, no use of the touchstone was required. Coins were typically minted by governments in a carefully protected process, and then stamped with an emblem that guaranteed the weight and value of the metal.

4. Representative money

As an example of representative money[4], the British 1896 note could be exchanged for five US Dollars worth of silver. The system of commodity money in many instances evolved into a system of representative money. This occurred because banks would issue a paper receipt to their depositors, indicating that the receipt was redeemable for whatever precious goods were being stored (usually gold or silver). It didn't take long before the receipts were traded as money, because everyone knew they were "as good as gold". Representative paper money made it possible the practice of fractional reserve banking, in which bankers would print receipts above and beyond the amount of actual precious metal on deposit.

So in this system, paper money and non-precious coinage had very little intrinsic value, but achieved significant market value by being backed by a promise to redeem it for a given weight of precious metal, such as silver and gold. This is the origin of the term "British Pound", for instance, it was a unit of money backed by a Tower pound of sterling silver, hence the currency Pound Sterling. For much of the nineteenth and twentieth centuries, many countries' currencies were based on representative money through use of the gold standard[5].

5. Fiat money

Fiat money[6] refers to money that is not backed by reserves of another commodity. The money itself is given value by government fiat (Latin for "let it be done") or decree, enforcing legal tender[7] laws, whereby debtors are legally relieved of the debt if they (offer to) pay it off in the government's money. By law the refusal of "legal tender" money in favor of some other form of payment is illegal. Fiat money is any money whose value is determined by legal means rather than the relative availability of goods and services. Fiat money may be symbolic of a commodity or government promises.

Fiat money, especially in the form of paper or coins, can be easily damaged or destroyed. However, it has the advantage in that the same laws that created the money can also define rules for its replacement in case of damage or destruction. For example, the US government will replace mutilated paper money by law if at least half of the bill can be reconstructed.

Governments through history have often switched to forms of fiat money in times of need such as war, sometimes by suspending the service they provided of exchanging their money for gold, and other times by simply printing the money that they needed. When governments print money more rapidly than economic growth, the money supply overtakes economic value. Therefore, the excess money eventually dilutes the market value of all money issued. This is called inflation.

In 1971 the United States finally switched to fiat money infinitely. At this point in time, many of the economically developed countries' currencies were fixed to the US dollar, and so this single step meant that much of the western world's currencies became fiat money based.

What Can Money Do for Us?

Consider this problem: You catch fish for your food supply, but you're tired of eating it every day. Instead you want to eat some bread. Fortunately, a baker lives next door. Trading the baker some fish for bread is an example of barter, the direct exchange of one good for another.

However, barter is difficult when you try to obtain a good from a producer that doesn't want what you have. For example, how do you get shoes if the shoemaker doesn't like fish? The series of trades required to obtain shoes could be complicated and time consuming.

Early societies faced these problems. The solution was money. Money is an item, or commodity, that is agreed to be accepted in trade. Over the years, people have used a wide variety of items for money, such as seashells, beads, tea, fish hooks, fur, cattle and even tobacco.

1.1.3 The Functions of Money 货币的职能

1. As a medium of exchange

It is as a medium of exchange that money makes a barter system irrelevant. Money overcomes the problems of a barter system and the need for a coincidence of wants. Money means a set of common prices can be established and the possibility to make up for and difference in value by the giving or receiving of "change". People can be paid their incomes in money and can pay money for the stuffs they want. The farmer can provide food to those wanting food and receive money from them in exchange for the food. The farmer then exchanges the money for a pair of shoes at a price the farmer is willing to pay. Such a process is much simpler and saves a great deal of travel, searching, and time.

Money helps bring simplicity and organization to our economy. It is something people are willing to accept in exchange for what they have produced and have available. Money is our medium of exchange.

2. As a measurement of value

One of the major problems of a barter system was the determination of value. Therefore, another vital function of money is, as a measurement of value whereby each item produced has its own determinable value. The price system is made possible by this function of money. Then this function may be regarded as the most basic of all the functions of money. After all, we must put a value on something before we make exchange for it or with it and tender money as a medium of exchange.

3. As a unit of account

Another function of money we noted was that it serves as a standard of value or a unit of account. That is, money serves as a common item in which the prices of all goods and services can be set and be set in the same unit of account. This function of money makes it possible to keep a set of accounts, to calculate profits, draft balance sheets and measure the national income.

The unit of account function of money is very closely associated with the measurement of value function mentioned above. Indeed, some authors treat the two functions as a single indivisible one.

4. As a store of value

Money has come to serve another important function, as a store of value (or wealth). Rather than using money for spending today, you can store (save) it for use in the future. If what we use as money is going to serve as a store of value, this can further limit what can serve as money. For example, suppose your income was paid in apples, but you didn't want to spend all your income right away; you wanted to save some of it to spend later. You're going to have some difficulty saving some of your "apple income". The apples will eventually rot, and no one is going to want rotten apples. Surely, you don't want this to happen to your money. You don't want it to lose its acceptability because you saved it. We want our money to enable us to save, that is, to postpone using some of our current income for use in the future. One of our goals in saving is usually to ensure that the value of our savings doesn't decrease over time. In fact, we usually hope that the value of our saved funds will increase. In modern economy, the value of savings can increase over time through wise investment and the earning of interest.

5. As a standard of deferred payment

Finally, money represents a standard of deferred payments. In modern societies, in stead of being settled in full and at once, many transactions are concluded by deferred payment. For examples, most house-buyers need to raise mortgage and take out insurance policies; and many people borrow for shorter periods by means of overdrafts on hire purchase or against credit cards. None of these would be possible unless money acts as a standard of deferred payment.

1.1.4　The Characteristics of Money　货币的特点

There are some general characteristics that are usually important for whatever serves as money in modern economy. They are as follows:

1. Generally acceptable

Throughout history, societies have used various items as the medium of exchange, everything from stones to shells to furs to gold. For one reason or another, these items became acceptable in some societies as forms of payment for goods and services. As soon as anything is generally accepted in a society as money, it can serve as a medium of exchange. That is the most important criterion for anything to serve as money — it must be generally acceptable. It is more important than intrinsic value — gold after all is measured in terms of money, not money in terms of gold. Therefore, acceptability is of primary importance.

2. Durable

To serve as an effective medium of exchange, money must be durable. Repeating our earlier example, we could have chosen to use apples as money and pay for everything in apples. But problems arise when the apples rot. Who wants to carry around rotten apples? Good apples tend to be eaten, and nothing could erode the value of your money more quickly than having it end up in your stomach.

Modern paper money does not last much longer than apples but is readily replaced by the government as it becomes worn out.

3. Not easily reproduced by people

What serves as money must not be easily reproduced by people. We could use chestnuts as money. They have intrinsic value and can last a long time. But, if we did, people would start growing chestnut trees, and we wouldn't be able to control the supply. Soon there would be so many chestnuts in use, and prices would be bid up so high, that you'd need a truck to carry the chestnuts to pay for bread and milk. We could use rocks, but everyone can simply pick up rocks from all over the place. Once again, we wouldn't be able to control the supply.

A word with different but close meaning to reproduce here is counterfeit. Money must be difficult to counterfeit since widespread forgery could also make the supply out of control and damage the economy.

4. Easily transportable

Money has to be easy to transport, convenient to handle, passing easily from one person to another. We could use elephants as money. But just think of all the problems at pay-day if elephant money was used to provide your wage or salary.

5. Divisible

Money must be divisible into usable quantities or fractions in order that the smallest transactions can be made. Imagine the difficulties you would incur to purchase something that had a price of 1/50 of an elephant. Not a pleasant thought. So, undoubtedly, divisibility is an important characteristic of good money.

6. Stable in value

Finally, money should be stable in value. In Germany in 1923 the monetary system collapsed and hyper-inflation was rife. Then money no longer had real meaning. Wage agreements had to be negotiated daily and a sack of paper money was insufficient to buy a loaf of bread.

However, today in many countries, levels of inflation running into two figures have been worrying enough and have created distortions in economic system. In recent years, for example, people tend to put money into property (such as houses and cars) because this seems to provide a better prospect of return than saving money.

1.1.5 The Types of Money 货币的类型

Money, in a modern society, takes two primary forms — cash and banking deposits.

Cash is composed of coins and paper money (paper notes) and can only be regarded as a small change of the modern monetary system. By far the largest part of the money now consists of bank deposits. Because bank deposits can be readily converted into notes and coins or transferred almost instantly from one person to another, and are considered more difficult to be counterfeited than cash, they are used much increasingly.

If we do not use our money to pay for current transactions, we can save it by placing it on deposit at a financial institution. There are mainly two kinds of savings deposits. They are term deposits[8] and checkable accounts (Note that checkable accounts are also referred to as demand deposits[9]). The kind of saving deposits where people deposit funds for a fixed, agreed-upon period of time such as one year, two years, or more years, is called term deposits. These savings deposits are not usually available for spending until the end of their term. The checkable accounts are those savings deposits for funds that savers can use whenever they want. Most notably, daily interest checkable accounts could be used trough checks in this way. However, checks are not money but only instruments for the payment of money and what could be regarded as money here is checkable deposits. Checkable deposits, then, are a somewhat different form of money from cash. Checkable deposits represent money and serve as a medium of exchange because, through the use of checks, they are readily accepted as payment for goods and services. Otherwise, a check is as good as cash because it is an instruction to your financial institution to transfer a particular quantity of funds from your account to the person or organization you identify on the check.

In fact, this simple division of bank deposits is not quite adequate for any sensible discussion because of the different nature of them. For example, some of them will be held by overseas investors and some may be saved by the national government. So we should access to the two terms of near money[10] and quasi-money[11]. The main elements of what is called near money are national savings bank deposit, loans at short notice to discount government securities and other governmental debts close to maturity. Near money must have a precise monetary value, must be highly liquid, and completely safe against loss. Quasi-money, on the other hand, consists of short-term instruments such as eligible bills and governments securities generally. Such instruments may fluctuate a great deal prior to maturity.

One means of making a payment is to use cash you have on hand. There are many merits of cash payment: cash can be used anywhere in the same country; it can be used for any purpose and among any individuals; cash payment is usually final and secret. However, cash payment also have a number of shortcomings including the difficulty of making remote payment, inflexibility of value units, the inconvenience and unsafety involved in storage and transporting. Therefore, making payments through the use of checks is becoming more and more common in modern economy, especially for large payments.

A recently emerged new kind of money in the form of smart cards[12] or store value cards[13] are introduced in the mid of 1990s, as a result of rapid development of information technology.

It is generally believed that we are moving towards a cashless world, hence banks are offering wider range of card products to customers to enable them pay non-cash money when purchasing commodities or services.

1.1.6 The Value of Money 货币的价值

As stated above, one of the important characteristics of money is the stability in value. However, in fact, the value of money will rise or fall in line with its purchasing power. If, as in our modern history, inflation predominates then money will generally buy less goods and services today than was the case a year ago. This may not be true of everything. The prices of some goods, for example, computers, have fallen dramatically in the recent year, and many domestic appliances, such as washing machine, freezers, TV sets, etc, are much cheaper in real terms than they were ten years ago.

Measuring the value of money, therefore, is not a easy task. The best known yardstick is the Index of Retail Prices and it is based on a large selection of commodities weighted in importance in relation to the average consumer. So the index includes expenditure on smoking and mortgage payments although these items will not necessarily form any part of some people's expenditure. Therefore, the index is nothing more than a numeric average of aggregate consumer spending.

In the example below, we consider an economy with just two commodities: A and B, each of which accounts for half of total spending. Hence, the index which includes them will give each of them equal weight. Assuming that over a year the price of A rises by 20% while that of B by only 5%. Because the two commodities are equally weighted, as shown in Table 1 – 1, the average price increase is 12.5%.

Table 1 – 1 A Simple Price Index（Case 1）

	Weight	Actual Prices		Relative Prices		Weighted Relative Prices	
		Year 1	Year 2	Year 1	Year 2	Year 1	Year 2
A	50	50	60	100	120	5,000	6,000
B	50	200	210	100	105	5,000	5,250
Price Indices						10,000	11,250
						100	112.5
The Average Price Increase						12.5%	

Let us suppose that A was three times more important in total spending than B. Then, in this case, A would be weighted 75% against a weighing of only 25% for B. In this situation, the greater weight allocated to A means that the greater increase in its price has a more remarkable effect on the price index. Therefore, it can be seen in the Table 1 – 2 that, by the same calculation to the former case, the average price increase becomes 16.5%.

It will be noted that food and clothing (two of the basic requirements of daily life) had become less important constituents of the average consumers' spending as the result of the increase of their income in recent years, but housing had become a bigger item. Associated with rising living standards, goods such as private cars, and other luxury items will be in greater demand.

Table 1 – 2   A Simple Price Index（Case 2）

	Weight	Actual Prices		Relative Prices		Weighted Relative Prices	
		Year 1	Year 2	Year 1	Year 2	Year 1	Year 2
A	75	50	60	100	120	7,500	9,000
B	25	200	210	100	105	2,500	2,625
Price Indices						10,000	11,650
						100	116.5
The Average Price Increase						16.5%	

1.2   The Circulation of Money
货币的流通

1.2.1   The Measurement of the Money   货币量的确定

The amount of money in the economy is measured according to varying methods or principles.

1. Narrow money & broad money

One of the above mentioned methods incorporates only money that people can use immediately to pay for goods and services, such as cash (sometimes may be represented by the term of M0) and the contents of checking accounts. This category of money is represented by the term of M1, and we also call it narrow money[14] since it is the narrowest measure of the money.

Another measure of the amount of money includes M1, plus savings and small time deposits, overnight repos[15] at commercial banks, and non-institutional money market accounts. This category of money is represented by the term of M2. Because it is not as narrow as M1, it is also referred to as broad money[16]. All the components of M2 are very liquid, and the non-cash components can be converted into cash very easily.

There is still another category of the money that includes M2 as well as all large time deposits, institutional money market funds, short-term repurchase agreements, along with other larger liquid assets. This is the broadest measure of money and it is represented by the term of M3 and sometimes also called the extended broad money.

2. Money stock & money flow

Money stock[17], also known as money supply, means the total supply of money in circulation in a given country's economy at a given time. There are several different measures for the money supply, such as M1, M2, and M3 which are explained in the previous section. The money supply is considered as an important instrument for controlling inflation. In order to control the money supply, the government has to decide which particular measure of the money supply to target. The broader the targeted measure, the more difficult it will be to control that particular target. However, targeting an unsuitable narrow money supply measure may lead to a situation where the total money supply in the country is not adequately controlled.

The term money flow[18] here, also referred to as the volume of money in circulation, means the total amount of the money held by all the participants in a given country's economy at a given time. It can be calculated according to the following formula:

The Volume of Money in Circulation = Money Supply × The Velocity of Money in Circulation

3. How money circulates

The treasury department[19] sends new paper money and coins to the central bank[20]; the Central Bank pay it to the commercial banks[21] and other depository financial institutions. Customers of these institutions withdraw cash as they need it. Once people spend their cash at department stores, grocery stores, supermarkets and so on, most of this money is eventually redeposited in depository financial institutions.

Besides spending cash for purchasing goods and service, people may spend their cash and deposits for the investment in the financial market through some non-bank financial institutions[22], such as security companies[23].

The employees of the stores, supermarkets, financial institutions and other businesses will be paid wages and then they can use the wages to pay for the stuffs they need.

Considering the country as a whole, it will pay money for its imports from and receive money for its exports to other countries.

Figure 1 – 1 simply illustrates how money circulates in the United States.

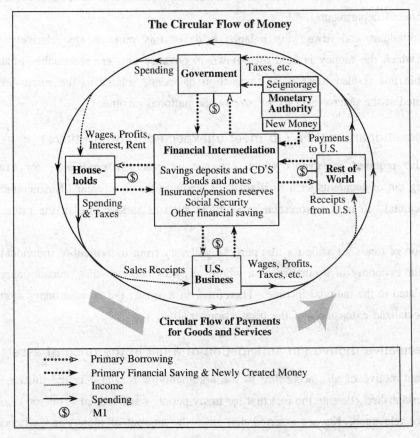

Figure 1 – 1   Circular flow of money in the US

1.2.2   Money Demand   货币需求

Money demand[24], of course, means the demand for money. Some people may think that the demand for money would be infinite. Who doesn't want more money? The key thing to remember is that wealth is not money. The collective demand for wealth is infinite as there is never enough to satisfy everyone's desires. However, money is a narrowly defined term which includes things like coins, paper currencies, bank deposits. It doesn't include things like stocks and bonds, or houses and cars. Since money is only one of these many forms of wealth, it has plenty of substitutes. Money demand theory deals with the desire to hold money rather than its substitutes. It is particularly associated with the work of the great English economist John Maynard Keynes.

Keynes identified three motives for holding money and we'll examine each of them in turn as follows.

1. The transaction motive (to meet day-to-day needs)

Consumers and firms require money to facilitate current transactions. The extent to which money is needed for this purpose depends on the needs of the individual or the firm in relation to the frequency with which income is received. A wage earner receiving $200 a week, all of it spent before the next pay-day has only this one motive — to hold it for transactions purposes; and his average requirement to meet his transactions needs will be $100. A salary earner on $1,200 a month may decide to set aside $200 each month in savings; he will therefore maintain an average balance of $500 ($1,000/2) a month for transactions purpose. Similarly, firms will require transactions balance and meet other regular commitments; and so do governments departments.

For most individuals and firms, the balance held for this purpose are relatively stable since the commitments for which the money is held are known in advance and are reasonably predictable. For the country as a whole this is also true. Thus transaction balances, related at the micro-level to individual incomes, are related at the macro-level to the size of the national income.

2. The precautionary motive (to meet unexpected future outlays)

Money is also required for events which can not be precisely predicted, for example, to meet expenditure arising out of accidents such as illness, or repair to the family car. Businessmen will also need additional liquid capital[25] to meet unforeseen expenditure such as sudden rise in the price of materials for production.

The proportion of funds set aside for this purpose will vary from individual to individual, and from firm to firm; but for the economy of a country as a whole, Keynes believed that precautionary balances could also be closely related to the national income. Therefore, in a sense, the precautionary motive is little more than a part (a specialized extension) of the transactions motive.

3. The speculative motive (in anticipation of a fall in the price of assets)

Most important motive of all, according to the arguments of Keynes, is the third — the speculative motive. This he established, despite the fact that for many people (and indeed firms too), only the first two motives have much relevance. Keynes asserted that since the amount of money in existence (chiefly bank deposits) greatly exceeds the demand for active balances[26] as he called the transactions and precautionary motives, there must be a third motive for holding money. Why though should some people wish to hold idle balances[27]?

Keynes looked at this phenomenon by reference to the price of bonds, i. e. gilt-edge securities[28]. The return or yield on such securities varies inversely with their prices. Thus, for example, at a price of \$30, 2.5% consols[29] will yield 8.33% (2.5/30 × 100% = 8.33%).

If investors believe that interest rates are likely to rise they will not invest at the current price but remain liquid money expecting the price of the stock to fall and the yield to rise. For example, at the price of \$20, the same security will yield 12.5% (2.5/20 × 100% = 12.5%).

Keynes regarded the demand for active balance as fixed relative to the quantity of money in the economy. It is completely interest-inelastic, because people have to hold money to buy stuffs which are necessary to daily life and for future emergencies such as car breakdown and job loss whatever the interest rate is. However, the demand for such balances will increase if the incomes rise up. The demand for speculative balances, argued by Keynes, is interest-elastic: the interest rate does have considerable impact on the demand for this kind of money.

Thus interest rates and investors' expectations about their future course are the important determinant of the demand for money. Figure 1−2 shows the demand for money, which Keynes called "liquidity preference[30]". It would be observed that, like all demand curves, it slopes downwards from left to right.

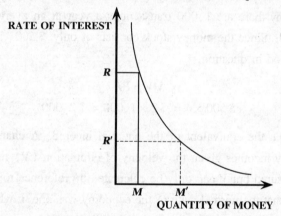

Figure 1 − 2   Liquidity preference

With the supply of money at *M* the rate of interest is *R*. An increase in the money supply to *M'* will cause interest rates to fall to *R'*. Eventually, the curve flattens out since below a certain level, the attraction of remaining liquid against that of holding bonds he considered to be overwhelming. At such a level, speculators will consequently believe that interest rates can move only one way — upward.

The volume of speculative balances then is determined by quite different considerations from those influencing the demand for active balances. Apparently, the size of the national income is not so important. The determining factor is the investors' expectations about future interest rates, which are highly volatile. Keynes' theory explained for the first time the paradox demand for idle balances in preference to interest-earning or tangible assets.

1.2.3   Money Supply   货币供应

Money supply[31] (also called monetary aggregates, money stock) is the total supply of money in circulation in a given country's economy at a given time. The money supply affects the interest rates. The two are related inversely, such that, as money supply increases interest rates will fall. When the interest rate equates the quantity of money demanded with the quantity of money supply, the economy is working at the money market equilibrium.

In the short term, Keynes regarded the money supply as fixed and was more interested in changes in the level of income. Keynes maintained that a change in income would alter the demand for active balances relative to that for speculative balances. Thus an increase in the level of income would drive up interest rates provided that the money supply was held constant.

Until Keynes' time, economists generally believed that while the money supply did not influence specific commodity prices it did, nonetheless, affect the overall price level. Keynes' views still command a very large measure of support although they have eventually been modified and refined by later economists. In more recent times, the Chicago School led by Milton Friedman, has made a forceful challenge to the Keynesians, emphasizing the greater importance they attach to the supply of money.

The germ of their ideas is the quantity theory of money initially developed by Irving Fisher. The quantity theory of money is based on the fundamentally simple equation: $MV = PT$ (M = the quantity of money supplied in the economy, V = the velocity of its circulation, P = the general level of prices, T = the total number of transactions in a given period).

The meaning of this simple equation can be understood if we look at a simple economic model. Supposing that in the economy there are 1,000 transactions a year at an average price of \$2 so that total turnover amounts to \$2,000. Since the money stock consists of only \$500, it can be seen that this money is used four times in the period in question.

$$MV = PT$$
$$\$500 \times 4 = \$2 \times 1,000 = \$2,000$$

MV and PT then are each the equivalent of the national income. A change in the money stock (M) leads to an increase in money incomes given the velocity of circulation (V) remains constant. M, P and T are all capable of being measured but V can only be calculated by reference to the other variables. Until the 1930s, economists believed that the normal state of the economy was one in which full employment existed; and that booms and slumps were merely hiccups in a well ordered economic system. It was therefore assumed that T remained fixed. This was also assumed to be the case with V since people change the pattern of their payments very slowly. So, if V and T can be considered fixed, an increase in the money stock (M) must lead to an increase in the overall level of prices (P).

Milton Friedman himself also directly challenged the Keynesian views on money with his radical redefinition of the quantity theory. In Friedman's view, although money has certain special qualities it is nevertheless possible to substitute a number of other assets — real assets as well as financial assets — for money. Thus in recent years house property and antiques have been considered better investments than gilt-edged stocks; and since the late 1950s investors generally have purchased ordinary shares in preference to gilts thus reversing the once traditional structure of yields. Today ordinary shares in general provide relatively low immediate returns but investors believe that over time company profits and dividends will increase.

The precise forms in which individuals choose to hold assets will obviously vary considerably, depending on taste, and convenience as well as on the money return. Owner-occupied homes, for example, are presumed to provide an implicit return equivalent to the rent which would otherwise be payable.

Friedman argues that an increase in the money supply will lead people to consider holding assets other than money and that increased demand for these assets will lead inexorably to an increase in the price level. This will then lead to an increase in money incomes (but not real incomes) as wage demands reflect past price increases and anticipate future ones.

Keynesians believe that there is a close relationship between the demand for money and the rate of interest, while the Monetarists who support the Friedman's views recognize no particular relationship between them. In their extreme forms neither theory seems completely tenable today. Both schools of thought contain an element of truth. However, because of the problems of defining the money supply and measuring the relative importance of different kinds of assets it may never be possible to ascertain precisely the relationship between the money supply, the rate of interest and the overall level of prices.

1.2.4 Inflation 通货膨胀

1. The definition of inflation

The definition of inflation[32] cannot be separated from that of the price level. Economists measure the price level by computing a weighted average of consumer prices. The value of the average is arbitrarily set equal to one (or one hundred) in a base year, and the index in any other year is expressed relative to the base year. For example, the value of the consumer price index in 2006 was 125, relative to a value of 100 in 2000 (the base year). That is, prices in 2006 were 25 percent higher on average than those in 2000.

Inflation occurs when the price level rises from one period to the next. The rate of inflation expresses the increase in percentage terms. Thus, a 2 percent annual inflation rate means that, on average, prices rose 2 percent over the previous year. Theoretically, the rate of inflation could be by the hour or the minute. For an economy suffering from hyperinflation, for example, Germany in the 1920s, this might be an appropriate thing to do (assuming the data could be collected and processed quickly enough). For the contemporary United States, which has never experienced hyperinflation, the rate of inflation is reported on a monthly basis.

2. Measuring inflation

The measurement of the price level is a difficult task and, therefore, so is the measurement of the inflation rate. For example, many economists believe that the consumer price index tends to overstate the inflation rate in recent decades because improvements in the quality of goods and services are not adequately reflected in the index. An index that held quality constant, according to this view, would show a smaller rate of price increase from year to year, and thus a smaller average rate of inflation.

It is important to recognize that a positive rate of inflation, as measured by a price index, does not mean that all prices have increased by the same proportion. Some prices may rise relative to others. Some might even fall in absolute terms, and yet, on average, inflation is still positive, and this means the overall level of prices rises up.

The distinction between absolute and relative price change is important in understanding the theory behind the effects of inflation on economic activity. In the simplest static (one-period) economic model of consumer behavior, a fully anticipated (understood and expected by consumers and producers) doubling of all prices — the prices of the various consumer goods and the prices of the various productive inputs (factors of production, like labor) — does not change the structure of relative prices and therefore should have no effect on the quantities of goods demanded. Similarly, the conventional model of producer behavior predicts that a doubling of all prices would not affect output price relative to the cost of production and therefore would not affect the quantity of goods supplied. The nominal value of GNP (Gross National Product) would double, but the real value would remain constant.

In such a model, money is said to be "neutral", and consumers and producers are free of "money illusion." In more complex, dynamic models, it is possible that a sustained, higher rate of inflation would alter consumers' desires for holds of money versus other assets (such as real estate) and this might change real economic activity.

When inflation is unexpected, however, it is entirely possible — indeed, almost inevitable — that real economic activity will be affected. Throughout American history there is evidence that money wages are "sticky" relative to prices; that is, changes in money wages lag behind (unexpected) changes in the price level. During the early years of the Great Depression of the 1930s, nominal hourly wages fell but not nearly as much as prices. With the real price of labor "too high, unemployment was the inevitable result. When inflation is unexpected, consumers or producers may react as if relative prices are changing, rather than the absolute price level. This can occur especially if the economy experiences a price "shock" in a key sector — for example, an unexpected rise in the price of oil — that sets off a chain of price increases of related products such as cars and petrochemicals, and a downturn in economic activity.

3. The causes of inflation

All of which begs the underlying question: What ultimately causes inflation? Although this is still a matter of dispute among economists in the details, most believe that inflation typically occurs when the supply of money increases more rapidly than the demand for money; or equivalently, when the supply of money per unit of output is increasing. This might occur within a single country. However, in a global economy today, it can also spill over from one country to another. The supply of money per unit of output can increase either because the velocity at which it circulates in the economy has increased or, holding velocity constant, because the stock of money per unit of output has increased.

This leads to another question: What factors determine the rate of growth of money supply relative to money demand? The demand for money depends on the overall scale of economic activity, along with interest rates, which measure the opportunity cost of holding money balances.

During the nineteenth century and part of the twentieth, many counties adhered to the gold standard. Under the gold standard, the money supply was guaranteed by holdings of gold, so the supply of money could grow only as rapidly as the government's holdings of gold. If these holdings increased more slowly than the demand for money, the price level would fall. Conversely, if holdings of specie increased more rapidly than the demand for money, the price level could rise. Generally, the latter would occur with the discovery of new deposits of gold within the territory of country or elsewhere, because gold could flow across international borders—as occurred in California in the late 1840s, or in South Africa in the late 1890s.

The main institutional determinant of the money supply in a single economy is the central bank. The central bank can affect the growth of the money supply in several ways. First, it can engage in open market operations, the buying and selling of government securities. When the central bank buys securities, it injects money into the system; conversely, when it sells securities, it pulls money out. Second, the central bank can alter certain features of the banking system that affect the ability of banks to "create" money. Banks take in deposits, from which they make loans. The supply of loanable funds, however, is larger than the stock of deposits because banks are required only to keep a fraction of deposits as reserves. The central bank can alter the bank reserve ratio, or it can alter the rate of interest that it charges itself to lend money to banks.

Most economists believe that the central bank, when deciding upon monetary policy, faces a short-run trade-off between inflation and unemployment. In the long run, unemployment tends toward a "natural" rate that reflects basic frictions in the labor market and that is independent of the rate of inflation. If the goal in the short run is to reduce unemployment, the central bank may need to tolerate a moderate inflation rate. Conversely, if the goal is to lower the inflation rate, this may require a slowdown in economic activity and a higher unemployment rate. Some economists believe that, rather than trying to regulate the economy, the central bank should increase the money supply at a steady, predictable pace.

It is sometimes argued that inflation is good for debtors and bad for creditors, and bad for persons on fixed incomes. A debtor, so goes the argument, benefits from inflation because loans are taken out in today's dollars, but repaid in the future when, because of inflation, a dollar will be worth less than today. However, to the extent that inflation is correctly anticipated, or rationally expected, the rate of interest charged for the loan, i. e., the nominal rate, will be the real rate of interest plus the expected rate of inflation. More generally, any fixed income contract expressed in nominal terms can be negotiated in advance to take proper account of expected inflation. However, if inflation is unanticipated, it can have severe distributional effects. The most typical example is that during the Great Depression millions of people lost their homes because their incomes fell drastically relative to their mortgage payments.

1.2.5   Deflation   通货紧缩

Deflation[33] is the opposite of inflation: a fall in the price level, and when the inflation rate (by some measure) is negative, the economy is in a deflationary period. For economists especially, the term has been and is sometimes used to refer to a decrease in the size of the money supply (as a proximate cause of the decrease in the general price level). However, this latter is now more often referred to as a "contraction" of the money supply. During deflation the demand for liquidity goes up, in preference to goods or interest. During deflation the purchasing power of money increases.

Deflation is considered a problem in a modern economy because of the potential of a deflationary spiral which may cause large falls in GDP and purchasing power, and its association with the Great Depression.

However, a deflationary bias is the norm under specie or specie backed money economies, as population and production tend to increase faster than the stock of specie. There are also episodes where there may be deflation in only a particular kind or type of goods, such as commodities during the great commodities depression of 1982 – 1998.

Deflation should not be confused with disinflation which is a slowing in the rate of inflation, that is, where the general level of prices is still increasing, but slower than before.

In Monetarists theory examined above, deflation is defined in terms of a rise in the demand for money, based on the quantity of money available. In this model of deflation, it is a contraction of the money supply (M) which reduces the velocity of money (V), and thus the number of transactions (T) falls and therefore the general price level (P) falls in response.

Deflation should not be confused with temporarily falling prices; instead, it is a sustained fall in general prices. In the classical IS-LM model this is caused by a shift in the supply and demand curve for goods and interest, particularly a fall in the aggregate level of demand. That is, there is a fall in how much the whole economy is willing to buy, and the going price for goods. Since this idles capacity, investment also falls, leading to further reductions in aggregate demand. This is the deflationary spiral. The solution to it is stimulus either from the central bank, by expanding the money supply, or by the fiscal authority to increase demand, and borrow at interest rates which are below those available to private entities.

In more recent economic thinking, deflation is related to risk, where the risk adjusted return of assets drops to negative, investors and buyers will hoard currency rather than invest it, even in the most solid of securities. This can produce the theoretical condition, much debated as to its practical possibility, of a liquidity trap. A central bank cannot, normally, charge negative interest for money, and even charging zero interest often produces less stimulative effect than slightly higher rates of interest. In a closed economy, this is because charging zero interest also means having zero return on government securities, or even negative return on short maturities. In an open economy, it creates a carry trade[34] and devalues the currency producing higher prices for imports without necessarily stimulating exports to a like degree. The experience of Japan during its 1988 – 2004 depression is considered to illustrate both of these problems.

In modern economies, as loan terms have grown in length and financing is integral to building and general business, the cost associated with deflation has grown larger. Since deflation discourages investment and spending, because there is no reason to risk on future profits when the expectation of profits may be negative and the expectation of future prices is lower, it generally leads to, or is associated with a collapse in aggregate demand. Without the "hidden risk of inflation", it may become more prudent just to hold onto money, and not to spend or invest it.

Deflation also occurs when improvements in production efficiency lowers the overall price of goods. Improvements in production efficiency generally happen because economic producers of goods and services are motivated by a promise of increased profit margins, resulting from the production improvements that they make. But despite their profit motive, competition in the marketplace will prompt those producers to apply at least some portion of these cost savings into reducing the asking price for their goods. When this happens, consumers pay less for those goods; and consequently deflation has occurred, since purchasing power has increased.

While an increase in the purchasing power of one's money sounds beneficial, it can actually cause hardship when the majority of one's net wealth is held in illiquid assets such as homes, land, and other forms of private property. It also amplifies the sting of debt, since — after some period of significant deflation— the payments one is making in the service of a debt represent a larger amount of purchasing power than they did when the debt was first incurred. Consequently, deflation can be regarded as a phantom amplification of a loan's interest rate.

This lesson about protracted deflationary cycles and the resultant hardships has been felt several times in modern history. During the 19th century, the Industrial Revolution brought about a huge increase in production efficiency, that happened to coincide with a relatively flat money supply. These two deflationary catalysts led, simultaneously, not only to tremendous capital development, but also to tremendous deprivation for millions of people who were ill-equipped to deal with the dark side of deflation.

Some ones argue that if there were no "rigidities" in an economy, then deflation should be a welcome effect, as the lowering of prices would allow more of the economy's effort to be moved to other areas of activity, thus increasing the total output of the economy. However, while there have been periods of 'beneficial' deflation (especially in industry segments, such as computers), more often it has led to the more severe form with negative impact to large segments of the populace and economy.

Most economists agree that the effects of modest long-term inflation are less damaging than deflation (which, even at best, is very hard to control). Deflation raises real wages which are both difficult and costly for management to lower. This frequently leads to layoffs and makes employers reluctant to hire new workers, increasing unemployment. However, in the last 5 years or so, real wages for the average worker has remained fixed or actually decreased, with little effect on unemployment.

Group Discussion ▶▶▶

1. Talk about the importance of money in modern economy.
2. Compare the monetary theory of Keynesian and Monetarists.
3. Discuss the inflation and deflation in the present world.

NOTES ▶▶▶

1　paper currency　纸币，钞票（亦用"paper money"、"paper note"、"bank note"、"bill"）
2　I.O.U.s　借据，欠条
3　peppercorn rent　徒有其名的租金
4　representative money　可兑现纸币
5　gold standard　金本位（若首字母大写，即"Gold Standard"，则指"国际金本位制度"）
6　fiat money　不兑现纸币
7　legal tender　法定货币
8　term deposit　定期存款（亦用"time deposit"、"fixed deposit"）
9　demand deposit　活期存款（亦用"current deposit"）
10　near money　近似货币
11　quasi-money　准货币
12　smart card　智能卡
13　store value card　储值卡
14　narrow money　狭义货币
15　repo　回购协议（"repurchase agreement"的缩写变体）
16　broad money　广义货币
17　money stock　货币存量
18　money flow　货币流量
19　treasury department　财政部
20　central bank　中央银行
21　commercial bank　商业银行
22　non-bank financial institution　非银行金融机构
23　securities company　证券公司

24 money demand　货币需求

25 liquid capital　流动资本（亦用"active capital"、"fluid capital"、"operating capital"、"working capital"、"floating capital"）

26 active balance　活动余额

27 idle balance　闲置余额

28 gilt-edge security　金边证券（即风险小回报高的证券，通常指国债）

29 consols　统一公债（由英国政府于1751年开始发行的长期债券）

30 liquidity preference　流动性偏好

31 money supply　货币供给

32 inflation　通货膨胀

33 deflation　通货紧缩

34 carry trade　套利交易

Chapter 2

Credit
信用

Learning Objectives

✔ To understand the concept of credit
✔ To know about the types of credit instruments and credit risks
✔ To grasp the concept of interest and interest rate
✔ To understand the determination of interest rate
✔ To learn the types and functions of interest rate

Opening Vignette

To Know Credit

Think of credit as a tool much like a hammer or a screwdriver. To use a tool correctly, it's important to know as much as you can about it. Here are some essential things you should know about credit.

What Is Credit?

Remember when you were younger, how fascinated you were whenever you saw someone using a credit card. Back then, it seemed like credit cards were magical squares of plastic that could easily and conveniently be used as a substitute for cash. If you haven't figured it out yet, here's one fact about credit that you must know: it's not a cash substitute, but rather a loan (and it could be considered as a debt) that you must pay back sometime in the future.

Credit is what you use to buy products or services today and pay for them at a later date. This includes credit cards, personal loans or mortgages, and familiar services such as your telephone and cable. In return for paying later for something you can enjoy today, you are often charged interest or service charges by the creditor (the lender who lend you the sum of money to buy the product or service).

Having credit lets you make purchases when you don't have cash available. Before a creditor will allow you to use credit, it must first believe that you can be trusted to repay the amount of credit you use. This is considered financial trustworthiness.

Creditors use a number of factors to determine your financial trustworthiness. The most commonly used factor is your credit history. How you have used credit in the past — your credit history — is considered to be the best way to predict how you will use it in the future. Your credit history is reported in your credit report and credit score. Therefore, it is of vital importance that you do pay later and on time, because your credit history will have an impact on your financial health now and in the future.

When you are a new debtor and do not have a credit history, the creditor might use other factors such as employment and salary to gauge your financial trustworthiness. Or, the creditor might require that someone who does have favorable credit agree to repay your charges if you fail to do so. In this case, the two of you share credit and the one who has favorable credit is in fact a guarantor.

How Does It Work?

To establish credit with a financial institution, you must first make an application for credit. The creditor will use identifying information, like your social security number, to look up your credit history. If the creditor determines that you are a trustworthy borrower, then it will extend credit to you.

Once you have been approved for credit, the creditor will give you guidelines, or terms, for using your credit. The terms include, but are not limited to, how often you should send payments for purchases, what happens if you are late on a payment, and the cost of using credit.

Usually, the creditor establishes a maximum amount of credit that you can use, a credit limit, based on your credit history. Your credit terms will outline what happens if you exceed this limit. In most cases, there is a monetary penalty.

When you've been approved for credit, the creditor provides you with a way to use this credit, e.g. a credit card. Periodically you will receive a statement from it detailing purchases you've made, interest charged, minimum payment amount due, and payment due date. As per your agreement with the creditor, you must make payments by the due date to avoid penalties.

Once I Get Credit, How Do I Keep It?

Keeping credit is easy. Just honor the terms of your agreement by making your payments. Missing payments, making late payments or frequently exceeding your authorized credit card limit will negatively affect your future credit privileges. Every form of credit you carry, including your Government Sponsored Student Loan, telephone bills and your credit card, is an important part of your credit history and can affect your credit rating.

Warm-up Questions

1. What do you think the credit is?
2. Why does the credit history matter so much?
3. How to keep your credit?

2.1 An Overview of Credit
信用概述

2.1.1 The Origin and Development of Credit 信用的产生与发展

1. The origin of credit

After the emergence of private ownership, the division of labor and surplus products grew increasingly. The private ownership and the division of labor caused different people to possess different products, and the surplus products made it possible for people to exchange for products.

As mentioned in the previous chapter, the exchange took the form of barter firstly. Afterward, because of the emergence of money, people could make exchange with money more easily. However, some problems did exist in the process of exchange with money. For instance, the potential buyer might have no money in hand to the moment when the seller sold his product. Supposed that the seller was acquainted very well with the potential buyer, he might sell his product to the latter and agreed to receive the payment from the buyer later. Such a transaction, in fact, was a credit transaction, which is also referred to as a sale on open account[1] or the deferred payment today.

With the development of economy and society, credit transactions went beyond the extent of exchange for products. Money, as the medium of exchange, got involved in the credit transactions, resulting in the lending and borrowing business. Thus, money and credit connected to form a new field in the economy — finance.

Reading Material

Credit Money

Credit money often exists in relation to other money such as fiat money or commodity money, and from the user's point of view is indistinguishable from it. Most of the western world's money is credit money derived from national fiat money currencies.

In a modern economy, a bank will lend all but a small portion of its deposits to borrowers, this is known as fractional reserve banking. In doing so, it increases the total money supply above that of the total amount of the fiat money (cash) in existence. While a bank will not have access to sufficient cash to meet all the obligations it has to depositors if they wish to withdraw the balance of their check accounts, the majority of transactions will occur using the credit money (checks and electronic transfers).

Strictly speaking, a debt is not money, primarily because debt can not act as a unit of account. All debts are denominated in units of something external to the debt. However, credit money certainly acts as a substitute for money when it is used in other functions of money (medium of exchange and store of value).

2. The reasons for using credit in modern society

In modern economy, credit is widely available and extensively used. Because credit includes a promise to pay, a debtor accepts the risks of borrowing to secure something of value, whether perceived or real, profitable or neutral. Borrowing extends one's purchasing power and ability to invest in capital assets to build wealth. But credit is not only used to increase wealth; credit may be necessitated by psychological and cultural factors as well.

The following are some of the most common reasons for using credit.

(1) Enjoyment. Credit has come to finance the enhancement of one's life style or quality of life through activities and purchases for enjoyment. Activities "profitable" to one's well being may translate into a more productive economic life. Enjoyment includes the financing of a new house, a luxury car, a higher education, etc.

(2) Utilitarian consumption. With the introduction of credit cards in the 1950s and the increase of home equity debt in the 1980s, the financing of daily consumption has greatly expanded. In fact, consumer credit[2] in 1990 was about four times that of 1975. Much of this debt was for convenience purchases, consumer goods, and services with a life of less than one year.

(3) Profit and wealth building. The profit incentive plays an important role in the accumulation of capital assets and in wealth building not only for companies — which generate profits through the introduction of capital improvements that must be financed over the long-term — but also for individuals. Individual buyers use a similar rationale when buying a house. They expect the purchase of a certain house in a certain location to be more "profitable" than renting or purchasing another house elsewhere. Although a home is not a factory, it is the production backdrop for the capitalist employee selling labor and services.

2.1.2　The Nature of Credit　信用的本质

Credit is a transaction between two parties in which one, acting as creditor or lender, supplies the other, the debtor or borrower, with money, goods, services, or securities in return for the promise of future payment. As a financial transaction, credit is the purchase of the present use of money with the promise to pay in the future according to a pre-arranged schedule and at a specified cost defined by the interest rate. In modern economies, the use of credit is pervasive and the volume enormous. Electronic transfer technology moves vast amounts of capital instantaneously around the globe irrespective of geopolitical demarcations.

In a production economy, credit bridges the time gap between the commencement of production and the final sale of goods in the marketplace. In order to pay labor and secure materials from vendors, the producer secures a constant source of credit to fund production expenses, i. e., working capital. The promise or expectation of continued economic growth motivates the producer to expand production facilities, employ more labors, and purchase additional materials. These create a need for long-term financing.

To accumulate adequate reserves from which to lend large sums of money, banks and insurance companies act as intermediaries between those with excess money reserves and those in need of financing. These financial institutions collect excess money through deposits and redirect it through loans into capital assets.

However, for individuals, when credit is talked about, it much likely refers to financial trustworthiness, i. e., how much someone will trust you with borrowed money.

In daily life, there are two kinds of credit commonly used: Item-based credit — these are usually fixed loans, such as a mortgage, personal, or car loans. They're used to buy one specific item that you normally would not be able to simply pay cash for (a house, a car, etc.). Revolving credit — these are your credit cards. They're referred to as "revolving" because you have a fixed amount of money you can access that you can spend as you wish. Once you repay the debt owed you can use that credit again.

Credit is something that needs to be repaid, and the different kinds of credit are usually repaid differently. Item-based credit, such as a housing loan, is usually repaid on a pre-determined schedule, which is usually in approximately equal amounts. With this kind of repayment the lender you borrowed from usually has a certain interest payment that needs to be made, which is agreed upon by the borrower and lender. This rate is how the lender makes a profit from lending money. Revolving credit, such as a credit card, can usually be repaid on a monthly basis or on an "as needed" basis (as long as the minimum monthly payment is met). So, if you have $1,000 in credit, you spend $300, and repay only $100, you'll have $800 in credit left with $200 left to pay. Again, the lender charges an interest rate which it uses to turn a profit on your credit.

Various credit instruments, which are more commonly known as financial instruments, will get involved in credit transactions. They will be examined in Chapter 5.

Credit is the potential to put yourself in debt; however, it also allows you to become financially trustworthy. It can be good or bad, depending on how responsible and proactive you are with your credit.

Reading Material

Testing Your Credit IQ

Find out how much you know about managing your money and credit by testing your credit IQ. Answer each of the following questions with the response that best describes you.

(1) When do you tend to pay your bills?
   a. When I receive them.
   b. As close to the due date as possible.
   c. I skip some payments.

(2) What portion of your credit card bills do you pay each month?
   a. Most of what I owe, if not all.
   b. Minimum payment due.
   c. I don't pay the bill.

（3）On average, how much of a balance do you carry on each of your credit cards?

 a. None — I pay it all off each month.

 b. Less than half of my available credit.

 c. I'm maxed out.

（4）How much of your monthly income goes to pay credit card bills?

 a. Less than 10%.

 b. Approximately 11% –20%.

 c. More than 20% or someone else pays my bills.

（5）Do you know how much total credit card debt you are carrying?

 a. Yes.

 b. I have a rough estimate.

 c. I'm afraid to add it up.

If you answered "a" to all of the questions, then congratulations! You're using credit wisely.

If you answered "b" to all of the questions, you should reevaluate your budget to identify ways to reduce your debt. You want to be prepared for what life sends your way — that includes making sure you have enough money for emergencies.

If you answered "c" to all of the questions, stop and reevaluate. Before you use your credit card again, examine your budget, financial status and credit obligations. If you are not the person paying the bill, you should still plan your spending with the person who is paying your credit card bills to make sure they can afford to pay — both your credit history and theirs are at risk.

2.1.3 The Types of Credit   信用的类型

Credit could be classified into different types by different criterion.

1. By the debtor's status

（1）Commercial credit [3]. It is credit which an individual or a business entity, such as a sole trader or a partner, obtains for business purposes not connected with the individual's domestic, household or family interests.

（2）Consumer credit. It is credit which an individual obtains when acting in a private capacity, and which is to be used primarily for domestic, household or family purposes.

2. By the nationalities of the creditor and the debtor

（1）Domestic credit. It is domestic credit when the creditor provides credit to domestic firms or individuals.

（2）International credit. It is international credit when the creditor provides credit to foreign debtors.

3. By the details of the credit agreement

（1）Credit sale [4]. Under credit sale, one can buy the goods at the present cash price and make the payment later. The buyer usually has to pay interest but some suppliers offer interest-free credit. Repayment is made in installments. The buyer is the legal owner of the goods as soon as the contract is made and the goods cannot be returned if he/she changes his/her mind. The supplier cannot repossess the goods if the buyer falls behind in repayments but can take court action to recover the money owed if the buyer is in arrears.

(2) Installment credit[5]. Installment credit is extended for the purchase of a specific product, repaid in regular monthly payments, and governed by a legally enforceable signed contract between buyer (debtor) and seller (creditor) that grants possession but not ownership of the good to the buyer. This is also referred to as a hire purchase (HP)[6].

(3) Mortgage[7]. A mortgage is a common example of a secured loan[8] under which the lender uses an asset (the borrower's house or insurance policy) as security for providing credit. This type of borrowing can be more cost effective in the long term because of the lower interest rate. Home mortgage loans, given by building societies or banks, enable individuals to buy a house. A mortgage is a loan while an installment credit agreement is not. Under a mortgage, both possession and ownership of the house transfer to the buyer; with an installment agreement, only possession transfers to the buyer. If a borrower defaults on or otherwise breaches a mortgage contract, the lender can place a lien on the house. This may necessitate sale of the house, but the lender does not take possession or ownership. An extra mortgage on the property, called a second mortgage (remortgage)[9], can be given, for example, for home improvements. The lender will charge a higher rate of interest on the remortgage. If you are a homeowner and you need to raise finance to refurnish your house, your first port of call should be to look to release equity from your property. A remortgage is a relatively inexpensive form of borrowing if the value of your property is greater than your current mortgage.

(4) Unsecured loan[10]. An unsecured loan is where the lender does not require any security for the credit it provides, and the borrower's application will be judged on the details provided in the application and information held by the Credit Reference Agency. The unsecured loan market is very competitive and it even pays to shop around.

(5) Pawnbroking[11]. it is credit under which one gives his/her jewellery or other possessions to the pawnbrokers, and then they lend him/her a small amount of money for a few days. The borrower then has to pay the money back to retrieve his/her goods; otherwise the pawnbrokers get to keep the items.

(6) Bank overdraft. If a depositor has a good relationship with his bank, the bank may be able to agree an attractive overdraft deal. A number of UK banks in attempt to win new customers are offering free overdraft facilities up to £2,500. This can be a very useful way of borrowing if you only require funds for a short period of time every month.

(7) Credit card[12]. Another relatively expensive way to borrow money is using a credit card. Credit cards are issued by banks, finance companies or shops. They can be used to buy goods or borrow money from a bank. You will get a monthly statement saying how much you owe (including interest) and will be told the minimum amount you must pay that month. You may also have to pay an annual fee.

2.1.4 Credit Risk 信用风险

Credit risk is the possibility of a loss occurring due to the debtor's failure to meet its contractual debt obligations. Credit risks take various forms.

1. Risks faced by lenders to consumers

Most lenders employ their own models (credit scoring) to rank potential and existing customers according to risk, and then apply appropriate strategies. With credits such as unsecured consumer loans or mortgages, lenders charge a higher price for higher risk customers and vice versa. With revolving credits such as credit cards and overdrafts, risk is controlled through careful setting of credit limits. Some credits also require security, most commonly in the form of property.

2. Risks faced by lenders to companies

Lenders will trade off the cost/benefits of a loan according to its risks and the interest charged. But interest rates are not the only method to compensate for risk. Protective covenants are written into loan agreements that allow the lender some controls. These covenants may be to:

(1) limit the borrower's ability to weaken his balance sheet voluntarily, e. g. , by buying back shares, or paying dividends, or borrowing further;

(2) allow for monitoring the debt by requiring audits, and monthly reports;

(3) allow the lender to decide when he can recall the loan based on specific events or when financial ratios like debt/equity, or interest coverage deteriorate.

3. Risks faced by companies

Companies carry credit risk when, for example, they do not demand up-front cash payment for products or services. By delivering the product or service first and billing the customer later, the company is carrying a risk between the delivery and payment.

Significant resources and sophisticated programs are used to analyze and manage risk. Some companies run a credit risk department whose job is to assess the financial health of their customers, and extend credit (or not) accordingly. They may use some programs to advise on avoiding, reducing and transferring risk. They also use third party provided intelligence. Companies like Moody's provide such information for a fee.

Credit risk is not really manageable for very small companies (i.e. , those with only one or two customers). This makes these companies very vulnerable to defaults, or even payment delays by their customers.

The use of a collection agency is not really a tool to manage credit risk; rather, it is an extreme measure closer to a write down in that the creditor expects a below-agreed return after the collection agency takes its share (if it is able to get anything at all).

Reading Material

Who Invented Credit Card?

Credit is a method of selling goods or services without the buyer having cash in hand. A credit card is only an automatic way of offering credit to a consumer. Today, every credit card carries an identifying number that speeds shopping transactions.

According to Encyclopedia Britannica, "the use of credit cards originated in the United States during the 1920s, when individual firms, such as oil companies and hotel chains, began issuing them to customers."

However, references to credit cards have been made as far back as 1890 in Europe. Early credit cards involved sales directly between the merchant offering the credit and credit card, and that merchant's customer.

Credit cards were not always been made of plastic. There have been credit tokens made from, metal plates, and celluloid, metal, fiber, paper, and now mostly plastic cards.

The inventor of the first bank issued credit card was John Biggins of the Flatbush National Bank of Brooklyn in New York. In 1946, Biggins invented the "Charge-It" program between bank customers and local merchants. Merchants could deposit sales slips into the bank and the bank billed the customer who used the card.

4. Risks faced by individuals

Individuals may also face credit risk in a direct form as depositors at banks or as investors/lenders. They may also face credit risk when entering into standard commercial transactions by providing a deposit to their counterparty, e. g. for a large purchase or a real estate rental. Employees of any firm also depend on the firm's ability to pay wages, and are exposed to the credit risk of their employer.

In some cases, governments recognize that an individual's capacity to evaluate credit risk may be limited, and the risk may reduce economic efficiency; governments may enact various legal measures or mechanisms with the intention of protecting individuals against some of these risks. Bank deposits, notably, are insured in many countries (to some maximum amount) for individuals, effectively limiting their credit risk to banks and increasing their willingness to use the banking system.

2.1.5   Credit Assessment   信用评估

In assessing credit risk from a single counterparty, a potential creditor must consider three issues.

(1) Default probability. What is the likelihood that the counterparty will default on its obligation either over the life of the obligation or over some specified horizon, such as a year? Calculated for a one-year horizon, this may be called the expected default frequency.

(2) Credit exposure. In the event of a default, how large will the outstanding obligation be when the default occurs?

(3) Recovery rate. In the event of a default, what fraction of the exposure may be recovered through bankruptcy proceedings or some other form of settlement?

When the credit quality of an obligation is talked about, this refers generally to the counterparty's ability to perform on that obligation. This encompasses both the obligation's default probability and anticipated recovery rate.

To place credit exposure and credit quality in perspective, recall that every risk comprise two elements: exposure and uncertainty. For credit risk, credit exposure represents the former, and credit quality represents the latter.

For loans to individuals or small businesses, credit quality is typically assessed through a process of credit scoring. Prior to providing credit, a bank or other lender will obtain information about the party requesting a loan. In the case of a bank issuing credit cards, this might include the party's annual income, existing debts, whether they rent or own a home, etc. A standard formula is applied to the information to produce a number, which is called a credit score. Based upon the credit score, the lending institution will decide whether or not to provide credit. The process is formulaic and highly standardized.

Many forms of credit risk — especially those associated with larger institutional counterparties — are complicated, unique or are of such a nature that it is worth assessing them in a less formulaic manner. The term credit analysis is used to describe any process for assessing the credit quality of such a counterparty. While the term can encompass credit scoring, it is more commonly used to refer to processes that entail human judgment. One or more people, called credit analysts, will review information about the counterparty. This might include its balance sheet, income statement, recent trends in its industry, the current economic environment, etc. They may also assess the exact nature of an obligation. For example, secured debt generally has higher credit quality than does subordinated debt of the same issuer. Based upon this analysis, the credit analysts assign the counterparty (or the specific obligation) a credit rating, which can be used by the lending institution to make credit decisions.

Many banks, investment managers and insurance companies hire their own credit analysts who prepare credit ratings for internal use. Other firms—including Standard & Poor's[13] and Moody's[14]— are in the business of developing credit ratings for use by investors or other third parties. Institutions that have publicly traded debt hire one or more of them to prepare credit ratings for their debt. Those credit ratings are then distributed for little or no charge to investors. Some regulators also develop credit ratings. In the United States, the National Association of Insurance Commissioners (NAIC) publishes credit ratings that are used for calculating capital charges for bond portfolios held by insurance companies.

The following exhibit indicates the system of credit ratings employed by Standard & Poor's.

(1) **AAA**: best credit quality—extremely reliable with regard to financial obligations.

(2) **AA**: very good credit quality—very reliable.

(3) **A**: more susceptible to economic conditions—still good credit quality.

(4) **BBB**: lowest rating in investment grade.

(5) **BB**: caution is necessary—best sub-investment credit quality.

(6) **B**: vulnerable to changes in economic conditions—currently showing the ability to meet its financial obligations.

(7) **CCC**: currently vulnerable to non-payment—dependent on favorable economic conditions.

(8) **CC**: highly vulnerable to a payment default.

(9) **C**: close to or already bankrupt—payment on the obligation currently continued.

(10) **D**: payment default on some financial obligation has actually occurred.

This is the system of credit ratings which Standard & Poor's applies to bonds. Ratings can be modified with + or – signs, so a AA – is a higher rating than is an A + rating. With such modifications, BBB – is the lowest investment grade rating. Other credit rating systems are similar.

The manner in which credit exposure is assessed is highly dependent on the nature of the obligation. If a bank has loaned money to a firm, the bank might calculate its credit exposure as the outstanding balance on the loan. Suppose instead that the bank has provided a line of credit to a firm, but none of the line has yet been drawn down. The immediate credit exposure is zero, but this doesn't reflect the fact that the firm has the right to draw on the line of credit. Indeed, if the firm gets into financial distress, it can be expected to draw down on the credit line prior to any bankruptcy. A simple solution is for the bank to consider its credit exposure to be equal to the total line of credit. However, this may overstate the credit exposure. Another approach would be to calculate the credit exposure as being some fraction of the total line of credit, with the fraction determined based upon an analysis of prior experience with similar credits.

Safeguard Your Credit

In addition to budgeting and using credit responsibly, the most important thing you can do to protect your credit is to keep your credit card information safe.

Be sure to notify creditors when you move or change your name. At a minimum, have your statements sent to an address where you know you will receive your mail. If you miss even one payment, it could lower your credit rating. And, be sure not to let your personal financial information falling into the wrong person's hands.

Financial institutions are making it easier to access and manage your account information online. Take advantage of these tools to monitor your information online and resolve potential problems before you receive your next account statement. Some institutions may offer e-mail alerts for a variety of account actions—profile changes, payment due dates, even alerts to advise you when you're close to reaching your credit limit.

Keep your personal information private when online. Look for a lock or key at the bottom left corner of your browser, a URL that begins with "https://", or the words "Secure Sockets Layer (SSL)". Don't provide your personal information to anyone calling or e-mailing you and claiming to be from your bank — respond using the contact information provided on your statement or the back of your credit card.

Report the loss or theft of your credit cards to the credit card issuers as soon as possible to void your lost card and receive a replacement card.

Credit risk modeling is a concept that broadly encompasses any algorithm-based methods of assessing credit risk. The term encompasses credit scoring, but it is more frequently used to describe the use of asset value models and intensity models in several contexts. These include supplanting traditional credit analysis; being used by financial engineers to value credit derivatives; and being extended as portfolio credit risk measures used to analyze the credit risk of entire portfolios of obligations to support securitization, risk management or regulatory purposes.

There are many ways that credit risk can be managed or mitigated. The first line of defense is the use of credit scoring or credit analysis to avoid extending credit to parties that entail excessive credit risk. Credit risk limits are widely used. These generally specify the maximum exposure a credit provider is willing to take to a counterparty. Industry limits or country limits may also be established to limit the sum of credit exposure a credit provider is willing to take to counterparties in a particular industry or country. Calculation of exposure under such limits requires some form of credit risk modeling. Transactions may be structured to include collateralization or various credit enhancements. Credit risks can be hedged with credit derivatives. Finally, firms can hold capital against outstanding credit exposures.

2.2 Interest and Interest Rate
利息与利率

2.2.1 A Brief Introduction to Interest and Interest Rate 利息与利率简介

1. The definition of interest & interest rate

Interest is the fee charged by a lender to a borrower for the use of borrowed money. The interest rate is often expressed as an annual percentage of the principal. It is calculated by dividing the amount of interest by the amount of principal. Interest rates often change as a result of inflation and monetary policies. For example, if a lender (such as a bank) charges a customer $90 in a year on a loan of $1,000, then the interest rate would be $90/1,000 \times 100\% = 9\%$.

2. The history of interest

Historically, charging interest was restricted by Jewish, Christian, Islam and other religions under laws of usury. This is still the case in the present Islam world, which mandates no-interest Islamic finance.

Usury (from the Medieval Latin *usuria*, "interest" or "excessive interest") was defined originally as charging a fee for the use of money. This usually meant interest on loans. After moderate-interest loans became an accepted part of the business world in the early modern age, the word has come to refer to the charging of unreasonable or relatively high rates of interest.

Usury (in the original sense of any interest) was denounced by a number of spiritual leaders and philosophers of ancient times, including Plato, Aristotle, Cato, Cicero, Plutarch, Aquinas, Moses, Philo and Gautama Buddha.

In the period from 1100 to 1500 AD, the church scholars differentiated between usury and interest, leading the shift in thought that labeled charging interest the same as theft. They made the first attempt at a science of economics and their main concern was usury; but this was not the same as just charging interest. It was generally not forbidden to earn interest if the lender was actually taking some risk, without a guaranteed gain. Interest could also be charged when the lender suffered some loss or passed up some opportunity by providing the loan. Usury was much more than charging interest — it was taking unfair advantage; it was an antisocial misuse of the money mechanism.

The pivotal change in the English-speaking world seems to have come with the legislative permission to charge interest on lent money: particularly the Act "In Restraint of Usury" of Henry VIII in England in 1545.

Later, in the modern age, the justification for charging interest evolved constantly in works promoting capitalism. The modern finance in which money and interest are the key factors, got furthest development in the advanced capitalist countries.

Reading Material

Credit Card Companies Sidestep Usury Laws

For hundreds of years, societies all over the world have protected borrowers by limiting interest rates charged by lenders. But in today's credit card market, American borrowers are on their own.

Less than half of all US states bother to cap credit card interest rates, and few credit card issuers are based in these states anyway. Most major credit card issuers are based in states without usury laws and without interest rate caps on credit cards. Banks and credit card issuers based in these states can charge any interest rate they wish — as long as the rate is listed in the cardholder agreement and the borrower agrees.

Thanks to a 1978 US Supreme Court decision, these the-sky's-the-limit rate policies dominate the credit card business. In Marquette vs. First Omaha Service Corp., the Supreme Court ruled that a national bank could charge the highest interest rate allowed in their home state to customers living anywhere in the United States, including states with restrictive interest caps. This means that the law in a lender's home state rules credit card interest rates no matter what kind of rate cap exists in a customer's state.

A funny thing happened after the Marquette ruling. Major credit card companies began relocating to states with liberal or no usury laws. New York-based powerhouse Citibank moved its credit card business to South Dakota in 1981. After that, many banks followed.

Therefore, to hang on to the credit card business, many other states loosened state usury limits. In the early 1980s, most states capped credit card interest rates between 12 percent and 18 percent. Today's caps are in the 18-percent to 24-percent range. Hawaii and the District of Columbia cap credit card interest rates at 24 percent, which isn't much of a cap at all.

One exception is the state of Arkansas. Arkansas' state constitution has kept a tight lid on interest rates for more than 125 years. Arkansas banks offer some of the lowest credit card rates in the country. "It's a wonderful thing for our consumers," says Todd Turner, a local consumer attorney. But all that may be changing, thanks to the Gramm-Leach-Bliley Financial Modernization Act, which the US Congress passed in 1999. The act allows state-chartered banks to charge interest rates equal to those charged by other banks operating in their state. "The banks are going to be increasing interest rates because they want to be able to offer the prevailing rate of their competitors," Turner says.

So, it seems that, there's no law stopping an issuer from charging you a super-high interest rate or an interest rate higher than you deserve.

Now the best advice may be to give up your credit card and begin to make payments by checks or general bank cards which can not be overdrawn. Do not give them chances to charge you usurious interest!

2.2.2　The Calculation of Interest　利息的计算

1. Time value of money

Supposing you have won a cash prize, and you have two payment options: (1) Receive $10,000 now; or (2) Receive $10,000 in three years. Which option would you choose?

If you're like most people, you would choose to receive the $10,000 now. After all, three years is a long time to wait. For most of us, taking the money in the present is just plain instinctive. So at the most basic level, the time value of money demonstrates that, all things being equal, it is better to have money now rather than later.

But why is this? A $100 bill has the same value as a $100 bill one year from now, doesn't it? Actually, although the bill is the same, you can do much more with the money if you have it now: over time you can earn more interest on your money.

Back to our example: by choosing option A and receiving $10,000 today, you are poised to increase the future value[15] of your money by investing and gaining interest over a period of time. For option B, you don't have time on your side, and the payment received in three years would be your future value and the present value[16] of the money would be less than $10,000. The timeline in Figure 2-1 illustrates this simply.

If you are choosing option A, your future value will be $10,000 plus any interest acquired over the three years. The future value for option B, on the other hand, would only be $10,000. It is necessary to find out how to calculate exactly how much more option A is worth, compared to option B.

The calculations of the future value and the present value depend on whether the interest is a simple or a compound interest[17].

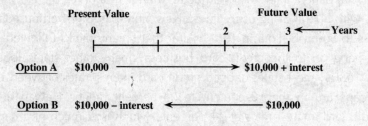

Figure 2-1 Time value of money

2. Simple interest

Simple interest is calculated on a principal sum, ignoring the interest on previously earned interest.

Still consider the above example, supposing the interest rate is a simple annual rate of 4.5%, then the future value of the amount of money under option A will be:

$$\$10,000 \times (1+3 \times 0.045) = \$11,350$$

Under option B, the present value will be:

$$\$10,000/(1+3 \times 0.045) = \$8,810.57$$

3. Compound interest

Compound interest is calculated not only on the initial principal but also the accumulated interest of prior periods. Nearly all economic calculations in practice involve compound interest.

Still the above example, but now the 4.5% is a compound interest rate. Then the future value of the amount of money under option A will be:

$$\$10,000 \times (1+0.045)^3 = \$11,411.66$$

The present value under option B will be:

$$\$ 10,000/(1+0.045)^3 = \$ 8,762.97$$

Here the formula to calculate present value is as follows:

$$PV = \frac{FV}{(1+r)^n}$$

This formula has four variables, each of which can be solved for: PV is the present value; FV is the future value; r is the rate at which the amount will be compounded each period; n is the number of periods.

The following formula is to calculate future value and it is similar and uses the same variables.

$$FV = PV \times (1+r)^n$$

2.2.3 The Structure of Interest Rates   利息的结构

So far we have discussed the interest rate as if there was only one single rate for all loans at any one time. However, it is known to all that this is not the truth. In fact, there are various interest rates in practice. Interest rates differ for many reasons as follows.

1. The risk involved

Loans to the government carry a lower rate of interest than equivalent loans to firms. This is because the risk of default is higher with the latter, and so borrowers have to compensate lenders for this. So, generally, the riskier the credit is, the higher the interest rate is.

2. The time period involved

In any loan transaction the lender is sacrificing liquidity. This means that he can not spend the money involved until the loan is repaid when its period expires. Therefore, the longer the loan period, the greater sacrifice the lender is making and the higher interest rate required.

3. The inflationary expectations

The interest rate is usually fixed in nominal terms, and its real value may therefore change if the price level changes. Let us take the following example to illustrate the consequences of this. A lends B $1,000 for one year, at an interest rate of 10%. This means that A will receive $1,100 repayment for the loan after a year. However, if the price level rises during the year, this sum would buy less than A thought it would when he agreed to provide the loan. Therefore, if A expected the price level to rise he would raise the interest rate, to protect the purchasing power of his money. We can witness this principle at work in the economy in general, with interest rates drifting upward if inflation is expected to increase.

4. The differential charged by financial institutions

A variety of financial institutions exist to bring borrowers and lenders together. For example, some banks may pay savers interest to absorb saving money, and in turn lend the money to borrowers. The interest rate which banks require borrowers to pay is higher then that banks pay to savers so that the banks can make profit. The differential between the two rates varies from market to market, and is likely to be affected by the degree of competition among financial institutions.

2.2.4 The Types of Interest Rate 利率的类型

1. Fixed interest rate & floating interest rate[18]

Fixed interest rates refer to those rates unchangeable over the life of the loan while those changeable are known as floating interest rates, or variable rates, adjustable rates.

2. Nominal interest rate & real interest rate[19]

The effect of inflation is not taken into account when deciding nominal interest rates. But real rates attempt to measure the value of the interest in units of stable purchasing power.

3. Benchmark interest rates & general interest rate[20]

Benchmark interest rate, also called base interest rate on which the other interest rates in the market are based, is the minimum interest rate investors will accept for investing in a nongovernmental security. In general, this is the yield that is being earned on the most recent on-the-run governmental security of similar maturity plus a premium. General interest rates refer to the general rates existing in the market.

4. Short-term interest rate & long-term interest rate[21]

The rate for the credit within a lifetime under a year is a short-term interest rate while over a year is a long-term interest rate.

5. Official interest rate, public interest rate & market interest rate[22]

Official interest rates, also referred to as legal interest rates, are decided by monetary authority such as the central bank or other equivalent governmental department, and public interest rates are concluded by some nongovernmental financial organization (e.g. banker's association) while market interest rates are of course set by the market itself.

2.2.5 The Determination of Interest Rate 利率的决定

The Loanable Funds Theory of Interest Rates, as an integral part of the classical tradition in nineteenth century economics, presented a model about the determination of interest rate which is shown in Figure 2 - 2. According to the model, in a competitive market, there will be the equilibrium interest rate when the demand for loanable funds equals the supply of loanable funds.

A change in either the demand or supply curves would lead to a change in the equilibrium interest rate. A rise in demand for loanable funds would shift the demand curve rightward, resulting in a higher interest rate. Similarly, a rise in the level of savings would shift the supply curve rightward, this time leading to a lower interest rate.

An alternative approach to the determination of interest rate was brought forward in the 1930s by Keynes. He stressed the fact that the interest rate was a monetary phenomenon, and that conditions in the money markets are likely to be major influence. The Keynes Theory has been stated in the Chapter 1.

However, different economists put forward different theories for determination of interest rate and every theory seems to make sense to some extent. Take a comprehensive look at these theories, it can be said that, the determinants of interest rate include the economic cycles, inflation, tax, the demand for and supply of capital, monetary and fiscal policy, foreign exchange rate, etc.

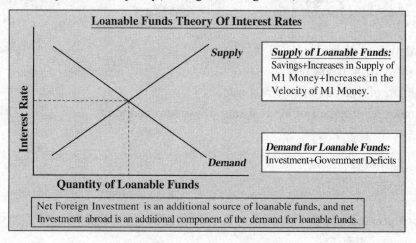

Figure 2 – 2   Equilibrium interest rate

2.2.6 The functions of Interest Rates   利率的作用

Interest rate, as one of the key levers in modern economy, performs great important functions on both macro and micro economy.

1. The functions of interest rates on macro economy

Interest rates have direct impact on savings and yields, and consequently regulate the supply of capital in the economy. For example, higher interest rates could attract more savings for banks and thus the banks have more capital to lend, thereby the total supply of capital will increase. Interest rates also affect the investment. For example, higher interest rates could increase the cost of investment for firms and compel them to reduce investment, and thereby the total investment in the economy will decrease; different interest rates for different industry could adjust the structure of investment. The changes in aggregate savings and investments will consequently result in changes in the aggregate supply and demand in the economy.

2. The functions of interest rates on micro economy

As far as individual company is concerned, interest rates could impact on the cost of and income from production, and thus push the company to promote management skills in order to maximize profit. As for individual consumer, interest rates may change his/her consuming expenditure and other economic behavior. For example, supposed that an individual consumer who has a stable annual salary income of $40,000, deposited $100,000 in bank for 5 years with an interest rate of 10%. Then he will have a total annual income of $50,000 during the 5 years. Such an annual income enables him to afford a tourist trip abroad every year. However, after 5 years, if the interest rate falls to 5%, his total annual income will decrease to $45,000 if he still choose to reserve his deposit in bank for 5 years. And this may make him turn to tour within domestic country for his yearly vacation. Again, another 5 years later, if the interest rate for 5 years' saving falls to 2% while the interest rate of 5 years' government bond is 5%, this man in question will probably draw his reserve money out of bank and use the money to buy the government bond.

Group Discussion

1. Talk about the nature of credit.
2. Discuss how to manage credit risks.
3. Tell the definition of interest and interest rate.
4. Discuss the major determinant of interest rate in modern economy.

NOTES

1	sale on open account	赊销
2	consumer credit	消费信贷
3	commercial credit	商业信贷
4	credit sale	赊销，先售后付交易
5	installment credit	分期还款信贷
6	hire purchase (HP)	分期付款购买
7	mortgage	抵押，抵押贷款
8	secured loan	担保贷款
9	second mortgage (remortgage)	二次抵押，再抵押
10	unsecured loan	无担保贷款
11	pawnbroking	典当
12	credit card	信用卡
13	Standard & Poor's	标准普尔公司
14	Moody's	穆迪投资服务公司
15	future value	终值
16	present value	现值
17	simple interest	单利；compound interest　复利
18	fixed interest rate	固定利率；floating interest rate　浮动利率
19	nominal interest rate	名义利率；real interest rate　实际利率
20	benchmark interest rate	基准利率；general interest rate　一般利率
21	short-term interest rate	短期利率；long-term interest rate　长期利率
22	official interest rate	官方利率；public interest rate　公定利率；market interest rate　市场利率

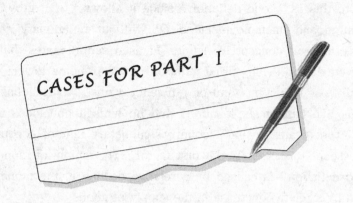

Good Deflation or Bad Deflation?
好的通货紧缩还是坏的通货紧缩？

What Is Deflation?

The Glossary of Economics Terms defines deflation as occurring "when prices are declining over time. This is the opposite of inflation; when the inflation rate (by some measure) is negative, the economy is in a deflationary period."

Deflation can occur because of a combination of four factors: The supply of money goes down; The supply of other goods goes up; Demand for money goes up; Demand for other goods goes down.

Deflation generally occurs when the supply of goods rises faster than the supply of money, which is consistent with these four factors. These factors explain why the prices of some goods increase over time while others decline. Personal computers have sharply dropped in price over the last fifteen years. This is because technological improvements have allowed the supply of computers to increase at a much faster rate than demand or the supply of money. So the suggestion to increase the money supply, if we're worried about deflation, is a good one, as it follows the four factors above.

Before we decide that the money authority should increase the money supply, we have to determine how much of a problem deflation really is and how it can influence the money supply. First let us look at the problems caused by deflation.

Why Is Deflation Bad?

Most economists agree that deflation is both a disease and a symptom of other problems in the economy. Luskin at Capitalism Magazine examines James Paulsen's differentiation of "good deflation" and "bad deflation". Paulsen's definitions are clearly looking at deflation as a symptom of other changes in the economy. He describes "good deflation" as occurring when businesses are "able to constantly produce goods at lower and lower prices due to cost-cutting initiatives and efficiency gains". This is simply the second factor "The supply of other goods goes up" on the above list of the four factors which cause deflation.

Paulsen refers to this as "good deflation" since it allows "GDP growth to remain strong, profit growth to surge and unemployment to fall without inflationary consequence". "Bad deflation" is a more difficult concept to define. Paulsen simply states that "bad deflation has emerged because even though selling price inflation is still trending lower, corporations can no longer keep up with cost reductions and/or efficiency gains". Luskin has difficulty with that answer, as it seems like half an explanation, and he himself concludes that bad deflation is actually caused by "the revaluation of a country's monetary unit of account by that country's central bank". In essence this is really the first factor "The supply of money goes down" from above list. So "bad deflation" is caused by a relative decline in the money supply and "good deflation" is caused by a relative increase in the supply of goods.

These definitions are inherently flawed because deflation is caused by relative changes. If the supply of goods in a year increases by 10% and the supply of money in that year increases by 2%, which are causing deflation, is this "good deflation" or "bad deflation"? Since the supply of goods has increased, we have "good deflation", but since the central bank hasn't increased the money supply fast enough we should also have "bad deflation". Asking whether "goods" or "money" caused deflation is like asking "When you clap your hands, is the left hand or the right hand responsible for the sound?" Saying that "goods grew too fast" or "money grew too slowly" is inherently saying the same thing since we're comparing goods to money, so "good deflation" and "bad deflation" are terms that probably should be retired.

Looking at deflation as a disease tends to get more agreement among economists. Luskin says that the true problem with deflation is that it causes problems in business relationships: "If you are a borrower, you are contractually committed to making loan repayments that represent more and more purchasing power — while at the same time the asset you bought with the loan to begin with is declining in nominal price. If you are a lender, chances are that your borrower will default on your loan to him under such conditions."

Curing Deflation by Printing Money

We finally get to the original question: "Is the problem that there is more to printing money than printing money? Is in fact the way printed money gets into circulation, that the central bank buys bonds, and thus gets money into the economy?" That's precisely what happens. The money the central bank gets to buy government securities has to come from somewhere. Generally it is just created in order for the central bank to carry out its open market operations. So in most instances, when economists talk about "printing more money" and "the central bank lowering interest rates", they're talking about the same thing. If interest rates are already zero, as in Japan, there is little room to lower them further, so using this policy to fight deflation will not work well. Fortunately interest rates in the US have not yet reached the lows of those in Japan.

The Quirky Nature of Credit
信用的诡异本质

One notable change in the fabric of American finance that is particularly striking over the years is the proliferation of credit and the growth of nonbank financing. The primary creditors of the nation's debtors are not banks, but are so-called nontraditional lenders—such as GE Capital, the financial services arm of General Electric (which, interestingly enough, provides 40 percent of GE's total earnings. And you thought GE made money by selling stuff!).

This was highlighted in a recent piece of Wall Street Journal, where it was pointed out that GE Capital's total assets of $425 billion exceed all but three banking conglomerates. According to the article, banks and thrifts contribute a proportionately smaller share of financing to the nation's credit market today compared to years past. The Journal comments, "Twenty years ago, banks and thrifts supplied 40 percent of the nation's credit. Ten years ago, it was 26 percent. Today, it is down to 19 percent."

Credit and finance have become the business of America, no longer dominated by banks, thrifts, and their ilk. The Wall Street Journal notes that approximately 40 percent of the earnings from the companies in the S&P 500 came from lending or other financial activities. Many retailers issue credit cards through banks that they own.

Consequently, the question arises as to what the consequences of such a trend might be, particularly given the quirky nature of credit, soaked as it is in a paper-based monetary system.

The Wall Street Journal reporter writes, "The benefits of this change in the financial underpinning of the economy were evident during the recession. As banks tightened lending standards, alternative lending and capital markets took up the slack."

He points to the well-publicized zero-percent-financing offers by auto manufacturers and to companies like Boeing Capital, which lent UAL $700 million to buy planes when the capital markets shunned them. The old guard of easy credit also helped grease the axles, as Fannie Mae's and Freddie Mac's assets have risen 21 percent and 35 percent, respectively, since the end of 2000. These two behemoths alone hold as much mortgage debt as all commercial banks combined. Bank assets, in contrast, rose "just 8 percent", the reporter ruefully tells readers.

So here, the unwritten assumption is that keeping the spigot of credit open is better than the alternative. Credit is the fuel that feeds spending, and spending, so the conventional thinking goes, is the key to economic growth. The more companies offering credit, the more readily available it becomes, making everybody better off. Easy credit means easy money, ergo prosperity.

For Every Creditor There Is a Debtor

One has to wonder if more credit is a good thing. After all, every dollar provided in credit creates a corresponding liability or debt. In theory, at least, debts must be repaid. The risks of debt and leverage become muted under the sunny optimism of boom-time economics. However, the realities of leverage do not change because they are ignored; like the fundamental forces of nature, suspension of belief does not diminish their power. Leverage in finance is similarly unrelenting.

The economist Benjamin Anderson explained the Great Depression in terms of a great excess of credit. He called cheap money the "most dangerous intoxicant known to economic life".

"Artificially cheap money," Anderson wrote, ". . . created a vast fabric of debt, internal and international. As the volume of this debt grew, its quality greatly deteriorated." He noted that "the period 1931 to March 1933 saw the progressive collapse of the unsound portions of this vast fabric of debt."

To take on a lot of debt is to exhibit a great deal of confidence about what lies ahead and in your ability to pay it back. It is also a matter of belief on behalf of the creditor. Debt, in essence, is a bet on a rosy future.

Since no one can predict the future, it is safe to say that no one can borrow infinitely, either, for the simple reason that there will be a limit to what a consumer—or business, or government—can borrow and yet still remain solvent. It is sort of a natural law of credit that as the volume of credit expands to more and more debtors, the quality of such credits deteriorate. Not everyone is creditworthy, and as the pool of credit widens, the fringes are shallower than the deeper center in terms of financial resources.

As Greenspan talks positively about the health of the US banking system, one also has to wonder whether a strong banking system matters, given its diminished role in providing credit. Consensus opinion holds that the Fed has some control over the money supply through its traditional means of manipulating bank reserves and interest rates. How much of that is cast into doubt, since non-banks are doing the bulk of the lending?

To his credit, the Journal reporter also notes that all this credit has a downside. Steve Galbraith, an investment strategist with Morgan Stanley, is quoted as saying, "Banks are not the place to be looking for the next blowup . . . because of the greater importance of these nonbank financial companies, odds are you'll get a hiccup in this area."

Which begs the question: What would the impact be if a GE Capital or Fannie Mae started to have financial difficulties? Would the effect be as deleterious as a failing banking behemoth? And would the Feds bail them out, too? In the span of less than a year, the government has, in one way or another, "saved" airlines, domestic steel manufacturers, domestic lumber producers, and, most recently, American farmers. How likely is it that the government will be able to resist saving Fannie Mae?

Some ones will advocate increased regulation of these non-banks to conform with, or exceed, existing banking standards. But these are superficial remedies for a problem that lies much deeper. We've had banking regulations and numerous supervising bodies for a long time, and that has not stopped financial crises from developing. The problem is the money itself.

The Satanism of Money and Credit

The quirky nature of credit is that it is not necessarily better in abundance. It's not like beer, butter, and bananas — where more means cheaper, and cheaper is good. Credit is like money; it represents buying power. Garet Garret called money's paradoxical quality the "Satanism of money". When it is plentiful enough, it is not worth enough, but when it is worth enough, it is not plentiful enough. The same sort of thinking applies to credit. More credit means more buying power, which means a bidding up of assets and a spark for an unsustainable boom.

Murray Rothbard wrote that "credit expansion always generates the business cycle process, even when other tendencies cloak its workings". Many economists and commentators point to the relatively low inflation rate during the boom years and the low-interest-rate environment of those years. "But prices may not rise because of some counteracting force," Rothbard notes. Indeed, productivity growth, an increase in the supply of goods, and an increase in the demand for dollars can absorb the increase in money, temporarily masking its inflationary effect.

The great merit of gold as money lies in the fact that the quantity of gold is limited by nature and by the amount of human energy and capital dedicated to mining it. As a result, gold holds its value. Wilhelm Ropke once wrote, "In the course of the centuries, no wager has been more of a certainty than that a piece of gold, inaccessible to the inflationary policies of governments, would keep its purchasing power better than a paper note." Gold acts as a natural limit to money, and for that it will always be the enemy of inflationists and governments.

The flaw in today's financial system is that these limits do not exist. Doug Noland, writing for PrudentBear. com, observed that the "... character of money and the contemporary credit-based system's ability to create uncontrolled quantities is a crucial ingredient in precarious financial excess." According to Noland, "the explosion of nonbank entities easily explains the relatively slow growth of bank assets in the midst of historic credit excess."

The fact is that you can't look just at banks or the Fed anymore. There are many more purveyors of credit than banks.

The state of American credit is already weakening. There are only eight AAA-rated companies left in America till 2002 (General Electric, UPS, AIG, ExxonMobil, Johnson & Johnson, Berkshire-Hathaway, Pfizer, and Merck), compared to 27 in 1990 and 58 in 1979. The first quarter of 2002 was one of the worst quarters on record for corporate bonds. Some 47 issuers defaulted on their debts, for a total of $34 billion in bad debt.

Personal bankruptcies are at record highs. More consumers filed for bankruptcy in 2001 than in any other year. Savings are low, and an increasing percentage of disposable income is being used to service debt.

Of course, these concerns also extend to government — the worst offender of all. The US government cannot control its appetite for spending on numerous various affairs around the globe, and year after year, it spends more than it takes in, going ever deeper into debt. Although the administration's alleges that the budget was balanced each year, government borrowing continues to reach new highs with each passing year.

As the Wall Street Journal reported, in March of 2002, total federal debt stood at $5.924 trillion, and the Bush administration was seeking to raise the limit to $6.7 trillion. As Representative Ron Paul observed, "the federal budget is essentially a credit card with no spending limit, billed to somebody else." Moreover, as Paul observes, politicians come and go, but "the benefits of deficit spending are enjoyed immediately by the politicians, who trade pork for votes and enjoy adulation for promising to cure every social ill."

The only solution to these problems—the explosion of credit and debt, the gradual destruction of the currency—is to wrest control of money from government hands and back into the market. Let the market decide what should be money. For centuries, gold was the money of choice, and there is a growing suspicion that it will be again.

The Interest Rates in Euro Area
欧元区利率

The charging of interest for lending money has not always been an acceptable practice. "Usury" is specifically condemned in both the Bible and in Shari'ah law, and modern Islamic banks still operate without interest.

In modern financial markets, however, the distinctions between interest, rent, profit and capital appreciation are not clear-cut. The current hotly-debated proposal on the taxation of interest within the EU has illustrated the difficulty of reaching legally precise definitions. In economic theory, interest is the price paid for inducing those with money to save it rather than spend it, and to invest in long-term assets rather than hold cash. Rates reflect the interaction between the supply of savings and the demand for capital; or between the demand for and the supply of money.

Interest rate can be expressed as a percentage payable (a "coupon"), usually per annum; or as the present "discounted" value of a sum payable at some future date (the date of "maturity"). There is an inverse relationship between the prevailing rate of interest at any one time, and the discounted value at that time of assets paying interest: i. e. bond prices fall when yields increase.

An important distinction must be made between "nominal" and "real" interest rates. A real rate of interest is the nominal — i. e. "coupon" — rate, less the rate at which money is losing its value. Calculating real rates, however, presents methodological problems, since there are significantly different ways of calculating rates of inflation.

Inflationary expectations, however, are one of the most important determinants of interest rates. Broadly, savers demand a real return from their investments. Changes in the forecasts of future inflation are therefore reflected in the current prices of assets.

Interest rates also reflect varying degrees of risk. A body with a rock-solid credit-rating, like the European Investment Bank, will be able to attract savings at a very much lower level of interest rates than corporate issuers of "junk bonds". Countries with high levels of existing debt may have to pay higher rates on government borrowing than countries where the risk of default is less. Indeed, the guarantee that "sovereign debt" will be repaid on maturity has frequently allowed governments to borrow at negative real rates.

Within any economy there will therefore be a multiplicity of interest rates, reflecting varying expectations and risks. The markets for different assets — physical and financial — will influence each other as savers shift their portfolios between cash, interest-bearing securities, equity in firms, complex derivatives, real estate, antiques, etc. Financial institutions and large corporations will behave differently from small savers and small businesses.

Experience in the Euro Area

Nominal interest rates in the countries of the euro area have been falling steadily since 1994, and in mid-1999 stood at historically low levels. This has enabled countries like Italy to cut dramatically the cost of servicing public debt. It has not, on the other hand, necessarily been the case with real interest rates which, in Germany during early 1999, were probably higher than nominal.

Euro area monetary policy effectively began on 3 December, 1998, when there was a coordinated reduction of key lending rates to 3% by the central banks of the participating countries. When the ESCB (European System of Central Banks) officially became responsible, this rate was confirmed "for the foreseeable future".

In the early months of 1999, however, a sizeable slowdown in economic growth, and persistently high levels of unemployment, led to growing political pressure for an interest rate reduction.

At the beginning of April in 1999 the key rate was indeed cut to 2.5%. Although M3 was growing at above target rate, inflationary pressures remained very low; but ECB (European Central Bank) President Wim Duisenberg made it clear at the time that "this is it!"

As the year progressed attention began to shift to the external value of euro. By early summer in 1999, it looked like falling to parity with the US dollar, and the euro was widely described as "weak". But when it came to July the exchange rate began to recover, and signs of higher economic growth appeared. Between July and September M3 also grew at nearly 6%, causing the ECB to talk of a "tightening bias" in monetary policy. On 4 November in that year the key interest rate rose again to 3%.

The evidence so far is that the ESCB has entirely carried out its mandate. Current inflation is well below the 2% "price stability" definition. More important, inflationary expectations, as indicated by bond yields, also remain low, while economic growth is picking up, and unemployment is falling.

There remain, however, some question marks over the utility of the 4.5% M3 reference level; over the degree to which financial markets have yet integrated; and over policy towards the external value of euro.

Conclusions

The globalization of the world's financial markets is increasing the pressure of external factors in the determination of domestic monetary policies. In addition, though the approaches of the world's major central banks towards the conduct of monetary policy differ in detail, there is broad agreement on fundamentals: the pursuit of price stability and the stability of financial markets. This is leading to the coincidence, of not the coordination, of central-bank-determined interest rate changes.

For the same reasons, real long-term interest rates are likely to converge on an international norm, the level of which will be determined by a complex interaction of both monetary and real factors, and in particular by the pace of technological advance.

PART II

Financial Institutions
金融机构

Chapter **3**

Banking Financial Institutions

银行类金融机构

Learning Objectives

- ✔ To understand the definition of bank
- ✔ To learn the basics about the central bank
- ✔ To understand the nature and operations of commercial banks
- ✔ To understand the creation of money
- ✔ To know about the specialized banks
- ✔ To know about the banking system in China

 Opening Vignette

How Banks Work

A bank is an institution that deals in money and its substitutes and provides other financial services. Banks accept deposits and make loans and derive a profit from the difference in the interest rates paid and charged, respectively.

Banks are critical to our economy. The primary function of banks is to put their account holders' money to use by lending it out to others who can then use it to buy houses, businesses, send kids to college ...

When you deposit your money in the bank, your money goes into a big pool of money along with everyone else's, and your account is credited with the amount of your deposit. When you write checks or make withdrawals, that amount is deducted from your account balance. Interest you earn on your balance is also added to your account.

Banks create money in the economy by making loans. The amount of money that banks can lend is directly affected by the reserve requirement set by the Federal Reserve (Fed). The reserve requirement is currently 3%–10% of a bank's total deposits. This amount can be held either in cash on hand or in the bank's reserve account with the Federal Reserve. To see how this affects the economy, consider the following example. When a bank gets a deposit of $100, assuming a reserve requirement of 10%, the bank can then lend out $90. That $90 goes back into the economy, purchasing goods or services, and usually ends up deposited in another bank. That bank can then lend out $81 of that $90 deposit, and that $81 goes into the economy to purchase goods or services and ultimately is deposited into another bank that proceeds to lend out a percentage of it.

In this way, money grows and flows throughout the community in a much greater amount than physically exists. That $100 makes a much larger ripple in the economy than you may realize.

Banking is all about trust (credit). We trust that the bank will have our money for us when we go to get it. We trust that it will honor the checks we write to pay our bills. The thing that's hard to grasp is the fact that while people are putting money into the bank every day, the bank is lending that same money and more to other people every day. Banks consistently extend more credit than the cash they have. That's a little scary; but if you go to the bank and demand your money, you'll get it. However, if everyone goes to the bank at the same time and demands their money (a run on the bank), there might be a serious problem.

Even though the Fed requires that banks keep a certain percentage of their money in reserve, if everyone came to withdraw their money at the same time, there wouldn't be enough. In the event of a bank failure, your money is protected as long as the bank is insured by the Federal Deposit Insurance Corporation (FDIC). The key to the success of banking, however, still lies in the confidence that consumers have in the bank's ability to grow and protect their money. Because banks rely so heavily on consumer trust, and trust depends on the perception of integrity, the banking industry is highly regulated by the government.

Banks are just like other businesses and sell their products for profit. Their products just happen to be money. Other businesses sell widgets or services; banks sell money — in the form of loans, notes and other financial products. They make money on the interest they charge on loans because that interest is higher than the interest they pay to their depositors.

The interest rate a bank charges its borrowers depends on both the number of people who want to borrow and the amount of money the bank has available to lend. As we mentioned in the previous section, the amount available to lend also depends upon the reserve requirement the Fed has set. At the same time, it may also be affected by the funds rate, which is the interest rate that banks charge each other for short-term loans to meet their reserve requirements.

Loaning money is also inherently risky. A bank never really knows if it'll get that money back. Therefore, the riskier the loan is, the higher the interest rate the bank charges. While paying interest may not seem to be a great financial move in some respects, it really is a small price to pay for using someone else's money. Imagine having to save all of the money you needed in order to buy a house. We wouldn't be able to buy houses until we retired!

Banks also charge fees for services like checking, ATM access and others. Loans have their own set of fees that go along with them. Another source of income for banks is investments and securities.

Warm-up Questions

1. What do you think the bank is?
2. How does a bank make money?
3. What are the differences between the bank and other business?

3.1　An Overview of Banking Financial Institutions
银行类金融机构概述

In financial business, a financial institution acts as an agent that provides financial services for its clients. Financial institutions fall under financial regulation from a government authority.

Financial institutions play an important role in the financial system of an economy. Generally speaking, they carry out three main functions. The first function is aggregation. Typically individuals save in relatively small amounts. It is the task of the financial institution to pool such small amounts together (the surplus) and to lend larger sums to those in deficit. The second is maturity transformation. In the case of the banks a large percentage of depositors' funds are on current account (technically repayable on demand) and most other deposits are relatively short term; whereas bank lending is often of longer duration. The third is risk transformation. A loan to the best of friends or the most reliable person can go wrong. However, financial institutions are experts at making loans and by spreading their activities they reduce the level of risk considerably.

In normal cases, the financial institutions are divided into two groups: banking financial institutions and nonbank financial institutions. The banking institutions, which mostly consist of various banks, are generally regarded as the base of the financial system.

It is common knowledge that a bank is a commercial or state institution that provides financial services, including issuing money in form of coins or paper notes, receiving deposits of money, lending money and processing transactions. A commercial bank (CB) accepts deposits from customers and in turn makes loans based on those deposits. Some banks (called banks of issue) issue banknotes as legal tender. Many banks offer ancillary financial services to make additional profit; for most banks also rent safe deposit boxes in their branches. Most banks are profit-making, private enterprises. However, some are owned by government, or are non-profit.

Reading Material

Global Banking

In the 1970s, a number of smaller crashes tied to the policies put in place following the depression, resulted in deregulation and privatization of government-owned enterprises in the

1980s, indicating that governments of industrial countries around the world found private-sector solutions to problems of economic growth and development preferable to state-operated programs. This spurred a trend that was already prevalent in the business sector, large corporations become to operate globally and dealing with customers, suppliers, manufacturing and information centers all over the world.

Global banking and capital market services proliferated during the 1980 – 1990s as a result of a great increase in demand from companies, governments, and financial institutions, but also because financial market conditions were buoyant and, on the whole, bullish. Interest rates in the United States declined from about 15% for two-year US Treasury notes to about 5% during the 20-year period, and financial assets grew then at a rate approximately twice the rate of the world economy. Such growth rate would have been lower, in the last twenty years, were it not for the profound effects of the internationalization of financial markets especially foreign investments in the US, particularly from Japan, who not only provided the funds to the US corporations, but also helped finance the federal government; thus, transforming the US stock market by far into the largest one in the world.

3.2 The Central Bank
中央银行

3.2.1 A Brief Introduction to the Central Bank 中央银行简介

1. What is a central bank

The central bank, also known as monetary authority or reserve bank, is an entity responsible for the monetary policy of its country or of a group of member states, such as the Federal Reserve System (Fed)[1] i n the United States or the European Central Bank (ECB) in the European Union. Central banks authorized by the government of the country. Its primary responsibility is to maintain the stability of the national currency and money supply, but more active duties include controlling subsidized loan interest rates and acting as a lender of last resort to the banking sector during times of financial crisis. Central banks may also have supervisory powers, to ensure that banks and other financial institutions do not behave fraudulently or recklessly. The central bank also is an indispensable part of the financial system, and is a bridge between the public sector (to which it belongs) and the private sector.

In some countries, the central bank is owed by the state. In other countries, it is a privately owned joint stock company which issues its own notes, subject to certainly legal restrictions. In either case, its function is to control the volume of credit by raising or lowering its rate of discount and by buying or selling securities on the market. Meanwhile, central banks undertake the negotiation of international monetary agreements.

Nearly every country around the world, and certainly every industrial nation, has a central bank, such as the Bank of Japan, the Reserve Bank of Australia. Commonly, basic models of central bank can be classified as the European type and the Federal Reserve type. The characters of European type are highly centralized and operating under the governor; the characters of Federal Reserve type are featuring detailed statute, decentralization of operations and policy making.

2. The history of the central bank

In Europe, prior to the 17th century most money was commodity money, typically silver or gold. Promises to pay, however, were widely circulated and accepted as value at least five hundred years earlier in both Asia and Europe. Probably, the medieval European Knights Templar ran the best known early prototype of a central banking system, as their promises to pay were widely regarded, and many regard their activities as having laid the basis for the modern banking system. At about the same time, Kublai Khan introduced fiat currency to China, which was imposed by force by the confiscation of specie.

Generally speaking, the oldest central bank in the world is the Riksbank, which was opened in 1668 with help from Dutch businessmen. This was followed by the Bank of England, created by Scottish businessman William Paterson in the City of London. The Bank of England is the first modern central bank, serving as the model for many others, such as the Bank of France, the Bank of Japan, as well as the US Federal Reserve. In some sense, the history of Bank of England represents the evolution of modern central banking policies. The Bank of England was established as a private bank in 1694 but by the mid-19th century had become largely an agency of the government. In 1946 the UK government nationalized the Bank of England. The Bank of France was established as a governmental institution by Napoleon in 1800. Then, on December 23, 1913, in the United States, the 12 Federal Reserve banks, together with the Board of Governors in Washington, D. C., constitute the Federal Reserve System, which was created by the US Congress through the passing of the Glass-Owen Bill, signed by President Woodrow.

3.2.2   The Nature of the Central Bank   中央银行的性质

1. Independence

In most countries the central bank is state-owned and has a minimal degree of autonomy, which allows for the possibility of government intervening in monetary policy. The term "independence" is usually defined as the central bank operational and managerial independence from the government. An "independent central bank" is one which operates under rules designed to prevent political interference; In addition, an independent central bank can run a more credible monetary policy, making market expectations more responsive to signals from the central bank. As we know, international organizations such as the World Bank, the International Monetary Fund (IMF) and the Bank for International Settlements (BIS)[2] are strong supporters of central bank independence. A good example is that, recently, both the European Central Bank and the Bank of England (1997) have been made independent and follow a set of published inflation goals so that markets know what to expect.

2. Difference between commercial bank and central bank

Central banks are non-commercial bodies. Compared with the commercial banks, there are several differences between them. These differences also reflect the central bank's nature in a way. In short, these differences include: a central bank's capital is owned by the state; second, a central bank does not accept ordinary commercial business - private or corporate; third, a central bank is not motivated by profit in the usual sense; fourth, a central bank's functions are altogether different from those of the commercial banks.

3.2.3   The Functions of the Central Bank   中央银行的职能

1. Issuing bank

Most of the central banks in the present world are responsible for the note issue. They print and issue banknotes which are ordained legal tenders by law in their countries. Although at one time the note issue was backed by gold, today, almost in every country and region, the whole of the issue is fiduciary. That is, not backed by gold.

2. Banker to the banks

In this category, the central bank's functions may be summarized as follows:

(1) Provision of notes and coins as required.

(2) All authorized institutions are required to keep a certain percentage of their eligible with the central bank as non-interest bearing deposits.

(3) Lender of last resort, that is, when there is a shortage of funds in the money market, central banks will normally give assistance to the financial institution. For most of the mature financial centers in the world, discount window facilities are made available by the central bank.

(4) Consultation and advice.

(5) Settlement of clearing house[3] indebtedness.

3. Banker to the government

As a banker to the government, the central bank is involved in some highly specialized operations as follows:

(1) Maintaining the central government accounts and those of government departments.

(2) Providing the temporary "ways and means" advances.

(3) Putting forward advice on a range of banking and related matters.

(4) Managing the government borrowing by means of the issues of treasure bills and gilt-edged stocks.

(5) Acting as the banker to overseas central banks and international organizations. In the world, most of the central banks work co-operates with a number of international bodies, such as the IMF, the World Bank and the Bank for international Settlements. In this connection, the central bank has the following functions: maintenance of working balances for the settlement of inter-government and trade indebtedness; settlement of their foreign exchange operations; management of their gilt-edged stocks and other funds; promotion of stability in international affairs.

(6) Other external functions of central bank. Many of the external functions of central bank are linked with government. The central bank's functions under this heading comprise: first, management of the exchange equalization account; this account holds the nation's gold and foreign currency reserves, the ultimate means of settling our international indebtedness; second, management of the exchange rate of a country; third, exchange control; exchange controls may be imposed to limit the flow of funds both into and out of a country, and so influence exchange rates. They may be applied to both current and capital movements.

3.2.4　The Central Bank in China　中国的中央银行

1. The evolution of the People's Bank of China

The People's Bank of China (PBC) is the central bank of the People's Republic of China. It is commonly known as the leading body of the Chinese banking system which includes state commercial banks and other banking institutions. Its branches can be found in the cities in China.

The People's Bank of China was established on December 1, 1948. Between 1949 and 1978 the People's Bank of China was the only bank in the People's Republic of China and was responsible for both central banking and commercial banking operations. In 1983, the commercial banking functions of the People's Bank of China were split off into four independent but state-owned banks. And the State Council promulgated that the People's Bank of China would function as the central bank of China. The Law of the People's Republic of China on the People's Bank of China passed by the Third Plenum of the Eighth National People's Congress on March 18, 1995 legally confirmed the People's Bank of China's central bank status.

2. The functions of the People's Bank of China

The entire capital of the People's Bank of China is contributed and owned by the state. Similar to other countries' central banks, the PBC is the bank of issue, the bank of bank and the state's bank. The People's Bank of China shall formulate and implement monetary policies, prevent and resolve financial risks and safeguard financial stability.

As stipulated in the People's Bank of China Law of the People's Republic of China, the People's Bank of China's functions are to:

- promulgate and implement the orders, rules and regulations that are related to its duties;
- formulate and implement monetary policies in accordance with the law;
- issue Renminbi and administer the circulation of Renminbi;
- hold, administer and operate the State's reserves of foreign exchange and gold;
- manage the national treasury;
- issue and honor treasury bonds and other government bonds for various financial institutions and organizations;
- open accounts for financial institutions in the banking industry according to needs;
- organize or assist in organizing a system for clearing among financial institutions in the banking industry;
- formulate the rules for payment and settlement in conjunction with the banking regulatory authority of the State Council;
- determine the amount, term, interest rate and method of lending to commercial banks according to the needs to implement monetary policies;
- regulate the gold market;
- safeguard the normal operation of the payment and clearing systems;
- regulate the inter-bank loans market and inter-bank bond market;
- implement foreign exchange control and regulate the inter-bank foreign exchange market;
- be responsible for carrying out surveys, statistics, analysis and forecasts of the financial industry;

- guide and plan the work of anti-money-laundering[4] in the financial industry and be responsible for monitoring the capital in anti-money laundering;
- engage in relevant international financial activities in the capacity of the central bank of the State;
- and other duties as prescribed by the State Council.

3.2.5 The Federal Reserve System in the US 美国联邦储备系统

The Federal Reserve Act of 1913 created the Federal Reserve System, commonly known as the Fed, which is the monetary authority in the US. Why it is called the Federal Reserve System and not the Federal Reserve Bank? The Fed was designed as a system because the Congress wanted a decentralized central bank. The decentralization was essentially geographic, reflecting people's desire for regional monetary independence.

The need for such regional autonomy has since dissipated, but the structure remains intact. The Fed's organizational structure is not very complicated. The nucleus of the Federal Reserve System is its Board of Governors, which meets in Washington, D. C. The Board consists of seven members, appointed by the President and confirmed by the Senate. Each serves a 14 year term. Appointments are staggered, one every other year, so that no President or Senate session can manipulate the composition of the board. This also ensures continuity. The Chairman is a board member appointed by the President to a four-year term. Chairmen may be reappointed, but normally they cannot serve longer than their 14 years on the Board. Typically, chairmen are reappointed for lengthy periods that overlap Republican and Democratic presidents. For instance, Alan Greenspan, the former Chairman who retired in early 2006 and exceptionally served longer than 18 years, was appointed by Ronald Reagan and continued into the old Bush and the Clinton and the current Bush administrations.

The Federal Reserve System consists of 12 District Federal Reserve Banks, each serving a region of the country. The larger District Federal Reserve Banks have smaller branches. Under this arrangement, a bank in a specific district would use its own District Federal Reserve as its central bank. In this way, banks in Nebraska, or Florida would not have to depend upon banking decisions made in New York. Figure 3 – 1 shows the geographic domain of the 12 District Federal Reserve Banks and their locations.

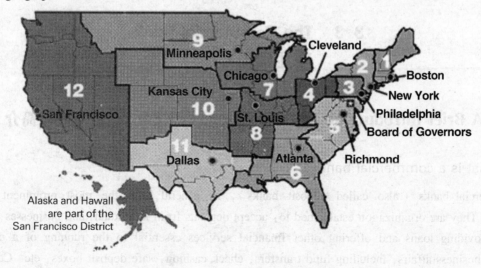

Figure 3 – 1 Federal reserve districts

The 12 District Banks make up the second tier of the Fed's structure. Each is managed by a board of nine directors, six chosen by the member banks of the district, the other three appointed by the Board of Governors. The President of each district bank is selected by its nine directors.

The Federal Reserve System is not owned by the government. Although created by and responsible to the Congress, the Fed pursues an independent monetary policy which at times can conflict with government's economic policy. For instance, the government may be pursuing a stimulative fiscal policy (lower taxes, increase government spending) while the Fed may be more interested in controlling inflation.

Each District Federal Reserve Bank is owned by all its member banks. Each member bank contributes 3% of its capital stock to the Federal Reserve Bank in its district and another 3% is subject to call by the Fed. These are what are known as the banks "reserve requirements". Of the more than 12,000 banks in the country, fewer than 5,000 are chartered nationally; the rest remain state-chartered. When the Act was first passed only nationally chartered banks could join the Fed. Nowadays, this is no longer the case and any bank can join.

All nationally chartered banks must be members of the Fed. The state chartered banks can choose to be or not be. Even though less than 13% of the state-chartered banks are members of the Federal Reserve System, along with nationally chartered banks hold more than 50% of all deposits in the US.

The Fed's main responsibility is to safeguard the proper functioning of the money system. Obviously, if it's going to do that job at all, it has to monitor the activities of the nation's financial institutions, anticipate what they will do, prevent them from doing some things, encourage them to do others, and do all this without interfering too much in the conduct of private business. Is this impossible? Some people think so. But these same people are unable to imagine a modern economy operating without a central bank.

The nerve center of the Fed is its Federal Open Market Committee. Here, the Fed exercises monetary control over the economy through its open market operations. The 12-person committee is composed of all seven members of the Board of Governors who each have one vote, as do the President of the New York Fed, and four District Presidents who rotate voting on the Committee. Its composition reflects the power of the Board, the unique position held by the New York District, and the Fed's commitment to regional representation.

3.3 The Commercial Bank
商业银行

3.3.1 A Brief Introduction to the Commercial Bank   商业银行简介

1. What is a commercial bank

Commercial banks (also called deposit banks), in general, are the most prominent financial institutions. They are organization established to: accept deposits from individuals and businesses; originate credit by providing loans and offering other financial services essential to the running of a customer's financial or business affairs, including fund transfers, check cashing, safe deposit boxes, etc. Commercial banks are also the most widely diversified in terms of both liabilities and assets. Their major source of funds used to be current deposits (checking accounts).

Furthermore, as a type of bank, the commercial bank has two possible meanings.

(1) Commercial banks are the term used for a normal bank to distinguish it from an investment bank; this is what people normally call a "bank". The term "commercial" was used to distinguish it from an investment bank. Since the two types of banks no longer have to be separate companies, some have used the term "commercial bank" to refer to banks which focus mainly on companies. In some English-speaking countries outside North America, the term "trading bank" has been used to denote a commercial bank.

(2) Commercial banking can also refer to a bank or a division of a bank that mostly deals with deposits and loans from corporations or large businesses, as opposed to normal individual consumers (retail banking).

2. The origin and development of commercial bank

The name "bank" derives from the Italian word "banco" (means "desk"), used during the Renaissance by Florentines bankers, who used to make their transactions above a desk covered by a green tablecloth.

In general, the history of banking is closely related to the history of money. As monetary payments became important, people looked for ways to safely store their money. As trade grew, merchants looked for ways of borrowing money to fund expeditions.

Banks probably predated the invention of money. The first banks were probably the religious temples of the ancient world, and were probably established sometime during the 3rd millennium BC. Deposits initially consisted of grain and later other goods including agricultural implements, cattle, as well as eventually precious metals such as gold, in the form of easy-to-carry compressed plates. Palaces and Temples were the safest places to store gold as they were constantly attended and well built. As sacred places, temples presented an extra deterrent to would-be thieves. There are extant records of loans from the 18th century BC in Babylon that were made by temple priests to merchants. By the time of Hammurabi's Code, banking was well enough developed to justify the promulgation of laws governing banking operations. According to the records, Pythius, who operated as a merchant banker throughout Asia Minor at the beginning of the 5th century BC, may be the first individual banker.

Modern Western economic and financial history is usually traced back to the coffee houses of London. The London Royal Exchange was established in 1565. At that time moneychangers were already called bankers, though the term "bank" usually referred to their offices, and did not carry the meaning it does today. There was also a hierarchical order among professionals; at the top were the bankers who did business with heads of state, next were the city exchanges, and at the bottom were the pawn shops or Lombard's. Some European cities today have a Lombard street where the pawn shop was located. In 1566, the Royal Exchange was built in London. This showed the new importance of banking, and particularly foreign exchange dealing, in England.

After the siege of Antwerp, trade moved to Amsterdam. In 1609 the Amsterdam Exchange Bank (Amsterdamsche Wisselbank) was founded which made Amsterdam the financial centre of the world until the Industrial Revolution. And it was established to provide a superior and more controlled service than that available from private bankers. Later its example inspires the establishment of the Bank of England. The Bank of England's establishment is usually considered as the initiative of the modern banks.

3.3.2　The Nature of the Commercial Bank　商业银行的性质

What is the nature of the commercial bank? Commercial banks are profit-seeking business. As we know, commercial banks are financial institutions that accept deposits from citizens and pay interest in return. Commercial banks share many common features with other companies. They are the profitable corporations. That is the primary nature of the commercial bank. Even if they are non-profit they do have to make money in their operation in order to pay expenses.

Generally speaking, the commercial banks make money in the following ways.

1. Charge interests on loans

Where do they get the money for the loans? The answer is from their depositors and from the central bank. They pay interests to depositors but charge a higher rate on money they lend out. For instance, banks may pay 2% on a savings account, but charge 9% in interest on a loan. In the case of money borrowed from the central bank, banks pay a percentage rate on money they borrow, called the discount rate. Then, banks loan that money and charge a higher rate on the loan than the rate that they paid.

In a word, banks raise funds by attracting deposits, borrowing money in inter-bank markets, or issuing financial instruments in money markets and capital markets. Banks then lend out most of these funds to borrowers. Banks make a profit from the differential between the level of interests they pay for deposits, and the level of interests they charges in their lending activities.

2. Operate on fractionalized deposits

Banks do not keep all of the depositor's money on hand, although they use depositor's money to make money by giving loans and earning interest. Banks have to take many measures to ensure that they remain profitable while responding to ever-changing market conditions. Especially in the past ten years in the United States, banks have taken a variety of measures in doing so. As a typical example, in 1999, the Gramm-Leach-Bliley Act allows the banks in the US to merge with investment companies and insurance houses. Merging banking, investment, and insurance functions enables traditional banks to respond to increasing consumer demands for "one-stop shopping" by offering compositive and integrated services, which are desired by the banks and will help to increase profitability.

3. Charge fees

It used to be the case that checking and savings accounts were free. Today, banks have fees for minimum deposit, per check fees and ATM fees. When ATMs were first introduced they were supposed to be able to replace bank branches, save banks operating expenses and that savings would be passed on to consumers. This has not happened. Instead, ATMs have become a revenue stream for banks as they charge up for every transaction. In some cases the consumer may get hit with a double whammy. If you use the ATM of a bank other than your own, both your bank and the ATM's bank may charge you a fee. Another example is that they increase the methods of payment processing available to the general public and business clients. These products include pre-paid cards, debit cards, credit cards, and smart-cards. These products make it easier for consumers to conveniently make transactions and smooth their consumption over time. However, with convenience there is also increased risk that consumers will mismanage their financial resources and accumulate excessive debt. Banks make money from card products through interest payments and fees charged on consumers and transaction fees on companies that accept the cards.

Reading Material

How Do ATMs Work?

An ATM is simply a data terminal with two input and four output devices. Like any other data terminal, the ATM has to connect to, and communicate through, a host processor. The host processor is analogous to an Internet service provider (ISP) in that it is the gateway through which all the various ATM networks become available to the cardholder wanting the cash.

The host processor may be owned by a bank or other financial institution, or it may be owned by an independent service provider. Bank-owned processors normally support only bank-owned machines, whereas the independent processors support merchant-owned machines.

3.3.3 The Operations of the Commercial Bank 商业银行的业务

1. The main operations of the commercial bank

Commercial banks raise funds by collecting deposits from businesses and consumers through checkable deposits, savings deposits, and time deposits. They make loans to businesses and consumers. They also buy corporate bonds and government bonds. Their primary liabilities are deposits and primary assets are loans and bonds.

Although the basic type of services offered by a bank depends upon the type of bank and the country, basic services provided usually include: taking deposits from their customers and issuing current or checking accounts and savings accounts to individuals and businesses; cashing cheques; extending loans to individuals and businesses, issuing credit cards , ATM cards , and debit cards; facilitating money transactions such as wire transfers and cashiers checks; storing valuables, particularly in a safe deposit box; consumer and commercial financial advisory services; pension and retirement planning; cashing and distributing bank rolls.

2. The types of deposits and loans

Usually, the deposits may further divide into demand deposit, time deposit and saving deposits. Demand deposit is an account from which deposited funds can be withdrawn at any time without any notice to the depository institution. This account allows you to "demand" your money at any time, unlike a time deposit, which cannot be accessed for a predetermined period (the loan's term). A time deposit, also known as a term deposit, is a money deposit at a banking institution that cannot be withdrawn for a certain "term" or period of time. Usually, the longer the term, the better the yield on the money. A certificate of deposit is a time-deposit product. A deposit of funds in a savings institution under an agreement stipulating that the funds must be kept on deposit for a stated period of time, or the institution may require a minimum period of notification before a withdrawal is made.

According to different standards, loans may be further divided into many different types. Usually, we know there are short-term, medium-term and long-term loans; or industry & commercial loans[5] , real estate loans[6], consumer loans, loans to financial institutions and other loans.

3. The balance sheet of the commercial bank

Hereunder, Table 3 – 1 is a sample balance sheet of a commercial bank.

Table 3 – 1   A sample balance sheet of a bank

Liabilities	$ m	%	Assets	$ m	%
Deposit and checking accounts	103,706	81.5	Cash and short-term funds Among:	20,092	15.8
			Cash in hand and with central banks Money at call and short notice Government treasury bills Other bills Certificates of deposit	1,822 10,946 2,943 1,973 2,408	
Other accounts	14,170	11.1	Items in course of collection	658	0.5
Loan capital	1,447	1.2	Investments	1,918	1.5
Shareholder's funds	7,893	6.2	Trading assets of securities business	7,807	6.1
			Advances	94,044	73.9
			Investments in associated companies	450	0.4
			Property and Equipment	2,247	1.8
	127,216			127,216	

From the above sample balance sheet, it will be noted that items are listed in order of liquidity, the very reverse of the usual method of presentation of a balance sheet. This is because for a bank, even more than for other concerns, liquidity is of paramount importance. Shareholders' funds and loan capital are also much smaller in relation to total assets than in balance sheets of other firms. In an industrial firm, this might be a sign of weakness but banks are very different kinds of institution. Of course, capital structure is very important and most of central banks in the world will have the power to regulate the capital ratios of the banks in their countries.

In the balance sheet of a commercial bank, the items of really vital importance are deposits and current accounts, cash and short-term funds and advances.

1) Deposits and checking accounts

A very large proportion of these will be current account deposits withdrawable on demand. It is a huge item (over 80% of total funds) and, theoretically, if there were a substantial demand by depositors for the return of their money this could cause an enormous strain on a bank's liquidity and force it to sell investments prematurely and call in its loans. However, it is unlikely that this would happen. This is because most withdrawals take place not for cash but by means of checks drawn on bank deposits, the significant part of the money supply today. For many banking institutions of considerable size, a large part of the withdrawal of some of its customers would be returned as deposits by others.

2) Cash and short-term funds

Referring to the further details of cash and short-term funds item listed in the above sheet, it can be concluded that less than one-sixth of its liquid funds (a very small proportion indeed of total funds) are earning no interest. Money at call or short notice represents funds advanced on a " call" basis (means " repayable on demand") traditionally to the discount houses but also to stock exchange firms, local authorities and other financial institutions. It will also include certificates of deposit, which although of fixed term, are readily negotiable in the money markets, and hence very liquid.

3) Advances

Advances are the least liquid of a bank's assets but the most profitable. Over recent years bank lending has become an even more important item in the balance sheet. Practically, the rise in bank lending is constrained by several factors.

(1) The level of deposits in the economy.

(2) The banks' ability to compete effectively for them.

(3) The requirements laid down by the government as to liquidity requirements including deposits with the central bank and the adequacy of a bank's capital base.

(4) The banks' attitude to risk in meeting this demand.

(5) The demand for advance.

4. Liquidity versus profitability

Bankers make a living by lending money and this can take a variety of forms. They must retain a measure of liquidity whether or not this is imposed upon them. By its very nature short-term lending (with the ability to call in the loan immediately) is not very profitable. However, since the banker must maintain a prudent degree of liquidity he will endeavor to achieve this as profitably as he can. Hence the item "money at call and short notice" and others similar to it in bank balance sheets. Absolute liquidity in the form of coins and notes generally accounts for less than 2% of total deposits. The other items of a bank's assets, with the exception of property and equipment, are all financial assets and, to a greater or lesser degree, considerably profitable.

5. The channels of financial transactions

As commercial banks, their financial transactions can be performed via many different channels, including:

(1) a branch, banking centre or financial centre — a retail location where a bank or financial institution offers a wide array of face to face service to its customers.

(2) ATM — a computerized telecommunications device that provides a financial institution's customers a method of financial transactions in a public space without the need for a bank teller or human clerk.

(3) mail — a part of the postal system which itself is a system wherein written documents typically enclosed in envelopes, and also small packages containing other matter, are delivered to destinations around the world.

(4) telephone banking — a service provided by a financial institution which allows its customers to perform transactions over the telephone.

(5) online banking — a term used for performing payments, transactions, etc. over the Internet through a bank, credit union or building society's secure website.

Top Ten Banks in the World Ranked by Market Capitalization

Rank	Country	Company	Market Capitalization (US)
1	United States	Citigroup	275 billion
2	China	ICBC	250 billion
3	United States	Bank of America	230 billion
4	United Kingdom	HSBC	200 billion
5	United States	JPMorgan Chase	165 billion
6	Japan	Mitsubishi UFJ	145 billion
7	Italy	Unicredit	130 billion (2007)
8	United States	Wells Fargo	120 billion
9	Switzerland	UBS	110 billion
10	United Kingdom	Royal Bank of Scotland	100 billion

Note: Figures in US dollars, and as at 26 July, 2006

3.3.4 The Creation of Money 货币的创造

1. How the banks create money

The banking system as a whole can create money (credit) by its lending and investing functions. It is required by law that banks have to keep a minimum cash reserve ratio against the deposits received from its customers. With this reserve system, banks will have adequate cash to meet withdrawal and thus to maintain the confidence of the depositors.

Suppose that, when a bank receives $100 from a depositor, it keeps a reserve ratio of 10% and lends out the rest (90%) or makes investment. If the banking system runs perfectly well, the total 90% (i. e. $90) will eventually come back. When the other bank receives this $90, it also keeps 10% and lends the rest out again. This sequence of activities will continue in the whole banking system until the amount becomes zero. Therefore, the total deposits in the banking system can be represented by:

$$\$ (100 + 90 + 81 + \dots)$$
$$= \$ 100 (1/0.1)$$
$$= \$ 1,000$$

The maximum increase in deposits is equal to the initial deposit times the banking multiplier. From the above formula, we find that the banking multiplier is the reciprocal of the reserve ratio. This is an over-simplified example, however, made for the sake of clarity.

2. Limitations on money creation

In practice, there are several limitations on money creation.

1) Monetary policy carried out by the central bank

To stabilize the national income at the full employment level without deflation or inflation, central banks carry out the monetary policies by the following instruments, which may limit the ability of banks to create money.

(1) Reserve ratio. If the central bank raises the required reserve ratio of the banks, banks have to keep a higher ratio of cash reserves against their deposits, thus limiting their ability to create money.

(2) Discount rate. Discount rate refers to the rate of the interest which the central bank charges on its loans to the commercial banks. As the interest rates usually follow the example of the central bank discount rate, therefore, if the central bank raises the discount rate, it will be more expensive for the commercial banks to borrow from the central bank and consequently the commercial banks will increase their interests on loans. The final result is that the people borrowing activities from commercial banks are restricted.

(3) Open market operation. In countries where there are active capital markets and a large amount of outstanding government bonds, central banks can control money and credit by buying or selling securities if it goes into the stock market to buy the bonds, it will decrease the money supply. Thus the banks will have less to create credit.

2) Legal requirement

Legal requirement such as cash ratio, liquidity ratio will affect the ability of the banking system in credit creation. For instance, if the banking system is required by law to raise the cash or liquidity ratio, then the banks would have to keep a greater amount of cash and liquid assets—non-profit earning assets. With assets which earn less profit, the ability to create credit is reduced.

3) Leakage of cash into circulation

In real life situations, people do not deposit their entire income into banks, instead, they keep part of it, more or less, as cash in hand. Also, they do withdraw cash from the bank constantly. All together these actions will reduce the reserves of the banking system and as a result its ability to create credit.

4) Supply of collateral security

When banks grant long-term loan to their customers, customers have to offer some kinds of collateral security to the banks as a guarantee that they will repay the loans. The collateral may be their fixed assets, including machinery, lands as well as buildings. The value of the collateral security must, of course, be higher than that of the loan. So once that standard of collateral security is specified, the supply of it is limited. If the standard is raised, the demand for banking loans will probably fall and therefore limite the credit creation ability of banking system.

5) Possibility of banks holding reserves above the legal minimum requirement

The law only requires banks to maintain in minimum reserve ratio. Of course, banks can keep a higher reserve for some purposes. If they do so, the banking multiplier will be reduced and consequently the total increase in deposits will be reduced.

6）Restriction of the multi-banking system

In the multi-banking system, every bank has to carry out more or less the same policy. In other words, a bank can not lend out too much or keep an exceedingly high reserve ratio.

3.3.5　The Risk Management of the Commercial Bank　商业银行的风险管理

Banks are susceptible to many forms of risks which have triggered occasional systemic crises. Banking crises have developed many times throughout history when one or more risks materialize for a banking sector as a whole. Prominent examples include the Japanese banking crisis during the 1990s, the bank run[7] occurred during the Great Depression.

Risk management is the human activity which integrates recognition of risk, risk assessment, developing strategies to manage it, and mitigation of risk using managerial resources. The strategies include avoiding the risk, transferring the risk to another party, reducing the negative effect of the risk, and accepting some or all of the consequences of a particular risk. Commonly, banks face many kinds of risks, including credit risk, liquidity risk, interest rate risk and etc. Each of the risks is sufficiently important to warrant separate treatment. Financial risk management focuses on risks that can be managed using traded financial instruments.

1. Credit risk

Credit risk is the risk that those who owe money to the bank will not repay. It stems because some bank borrowers may not be able to repay their loans. Moreover, many of these loans are made to borrowers whose performance is difficult to monitor and whose risk is difficult to assess. That is, they are loans characterized by the asymmetric information problems of adverse selection and moral hazard. The primary way to reduce credit risks is by monitoring the behaviors of clients who wish apply for credit in the business. Particularly, the riskier loans should be charged a higher interest rate and/or face higher collateral requirements. This helps to offset the losses from bad loans.

2. Liquidity risk

Liquidity risk is the risk that many depositors will request withdrawals beyond available funds. It stems because transactions deposits and saving accounts can be withdrawn at any time. Thus when withdrawals significantly exceed new deposits over a short period, banks must scramble to replace the shortfall in funds. Commonly, bankers solved this liquidity problem by having lots of government bonds on hand that they could easily sell for cash. Therefore, it is not surprising that the ratio of cash plus securities to total assets is a traditional measure of bank liquidity.

3. Interest rate risk

Interest rate risk is the risk that the bank will become unprofitable if rising interest rates force it to pay relatively more on its deposits than it receives on its loans. For instance, if interest rates increase a bank whose assets have a longer maturity than its liabilities will suffer a decline in net interest margin because the bank has to pay higher rates to renew its deposits before it gets a chance to replace its low-yielding assets. Additionally, the present value of its assets will decline by more than the present value of its liabilities because long-term securities are more sensitive to changes in interest rates than short-term securities.

Therefore, interest rate risk affects both the income statement and the market value of assets and liabilities on the balance sheet of a bank. There are many measures to avoid the interest rate risk. The simplest and most commonly used measure is the one-year reprising gap. Banks also can reduce their interest rate risk by changing the maturities of their assets or liabilities.

3.3.6 The Commercial Banks in China 中国的商业银行

1. Introduction

In China, according to the Law of the People's Republic of China on Commercial Banks and the Company Law of the People's Republic of China, the commercial banks are those corporate legal entities which are established to absorb public deposits, make loans, arrange settlement of accounts and engage in other businesses in accordance with this law. Although Chinese commercial banks do not take participation in the note issue, they manage it.

Examples of large commercial banks in China are: the Bank of China (BC), the Industrial and Commercial Bank of China (ICBC), the China Construction Bank (CCB) and the Agricultural Bank of China (ABC). These four banks differ from most foreign commercial banks, because they are state-owned. However, because these banks are now responsible for their own profitability and compliance with the banking regulations, they are practically like the general foreign commercial banks. Through years of reform efforts, China has developed a banking system consisting mainly of the wholly state-owned commercial banks and joint-equity commercial banks (such as the Bank of Communications[8]) under the supervision of the People's Bank of China and the China Banking Regulatory Commission (CBRC)[9].

2. The role of commercial banks in China

The commercial banks play a unique role in the Chinese economy through mobilizing savings, allocating capital funds to finance productive investment, transmitting monetary policy, providing a payment system, and transforming risks. The functions of commercial banks in China are as follows:

(1) To play a key role in facilitating efficient allocation of scarce financial resources by channeling savings to productive investments.

(2) To serve as a principal repository of liquid funds for the public. The safety and availability of such funds for transactions and other purposes are essential to the stability and efficiency of the financial system.

(3) To serve to transmit the impulses of monetary policy to the whole financial system and ultimately to the real economy.

(4) To provide the indispensable national payments mechanism for the development of modern financial and business systems.

(5) To reduce risks through aggregation (the banking system as a whole).

With the continuous development of China's economy, commercial banks will be playing a more and more important role in daily lives.

3. The business scope of a commercial bank in China

In China, commercial banks work under the principles of fluidity, safety, and efficiency, with full autonomy, and assume sole responsibility for their own risks and with self-restraint.

In accordance with the Law of the People's Republic of China on Commercial Banks, a commercial bank may operate the following businesses in part or in whole: absorbing public deposits; providing short-term, medium-term and long-term loans; handling acceptance and discount of negotiable instruments; arranging settlement of both domestic and overseas accounts; undertaking inter-bank borrowing or lending; engaging in bank card business; issuing credits and guarantees; purchasing and selling government bonds as agents; issuing, buying and selling financial bonds; buying and selling foreign exchange by itself or as agents; offering safe boxes services; handling receipts and payments and insurance business as agents; and other businesses as approved by the banking regulatory authority.

3.4   The Policy Bank
政策性银行

3.4.1   A Brief Introduction to the Policy Bank   政策性银行简介

A policy bank commonly refers to a policy financial institution established and owned by the state. Its business scope is determined by the state in line with the needs of national economic development. Its main target is to promote economic and social development. It obtains its financial resources from the state treasury, or through issuing of financial bonds and borrowing from the central bank, and etc.

There are many policy banks that contribute much to their counties' national economies in the present world. For example, the Development Bank of Japan (DBJ) is an important policy bank in Japan and it aims to provide long-term financing and other policy-based schemes to qualified projects as a supplement and inducement to the lending and other services provided by ordinary financial institutions. By doing so, it promotes the upgrading, vitalization and sustainable development of the economy and society, the creation of self-reliant regions and the realization of an enhanced quality of life.

3.4.2   The Policy Banks in China   中国的政策性银行

At present, China has three policy banks.

The China Development Bank (CDB)[10] is the first policy bank in China, which was founded in March 1994. The China Development Bank is under the direct jurisdiction of the State Council of China. As a development-oriented financial institution of the government, China Development Bank has been a major player in long-term financing for key projects and supportive construction in infrastructure and pillar industries, which are vital to the development of the national economy. The main missions of the CDB include: supporting the development of infrastructure, basic industries and pillar industries; promoting coordination in regional development and industry restructuring; promoting international cooperation and sharing development experiences.

The Export-Import Bank of China (China Exim Bank)[11] is a fully government-owned policy bank under the direct leadership of the State Council. Its primary task is to implement the state policies in foreign trade and economy, and provide policy financial supports in order to promote the export of Chinese mechanical and electronic products and high-and new-tech products, to support Chinese companies with comparative advantages to "go global" for offshore construction contracts and overseas investment projects, to develop and strengthen the relationships with foreign countries, and to enhance Sino-foreign economic and technological cooperation and exchanges.

The Agricultural Development Bank of China (ADBC)[12] is a state-owned agricultural policy bank under the direct administration of the State Council. The primary aim of the bank is to promote development of agriculture and rural areas through the following activities: raising the funds for agricultural policy businesses based on the state credibility in accordance with the laws, regulations, and policies; undertaking the agricultural policy credit businesses specified by the central government and the agriculture-related commercial businesses approved by the regulatory authority; and serving as an agent for the state treasury to allocate the special funds for supporting agriculture.

3.5 Other Banks
其他银行

In the present world, especially in those counties having well-developed financial systems, there are also some other banks which differ from the normal banks mentioned above. Some of them are listed as follows (Note that they may be regarded as banks in some countries while not in others).

(1) Community banks[13]—locally operated financial institutions that empower employees to make local decisions to serve their customers and the partners.

(2) Community development banks[14]—regulated banks that provide financial services and credit to underserved markets or populations.

(3) Savings banks—depository financial institutions that primarily accept consumer deposits and make home mortgage loans. In Europe, savings banks take their roots in the 18th century. Their original objective was to provide easily accessible savings products to all strata of the population. In some countries, savings banks were created on public initiative, while in others socially committed individuals created foundations to put in place the necessary infrastructure. Nowadays, European savings banks have kept their focus on retail banking: payments, savings products, credits and insurances for individuals or small and medium-sized enterprises. Apart from this retail focus, they also differ from commercial banks by their broadly decentralized distribution network, providing local and regional outreach and by their socially responsible approach to business and society. In the US, savings banks are also known as mutual savings banks or savings and loan associations, supervised by the Federal Housing Finance Board (FHFB) and insured by the Savings Association Insurance Fund (SAIF), a unit of the Federal Deposit Insurance Corporation (FDIC).

(4) Postal savings banks—savings banks associated with national postal systems.

(5) Private banks— the banks only manage the assets of high net worth individuals.

(6) Building societies and Landesbanks—financial institutions principally conduct retail banking relating to house purchase.

Reading Material

China to Establish Postal Savings Bank

The State Council of China has given the nod to a new Chinese bank to be known as the National Postal Savings Bank, which will be based on the existing savings deposit business at far-flung postal stations, a senior banking official revealed Wednesday.

Vice Chairman Cai Esheng of the China Banking Regulatory Commission said on a finance forum in Beijing the new bank will provide "basic services" to millions of rural dwellers.

Postal savings services began in 1986 with the establishment of the China Post Savings and Remittance Bureau. By the end of 2005, CPSRB had a deposit balance of 1. 3 trillion yuan RMB (approximately US$162 billion), making it the fifth largest savings institution, just after the "Big Four" state banks.

Group Discussion

1. Talk about the role of the central bank in an economy.
2. Tell the nature and operations of commercial banks.
3. Describe the creation of money.
4. Discuss the risk management of commercial banks in China.
5. Say something about the policy banks in China.

NOTES

1	Federal Reserve System (Fed)	美国联邦储备系统
2	Bank for International Settlements (BIS)	国际清算银行
3	clearing house	票据交换所（亦用"clearinghouse"）
4	anti-money-laundering	反洗钱
5	industry & commercial loans	工商企业贷款
6	real estate loans	不动产贷款
7	bank run	银行挤兑
8	Bank of Communications	交通银行
9	China Banking Regulatory Commission (CBRC)	中国银行业监督管理委员会
10	China Development Bank (CDB)	国家开发银行
11	Export-Import Bank of China (China Exim Bank)	中国进出口银行
12	Agricultural Development Bank of China (ADBC)	中国农业发展银行
13	community bank	地区银行
14	community development bank	地区开发银行，地区发展银行

Chapter 4

Non-bank Financial Institutions
非银行金融机构

Learning Objectives

- ☑ To understand the definition of nonbank financial institution
- ☑ To learn the functions and operations the insurance company
- ☑ To learn about the investment institution
- ☑ To know about other nonbank financial institutions
- ☑ To konw about the major nonbank financial institutions in China

 ## Opening Vignette

What Is the NBFI?

NBFI, the abbreviation for nonbank financial institution, refers to the financial institution that accumulates funds by borrowing from the general public and lends the same to meet specialized financing needs, but is prohibited to accept such deposits payable either on demand or by check, draft, etc., and operates checking accounts for which its liabilities are not a part of the money supply. The first nonbank financial institution (NBFI) was a fire insurance company established in 1680 in London.

Although all financial institutions have a common basis for their operations and some role with respect to lender-borrower relationships, there are some fundamental differences between the banks and NBFIs. The liabilities created by the banks are unique in that these liabilities are themselves "spendable", i. e., the deposits in banks are used as money by the holders of the deposits; whereas the liabilities of a NBFI, such as an insurance company cannot be used in this way. Banks can actually increase the total volume of spending in the economy by their capacity to create money and thereby increase the money in circulation. But the nonbank financial institutions do not have that capacity and they are merely "honest brokers" and transmitting funds, which have been created elsewhere, e. g. , by the banking system. The NBFI, such as a leasing company, receives additional funds and is capable of adding to its mortgage lending by withdrawing from its larger demand deposits kept with the deposit money bank. The leasing company thus adds to the volume of credit and enables additional spending (e. g. , on house purchase) to take place. The combination of financial assets created by the banks and NBFIs for ultimate lender varies depending on the origin of the asset.

In general, the operations of NBFIs are also regulated by the central bank. The grant of authority to engage in borrowing from the general public is normally based on such factors as minimum capital requirement, quality of management, compliance with the concerned laws, rules, and regulations, and stability of financial standing. NBFIs may provide loans to their members and the general public up to a certain amount and may also engage in trust functions with prior permission of the central bank. In normal cases, they are not allowed to engage in foreign exchange transactions.

NBFIs are specialists of the intermediation process and their origins can be traced to the development of specialized financial institutions. Some survived centuries of changing economic and financial developments. Others appeared in response to special opportunities or needs and have disappeared just as quickly. Their survival and existence depend upon their ability to offer contracts that serve the needs of specialized customers, maintain a spread between the rate they pay for funds and the rate they receive that will support their costs, and meet commitment to suppliers of funds.

The nonbank financial sector has a wide diversity of institutions. Despite their importance as alternative sources of finance to the commercial banks, their liabilities may nevertheless be regarded as "near money". The most important NBFIs in those most developed countries largely include hire purchase companies, leasing companies, mortgage companies, insurance companies, pension funds, investment banks/companies, investment trusts, security dealer/ brokers, pawn shops, central provident fund (CPF), discount houses, securities companies, fund managers, venture capital companies, stock exchanges, and factoring companies.

 Warm-up Questions

1. **What do you think about the NBFIs?**
2. **What are the differences between the banks and the NBFIs?**
3. **How much do you know about the NBFIs in China?**

4.1　An Overview of Non-bank Financial Institutions
非银行金融机构概述

Nonbank financial institutions are financial institutions that provide banking services without meeting the legal definition of a bank, that is, one that does not hold a banking license. Their operations are, regardless of this, still exercised under banking regulation.

Non-bank Bank

In the US, a non-bank bank refers to a financial institution that provides most of the services of a bank but is not a member of the Federal Reserve System and does not have a charter from a state banking agency. A non-bank bank may offer credit cards, consumer and commercial loans, savings accounts, and accounts with services similar to bank checking accounts. By avoiding government regulation, such businesses may be able to be more innovative and profitable than traditional government–regulated banks.

However this depends on the jurisdiction, as in some jurisdictions, such as New Zealand, any nonbank financial institutions can do the business of banking, and there are no particular banking licenses issued.

Nonbank institutions frequently act as suppliers of loans and credit facilities, supporting investments in property, providing services relating to events within peoples lives such as wealth management, retirement planning and funding private education. However, in normal cases, they are not allowed to take deposits from the general public and have to find other means of funding their operations such as issuing debt instruments.

In most countries, the nonbank financial institutions mainly consisted of the insurance company, the investment institution, the trust company[1], the financial leasing company[2] the finance company[3], and etc.

4.2 The Insurance Company
保险公司

4.2.1 A Brief Introduction to the Insurance Company 保险公司简介

1. What is the insurance company

Literally, insurance is a form of risk management primarily used to hedge against the risk of a contingent loss. In modern economics, insurance is defined as the equitable transfer of the risk of a potential loss, from one entity to another, in exchange for a premium. The insurer (insurance company) is the company that sells the insurance. Insurance rate is a factor used to determine the amount of the premium to be charged for a particular insurance coverage. For example, an insurance company will pay to repair or replace the property if it is damaged or stolen. How much an insurer will pay in the event of a claim depends on how much insurance the policyholder has bought. The amount may also depend on the conditions that led to the damage.

2. Insurance companies as financial institutions

In developed countries, insurance companies are among the most important financial institutions. They make a significant contribution to the economic growth, both as investors in their economies and as employers. Life and health insurance companies invest their assets in other businesses and industries, as well as in mortgage loans. These investments help provide the funds that other businesses need to operate and grow and that individuals need to purchase homes. Insurance companies also invest in social programs that help improve the quality of lives for all people. For instance, life and health insurance companies invest money to provide support to charitable organizations.

Nowadays, the distinctions between these financial institutions have become more and more confusable. In developed countries, especially in the United States and Canada, laws have been changed so that each type of financial institution can now offer a wider variety of products. Banks now may offer insurance products and investment products, in addition to the usual checking and savings accounts. Insurers have begun to offer a wider variety of insurance or non-insurance products, such as savings plans, funds, and mortgage loans. In a word, today, various financial institutions are competing fiercely with one another to provide a wide range of financial services to consumers.

3. The origin and development of insurance companies

Insurance is an ancient idea. It can be said that insurance appears simultaneously with the appearance of human society. At that time, insurance was in the form of people helping each other. For example, if a house burned down, the members of the community helped build a new house. The member who did not help would never get help from the others if his own house burned on some day.

Early methods of transferring or distributing risk were practiced by Chinese and Babylonian traders as long ago as the 3rd and 2nd millennia BC, respectively. Chinese merchants traveling treacherous river rapids would redistribute their wares across many vessels to limit the loss due to any single vessel's capsizing. The Babylonians developed a system which was recorded in the Code of Hammurabi, and practiced by early Mediterranean sailing merchants. If a merchant received a loan to fund his shipment, he would pay the lender an additional sum in exchange for the lender's guarantee to cancel the loan should the shipment be stolen.

Then, the Greeks and Romans introduced the origins of life and health insurance in 600 AD when they organized guilds called "benevolent societies" which cared for the families and paid funeral expenses of members upon death.

Up to the end of the 17th century, London's growing importance as a center for trade increased demand for marine insurance. In the late 1680s, Mr. Edward Lloyd opened a coffee house that became a popular haunt of ship owners, merchants, and ships' captains, and thereby a reliable source of the latest shipping news. It became the meeting place for parties wishing to insure cargoes and ships, and those willing to underwrite such ventures. Today, Lloyd's of London[4] remains the leading market (note that it is not an insurance company) for marine and other specialist types of insurance, but it works rather differently than the more familiar kinds of insurance.

Insurance as we know it today can be traced to the Great Fire of London, which in 1666 devoured 13, 200 houses. In the aftermath of this disaster, Nicholas Barbon opened an office to insure buildings. In 1680, he established England's first fire insurance company, "The Fire Office", to insure brick and frame homes.

The first insurance company in the United States underwrote fire insurance and was formed in Charles Town (modern-day Charleston), South Carolina, in 1732.

Benjamin Franklin helped to popularize and make standard the practice of insurance, especially against fire in the form of perpetual insurance. He founded the Philadelphia Contributionship for the Insurance of Houses from Loss by Fire in 1752. Franklin's company was the first to make contributions toward fire prevention. Not only did his company warn against certain fire hazards, it refused to insure certain buildings where the risk of fire was too great, such as all wooden houses.

Nowadays, the global insurance industry has developed to a new stage. Insurance industries flourish in most countries all over the world.

4.2.2　The Functions of the Insurance Company　保险公司的职能

1. Risk transfer

The primary function of insurance is to serve as risk transfer mechanism. For example, to a motor vehicle owner, the motor vehicle may be stolen, or damaged in an accident which may also result in serious injury to the passengers in the vehicle or other people. The owner can transfer the financial losses to the insurance company by purchasing corresponding insurances.

2. Creation of the common pool

An insurance company sets itself up to operate a common pool of fund. By collecting premiums from all enterprises and individuals that wish to transfer the risks to it, an insurer can spread the cost of the few losses that are expected to occur among all the insured. It takes contributions, in the form of insurance premiums, from many people and pays the losses of the few. The contributions have to be enough to meet the total losses in any one-year and cover the other costs of operating the pool, including the profit of the insurance company. Even after taking all these costs into account, insurance is still a very attractive business in normal cases.

In operating the common pool, the insurance company benefits from the law of large numbers that is also called the law of average, which briefly means that any risk must have a large number of homogeneous exposure units and, as the number increases, the actual results are increasingly likely to become close to expected results.

4.2.3　The Operations of Insurance Company　保险公司的业务

1. The business model of the insurance company

Insurance companies make money in two ways: through underwriting—the process by which they select certain risks to insure and decide how much premiums to charge for accepting these risks; and by investing the premiums they collect from the insured. The profit formula of insurance companies may be expressed as follows:

Profit = Earned Premium + Investment Income - Incurred Loss - Underwriting Expenses

In order to earn premiums, insurers must frame reasonable insurance policies, which is the most difficult aspect of the insurance business. Insurers use actuarial science to quantify the risks they are willing to assume and the corresponding premiums they would like to charge. Actuarial science uses statistics and probability to analyze the risks associated with the range of perils covered, and these scientific principles are used to determine an insurer's overall exposure. Upon termination of a given policy, the amount of premium collected and the investment gains thereon minus the amount paid out in claims is the insurer's underwriting profit on that policy. Of course, from the insurance company's perspective, some policies are winners (that is, the insurance company pays out less in claims and expenses than it receives in premiums and investment income), whereas some are losers (that is, the insurance company pays out more in claims and expenses than it receives in premiums and investment income). For example, in the US, property and casualty insurers currently make the most money from their auto insurance line of business. Generally better statistics are available on auto losses and underwriting on this line of business has benefited greatly from advances in computing. Additionally, property losses in the US, due to natural catastrophes, have exacerbated this trend.

An insurance company's underwriting performance is measured in its combined ratio—the loss ratio is added to the expense ratio to determine the company's combined ratio. The combined ratio is a reflection of the company's overall underwriting profitability. A combined ratio of less than 100% indicates profitability, while anything over 100% indicates a loss.

In addition, insurance companies can earn investment profits on float. Float (available reserve) is the amount of money, at hand at any given moment, which an insurer has collected in insurance premiums but has not been paid out in claims. Insurance companies start investing insurance premiums as soon as they are collected and continue to earn interest on them until claims are paid out.

2. The types of insurance

In theory, any risk that can be quantified can potentially be insured. Specific kinds of risk that may give rise to claims are known as "perils". An insurance policy will set out in detail which perils are covered by the policy and which is not. Some important types of insurances are stated as follows.

Life insurance or life assurance is a contract between the policy owner and the insurer, where the insurer agrees to pay a sum of money upon the occurrence of the policy owner's death. In return, the policy owner (or policy payer) agrees to pay a stipulated amount called a premium at regular intervals.

Property insurance provides protection against most risks to property, such as fire, theft and some weather damage. This includes specialized forms of insurance such as fire insurance, flood insurance, earthquake insurance, home insurance or boiler insurance.

Health insurance is a type of insurance whereby the insurer pays the medical costs of the insured if the insured becomes sick due to covered causes, or due to accidents.

Social insurance is where people receive benefits or services in recognition of contributions to an insurance scheme. It primarily refers to social welfare service concerned with social protection, or protection against socially recognized conditions, including poverty, disability, old age, unemployment and others. But a summary of its essence is that it is a collection of insurance coverage (including components of life insurance, unemployment insurance, health insurance, disability income insurance, and etc.), plus retirement savings that mandates participation by all citizens. By forcing everyone in society to be a policyholder and pay premiums, it ensures that everyone can become a claimant when or if he or she needs to. Along the way this inevitably becomes related to other concepts such as the welfare system.

Casualty insurance is a type of insurance which policies are written to cover losses that are the direct result of an unforeseen accident. It may include marine insurance for shipwrecks or losses at sea, auto liability insurance[5] for car accidents and etc.

Liability insurance is designed to offer specific protection against third party claims, that is, the payment is not typically made to the insured, but rather to someone suffering loss who is not a party to the insurance contract.

Marine insurance covers the loss or damage of ships and cargo, and any transport or property by which cargo is transferred, acquired, or held between the points of origin and final destination.

Vehicle insurance (or car insurance, auto insurance, motor insurance) is the insurance people can purchase for trucks, cars, and other vehicles. Its primary use is to provide protection against losses incurred as a result of traffic accidents.

Credit insurance is an insurance policy associated with a specific loan or line of credit which pays back some or all of any money owed should certain things happen to the borrower, such as disability, death, or unemployment.

Crop insurance is purchased by agricultural producers, including farmers, ranchers, and others to protect themselves against either the loss of their crops due to natural disasters, such as drought, floods, hail, or the loss of revenue due to declines in the prices of agricultural commodities.

4.2.4 The Types of the Insurance Company 保险公司的类型

1. Life insurance companies vs. non-life insurance companies

According to the scope of business, insurance companies may be divided into life insurance companies and non-life (or general) insurance companies.

Life insurance companies sell life insurance, annuities and pensions products while non-life insurance companies sell other types of insurance. Commonly, non-life insurance companies can be further divided into standard line insurance companies and excess line insurance companies.

In the US, standard line insurance companies are main insurers. These are the companies that typically insure the autos, homes or businesses. They usually use pattern policies without variation from one person to the next and have lower premiums than excess line insurance companies and can sell directly to individuals. They are regulated by state laws that can restrict the amount of the premium they can charge for insurance policies. Excess line insurance companies typically insure risks not covered by the standard lines market. They are broadly considered as non-admitted insurers which are not licensed in the states where the risks are located. These companies have more flexibility and can react faster than standard companies because of the fewer regulations than those on standard insurance companies. State laws generally forbid the insurance placed with excess line agents and brokers to be available through standard licensed insurers.

2. Reinsurance companies

Reinsurance companies[6] are insurance companies that sell policies to other insurance companies, allowing them to reduce their risks and protect themselves from very large losses. The reinsurance market is dominated by a few very large companies, with huge reserves. A reinsurer may also be a direct writer of insurance risks as well.

3. Mutual insurance companies vs. stock insurance companies

Insurance companies can be classified into mutual insurance companies and stock insurance companies by their different proprietors. This is more of a traditional distinction as true mutual insurance companies are becoming rare. Mutual insurance companies are owned by the policyholders, while stock companies are owned by their stockholders (who may or may not own the policies).

4. Captive insurance companies

Captive insurance companies[7] may be defined as limited-purpose insurance companies established with the specific objective of financing risks emanating from their parent corporations. This definition can sometimes be extended to include some of the risks of the parent corporations' customers. In other words, it is an in-house self-insurance vehicle. Captive insurance companies may take the form of a "pure" entity (which is a 100% subsidiary of the self-insured parent company); of a "mutual" captive (which insures the collective risks of members of an industry); and of an "association" captive (which self-insures individual risks of the members of a professional, commercial or industrial association). They represent commercial, economic and tax advantages to their sponsors because of the reductions in costs that they help create and for the ease of insurance risk management and the flexibility for cash flows that they generate. In addition, they may provide coverage of risks which is neither available nor offered in the traditional insurance market at reasonable prices.

The types of risk that a captive company can underwrite for their parents include property damage, professional indemnity, public and products liability, employees' benefits, employers' liability, motor and medical aid expenses. The captive company's exposure to such risks may be limited by the use of reinsurance.

4.2.5　The Insurance Companies in China　中国的保险公司

In China, an insurance company is legally defined as a commercial insurance company that is established with the approval of China's insurance regulatory authority and registered according to law, including direct insurance company and re-insurance company. An insurance company shall be established as either a stock company with limited liability or a wholly state-owned company.

As early as in 1876, the government of Qing dynasty ordered the Commercial Bureau to set up Renhe Insurance Company. This was the first Chinese insurance company established with national capital.

Ratified by Financial Committee of the State Council, the People's Insurance Company of China (PICC) was established in Beijing in 1949. The establishment of PICC marked the start-up of China's insurance industry.

The Ping An Insurance Company of China (Ping An of China), which was established in Shenzhen in 1988, is the first joint-stock insurance company in China.

The China Pacific Insurance Company (CPIC) was founded in 1991 and held by the Bank of Communications.

There are also some smaller insurance companies established in China in recent years, such as the Tai Kang Life Insurance Company, New China Life Insurance Company and etc.

According to the Insurance Law of the People's Republic of China, the business scope of the insurance company may be summarized as follows: property insurance business, including property loss insurance, liability insurance, credit insurance and etc.; personal insurance business, including life insurance, health insurance, accidental injury insurance, etc. In addition, subject to the approval of the insurance regulatory authority, insurance companies may engage in the following reinsurance business for insurance business prescribed in the preceding clause, including ceding reinsurance[8] and assuming reinsurance[9].

4.3 The Investment Institution
投资机构

4.3.1 Investment Bank 投资银行

1. What is an investment bank

An investment bank is a financial institution that can act as an agent or underwriter for companies that wish to issue securities or equity. Usually, the term investment bank is commonly used in the US and some Continental countries, and in other countries, it has different names. For instance, it is called the securities company in Japan while the merchant bank in England. Moreover, they may be categorized into the group of banking financial institutions in some counties.

An investment bank assists companies and governments and their agencies to raise money by issuing and selling securities in the primary market. It helps public and private corporations in raising funds in the capital markets (both equity and debt), and in providing strategic advisory services for mergers, acquisitions and other types of financial transactions. The investment bank also acts as intermediary in trading for clients.

The leading investment banks in the present world include the Morgan Stanley and the Goldman Sachs, which are said to be in the Bulge Bracket[10].

2. The difference between investment banks and commercial banks

Investment banks differ from commercial banks fundamentally, for they do not accept deposits of or provide loans to individuals. However, in recent years the lines between the two groups have become blurry, especially as commercial banks have offered more investment banking services. In the US, the Glass-Steagall Act, initially created in the wake of the 1929 market crash, required that commercial banks only engage in banking activities (i.e. accepting deposits and making loans, and other fee based services), whereas investment banks were limited to capital markets activities. The Glass-Steagall Act was repealed by the Gramm-Leach-Bliley Act in 1999. By now, this separation is no longer mandatory.

3. The difference between investment banks and brokerages

An investment bank also differs from a brokerage. Generally, brokerages assist in the purchase (not the issue) and sale of stocks, bonds, as well as funds. Some firms, however, operate as both brokerages and investment banks; this includes some of the best known financial services firms in the world.

4. The functions of investment banks

The primary functions of investment banks are to act as advisers to governments and corporations seeking to raise funds, and intermediaries between these issuers of securities and institutional or individual investors.

As they take various forms, investment banks have come to fill a variety of roles, which include: underwriting and distributing new security issues; offering brokerage services to public and institutional investors; providing financial advice to corporate clients, especially on security issues, as well as mergers and acquisitions deals; providing financial security research to investors and corporate customers; market-making, in particular securities; and in some countries, investment banks have also moved into foreign currency exchange, private banking and etc.

A key role of the investment bank is to help companies in raising money. There are two means of fund-raising which investment bankers typically engage in: via the capital markets and through private placements.

Investment banks can help raise funds in capital markets in two ways. They can sell the company's equities in the stock market in an initial public offering (IPO)[11] or secondary offering, or they can advise on debt securities issues to the public markets. These issues and sales are tightly regulated by governing bodies such as the Securities and Exchange Commission (SEC), in the US, the largest such regulatory body in the world.

Investment banks may also advise companies on private placements which refer to the purchases or sales of corporate securities by private companies or individuals. Types of private placement transactions generally include venture capital investments, strategic investments, private debt placements, divestitures, acquisitions and etc.

Investment banks create value for their clients through three primary ways: first, they create a competitive environment for the company's securities; second, they possess an extensive network of industry and financial contacts; third, they have great and current knowledge about transaction structuring, comparable market events and legal processes.

5. The main operations of investment banks

The large and global investment banks typically have several business units: (1) corporate finance, concerned with advising on the finances of corporations, including mergers, acquisitions and divestitures; (2) research, concerned with investigating, valuing, and making recommendations to clients — both individual investors and larger entities such as hedge funds and funds — regarding shares and corporate and government bonds; (3) sales and trading, concerned with buying and selling shares either on behalf of the clients or for the bank itself.

Corporate finance, is the traditional aspect of investment banking which involves helping customers raise funds in the capital market and advising on mergers and acquisitions. Commonly, the highest profit margins come from advising on mergers and acquisitions. Investment banks have had a palpable effect on the history of global business, as they often proactively meet with the executives of corporations to encourage deals or expansion.

Research, is the division which reviews companies and writes reports about their prospects, often with "buy" or "sell" ratings. Although in theory, this operation would make the most sense at a stock brokerage where the advice could be given to the brokerage's customers, in fact, research has historically been performed by investment banks. The primary reason for this is the investment bank must take responsibility for the quality of the company that they are underwriting vis-a-vis the prices involved to the investors.

Sales and trading, is often the most profitable area of an investment bank, often responsible for a much larger amount of revenue than the other divisions. In the process of market making, investment banks will buy and sell stocks and bonds with the target of making an incremental amount of money on each trade. The primary job of an investment bank's sales force is to call on institutional investors to buy the stocks and bonds underwritten by their own bank. Another task of the sales force is to sell to institutional investors the stocks, bonds, commodities, or other things the bank might have on its books. These sales are on a caveat emptor basis.

Management of the investment bank's own capital, or proprietary trading, is often one of the biggest sources of profit. For example, the bank may arbitrage stock on a large scale if it see a suitable profit opportunity or it may structure its books so that it can make a profit from a fall in bond price or yields.

4.3.2 Investment Company 投资公司

The investment company is also a financial intermediary providing assistances and services for the investor, which may be regarded as the same as the investment bank in some cases.

In the US, an investment company refers to a company whose main business is holding securities of other companies purely for investment purposes. The investment company invests money on behalf of its shareholders who in turn share in the profits and losses. According to the US securities law, investment companies can be roughly classified as follows: the open-end management investment company[12] (which operates the open-end funds[13] and commonly known as mutual funds[14] in the US), the closed-end management investment company[15] (operating the close-end funds[16]), the UITs (unit investment trusts)[17] and others.

Hereinto, the management investment companies mostly operate the fund which is a form of collective investment that pools money from many investors and invests their money in bonds, stocks, short-term money market instruments, and/or other securities. Each investor in the fund gets a slice of the total pie. The fund will have a fund manager who is responsible for investing the pooled money into specific securities. By pooling money together in a fund, investors can purchase stocks or bonds with much lower trading costs than if they tried to do it on their own. But the biggest advantage to funds is diversification. There are many types of funds, such as aggressive growth fund[18], balanced fund[19], hedge fund[20], and an investment company may operate a variety of funds simultaneously.

4.3.3 The Investment institutions in China 中国的投资机构

Chinese investment banks have not yet appeared in the global arena until the China International Capital Corporation Ltd. (CICC)[21] was established in 1995. It is the first joint venture investment bank in China and has a registered capital of US$125 million.

Investment banking is at the core of CICC's professional services. The Investment Banking Department (IBD) of CICC offers a wide range of world-class financial advisory and capital-raising services to leading Chinese companies, multinationals and government institutions. IBD services include equity and debt capital raising, corporate restructuring, mergers and acquisitions in both domestic and international capital markets.

In addition, some famous transnational investment banks have also begun operations in China in recent years, such as Morgan Stanley and etc.

In China, there are also some investment companies (including securities companies), which engage in part of investment bank's business and play an important role in financial system. In Sept., 2007, the biggest Chinese investment company — China Investment Corporation Ltd.[22] was founded in Beijing.

According to the Securities Law of the People's Republic of China, the term securities company refers to a limited-liability company or stock-limited company that engages in business operation of securities. Securities companies may undertake some or all of the following business operations upon the approval by the securities regulatory authority: securities brokerage; underwriting and recommendation of securities; securities investment consulting; financial advising relating to activities of securities trading or securities investment; securities asset management; self-operation of securities; and any other business operation concerning securities.

4.4   Other Non-bank Financial Institutions
其他非银行金融机构

4.4.1   Trust Company   信托公司

1. A brief introduction

A trust company is a non-bank financial institution, which is considered by some authors as the origin of the investment bank. It is usually owned by one of the following three types of structures: an independent partnership, a nonbank corporation or a bank.

The term "trust" refers to the ability of the institution's trust department to act as a trustee — someone who administers financial assets on behalf of another. The assets are typically held in the form of a trust — a legal instrument that spells out the beneficiaries and what the money can be spent for.

2. The operations of the trust company

The trust company's main operations generally cover the following aspects.

(1) Escrow services. The trust company may provide escrow services, invest education, retirement funds and etc.

(2) Asset management. A trust department can provide investment management, including securities market advice, investment strategy and portfolio management, management of real estate and safekeeping of valuables.

(3) Estate administration[23]. A trust company can be nominated as an executor or personal representative in a last will and testament. The responsibilities of an executor in settling the estate of a deceased person include settling claims for debt and taxes, collecting debts, accounting for assets to the courts as well distributing wealth to beneficiaries.

(4) Corporate trust services[24]. Corporate trust services are the services which assist, in the fiduciary capacity, in the administration of the corporation's debt.

According to the different implement modes of trusts, trusts may be divided into revocable trusts and irrevocable trusts. The revocable trust is the one in which assets remain under the ownership of the client and the trustee acts solely as a hired manager. As the client still owns the property, there are normally no tax advantages involved in this arrangement. The irrevocable trust is often used for charitable purposes by millionaires or organizations as well as for the management of inheritances. As the benefactor relinquishes control of the assets upon creating the trust, any charitable activities incur tax benefits even while the assets are invested to provide a financial endowment for later use by the charitable foundation. This approach has been successfully used by foundations established by well-known and wealthy families such as the Fords and the Carnegies.

3. Trust companies in China

In China, the trust company is known as the trust and investment corporation[25] and the China International Trust and Investment Corporation (CITIC)[26] is the most famous.

According to the relative laws of China, the trust and investment corporation may engage in the following businesses: holding of funds, movables and immovables, and other property in trust upon entrustment; engaging in investment fund business; engaging in such intermediary business as the restructuring and acquisition of corporate assets, project financing, corporate financial management, financial consulting, and etc.; engaging in the distribution of bonds such as sovereign bonds, policy bank bonds and corporate bonds; acting as an agent in the management, use and disposal of property; keeping custody on the behalf of others; business of credit certification, investigations of creditworthiness and economic consultancy; using its own property to provide security for third parties; and accepting charitable trusts.

4.4.2 Financial Leasing Company   融资租赁公司

1. A brief introduction

A financial leasing company refers to any nonbank financial institution that is principally engaged in financial leasing businesses, including financial lease and leaseback.

The financial lease means any transaction in which the lessor, at the request of the lessee, acquires the leased property from the supplier and leases it to the lessee for the latter's possession and use in return for payment of rent by the lessee. The leased property in a financial lease transaction is often a fixed asset.

Leaseback is a type of financial lease in which the lessee itself is also the supplier of the leased property. The lessee sells its own property to the lessor, and then leases back the very property from the lessor by entering into a leaseback contract with the lessor.

2. Financial leasing companies in China

China Leasing Company Ltd.[27], the first financial leasing company in China, was established in 1981. Since then, sever other financial leasing companies was funded successively.

According to the Procedures for Administration of Financial Leasing Companies, the businesses of financial leasing companies cover: financial leasing business; inter-institution borrowing; financial consultation; borrowing from financial institutions; overseas foreign exchange borrowing; receiving of lease security deposits from the lessees; assignment of rental receivables to commercial banks; issuing financial bonds; taking-up fixed deposits of over one year from shareholders; realization of the residual value in leased property and disposition of business; and other businesses approved by the regulatory authority. It should be stressed that Chinese financial leasing companies are not allowed to take up any deposits from bank shareholders.

4.4.3 Finance Company 金融公司

1. A brief introduction

A finance company makes small loans with funds obtained from invested capital, surplus, and borrowings. It is a nonbank financial institution which mainly provides consumption loans, auto loans, and etc.

The finance companies can be broadly categorized as commercial finance companies and consumer finance companies. Commercial finance companies make commercial loans usually on a secured (collateralized) basis. Consumer finance companies primarily make consumer loans. Some of them specialize in credit card financing and are referred to as specialized finance companies.

The loans made by finance companies have traditionally been riskier than those made by commercial banks. Because much of their lending is short term, finance companies raise substantial amounts of fund by issuing the commercial papers in the money market. In fact, they are commonly considered as the largest category of commercial paper issuers. In the US, some of the most successful financial institutions are finance companies. The classic example is the General Electric Capital Corporation.

Some finance companies are referred to as captive finance companies. For example, General Motors Acceptance Corporation is the finance company subsidiary of General Motors (GM). Its principal operation is to finance car loans and lease to purchasers of GM cars and finance the inventory of GM dealers.

2. Finance companies in China

At present, there are some finance companies operating in China. For example, Mercedes-Benz Auto Finance Ltd. (MBAFC), headquartered in Beijing, which started business in November, 2005, is a company of the Daimler Financial Services Group, one of the world's largest automotive financial service providers worldwide. MBAFC is the dedicated finance and insurance source of Daimler AG's automotive products, offering a broad range of automotive finance and insurance solutions for dealers and customers in China.

As licensed by the relative regulatory authority, the finance companies in China may engage in the following business activities: taking deposits with maturity of no less than three months from its shareholders in the mainland of China; extending loans; making investments; discounting bill of exchange; financial leasing; agency business; borrowing from financial institutions; providing guarantees; transferring and selling receivables; and others.

Reading Material

What Is an Auto Finance Company?

An auto finance company is usually a wholly-owned subsidiary or an affiliate of an automotive manufacturer. Its purpose is to help consumers purchase the brands' products. For instance, Mercedes-Benz Auto Finance Ltd. is readily to finance consumers to buy the Mercedes-Benz cars.

What is the difference between an auto finance company and a bank? To the consumer, both provide money. The major difference is the way in which interest and fees are charged. Auto finance companies charge an interest rate that includes all fees. Many banks have a lower interest rate, but charge the customer additional fees which raise the effective interest rate.

4.4.4 Financial Asset Managing Company 金融资产管理公司

1. A brief introduction

A financial asset managing company is a financial intermediary whose major operation is to purchase, manage and dispose of non-performance loans (NPL) acquired from financial institutions, and its operational target is to preserve the asset value and maximize the recovery value.

2. Financial asset managing companies in China

Since the 1990s, especially after the Asian financial crisis, great attention has been given to the non-performing assets of financial institutions.

Before 1993, Chinese banks had never set up a bad debt provision and never written off bad debts, which resulted in a constant accumulation of bad debts and, in turn, financial exposure. The non-performance loan is undoubtedly a major hidden risk to the banks. Having learned overseas experiences and lessons, the Chinese government decided to set up financial asset management companies for integrated management and disposal of the non-performing loan acquired from commercial banks. The founding of the financial asset management company is an important measure to dispose non-performing assets, and is of great significance to take precautions against and dissolve financial risks.

In 1999, four financial asset managing companies were authorized to set up in China. They are the China Huarong Asset Management Corporation (CHAMC), the China Great Wall Asset Management Corporation (CGWAMC), the China CinDa Asset Management Corporation (CINDA), and the China Orient Asset Management Corporation (COAMC).

According to the Administrative Rules Governing the Financial Asset Managing Company, the financial asset managing company's major businesses include: debt collection; debt-equity swap and temporary share holding; bond issuing and borrowing from other financial institutions; financial and legal consultancy, asset and project appraisal; asset leasing, transfer and restructuring; initial public offerings recommendation for the enterprises under its management, bond and stock underwriting; and other businesses approved by the regulatory authority.

4.4.5 Credit Union 信用合作社

1. A brief introduction

Credit unions[28], also known as credit cooperatives, are financial institutions owned cooperatively by groups of persons having a common business, fraternal, or other interest. They make small loans to their members out of funds derived from the sale of shares to members.

Credit unions are owned and operated by and for their members. They are usually organized by a union or employers to serve employees. They are not-for-profit, and exist to provide a safe, convenient place for members to save money and to get loans at reasonable interest rates. Credit unions include rural credit cooperatives (RCCs) and urban credit cooperatives (UCCs).

The credit union typically pays higher dividend (interest) rates on shares (deposits) and charge lower interest on loans than banks. However, credit union revenues (from loans and investments) do need to cover operating expenses and dividends (interest paid on deposits) in order to maintain solvency.

The credit union offers many of the same financial services as banks, including savings accounts, credit cards, share draft (checking) accounts, share term certificates (certificates of deposit) as well as online banking.

2. The history of credit unions

The first cooperative was organized in 1844 by a group of workers in Rochdale, England. Friedrich Wilhelm Raiffeisen founded a credit society in Germany in 1849, but it depended on the charity of wealthy men for its support. Then he organized a new credit union in 1864 in accordance with the principles which are still in practice today. Germany's credit societies and similar institutions founded in Italy were the forerunners of the modern large cooperative "banks" in Europe.

Credit unions now have expanded around the globe, and their spectacular growth has made them been an important part of the global financial system. Today, credit unions are regularly gaining market shares in retail banking in various European countries. In the US, credit unions have gained popularity as an alternative financial resource for many consumers.

3. The difference between credit unions and banks

What makes a credit union different from a bank? Like other financial institutions, credit unions are closely regulated and they operate in a very prudent manner. For instance, in the US, the National Credit Union Share Insurance Fund administered by the National Credit Union Administration (NCUA), an agency of the federal government, insures deposits of credit union members at more than 9,000 federal and state-chartered credit unions nationwide. Deposits are insured up to $100,000; and also, the credit union accepts deposits and makes loans.

Debate on the Credit Union

From the viewpoints of different authors, credit cooperatives may be considered as non-profit organizations, or alternatively as for-profit enterprises making a profit for their members (who receive any profits earned by the cooperative in the form of dividends paid on savings or reduced interest rates on loans).

This debate comes from the credit unions' unusual organizational structure, which attempts to solve the "principal & agent" problem by ensuring that the owners and the users of the institution are the same people.

No matter whether it is or not for-profit, in normal cases, a credit union can not accept donations and must be able to prosper in a competitive market economy.

Unlike banks, credit unions are not in business to make a profit. The treasurer of a Midwestern Credit Union said that credit unions were "not for profit, not for charity, but for service," and that philosophy still holds true today. On the contrary, banks are owned by groups of stockholders who are interested in earning a healthy return on their investments.

In short, the positive aspect of credit unions is that they make low interest loans to their members. Because they are non-profit, member service organizations.

4. The rural credit cooperatives (RCCs) in China

In 2002, China's four state-owned commercial banks — the Industrial and Commercial Bank of China, the Bank of China, China Construction Bank and the Agricultural Bank of China closed their outlets in rural areas successively to focus on more profitable businesses in big cities. This has left the mission of financing agricultural needs with RCCs and RCCs have become more important lenders in the rural financial market.

China has achieved phenomenal progress in the reform of its rural credit cooperatives over the past several years. The China Banking Regulatory Commission (CBRC) statistics revealed that by March in 2005, the capital adequacy ratio of China's rural credit cooperatives grew 10. 94 percentage points since the end of 2002. The first eight provinces to start reforming rural credit cooperatives have found their capital adequacy ratios had risen as high as 8. 65% at the end of last year.

With an aggregated deposit balance of 3. 064 trillion yuan as of June in 2005, China's rural credit cooperatives have become the fourth group of financial institutions to break through the deposit record of 3 trillion yuan. The top three are the Industrial and Commercial Bank of China, the Agricultural Bank of China and the China Construction Bank.

To a large agricultural country like China, RCCs play an important role in rural development. Therefore, it is of vital significance for China to make further reform on RCCs and maintain their sound operation.

4.4.6   Pension Fund   退休养老基金

1. A brief introduction

Pension fund is a fund established by an employer or a body authorized by the government to facilitate and organize the investment of employees' retirement funds contributed by the employer and employees.

The pension fund is a common asset pool meant to generate stable growth over the long term by investing those funds safely and profitably, and provide pensions for employees when they reach the end of their working years and commence retirement.

Pension funds are commonly run by some sort of financial intermediary for the company and its employees, although some larger corporations operate their pension funds in-house. Pension funds control relatively large amounts of capital and represent the largest institutional investors in many nations.

Pension fund may be classified as open or closed pension funds, public or private pension funds.

Open pension funds support at least one pension plan with no restriction on membership while closed pension funds support only pension plans that are limited to certain employees. Closed pension funds are further sub-classified into: single employer pension funds, multi-employer pension funds, related member pension funds, individual pension funds.

The public pension funds refer to those pension funds operating under public law while the private pension funds under private law.

2. Social security funds in China

China social security funds consist of pension, unemployment, health, and occupational injury insurance, and the annual income of the social security funds increased about 20% year-on-year to 696 billion yuan in 2005.

Thereinto, the pension fund was set up in 2000 by the Chinese Government as a strategic reserve for its ageing population, and its total asset was valued at 201.02 billion yuan by the end of 2005. The fund mainly comes from budgetary allocation from the Ministry of Finance, revenues from sales of shares of State-owned firms listed overseas.

The pension fund has been permitted to begin to invest overseas as of May 1, 2006 under the provisional regulations governing the overseas investment of the pension fund, which became effective on the same day and was approved by the Ministry of Finance, the Ministry of Labor and Social Security and the People's Bank of China.

Overseas investment will help the fund to explore more investment opportunities, diversify investment risks and maintain and increase the value of the fund.

Group Discussion

1. Discuss the differences between the NBFIs and the banks.
2. Talk about the functions and operations of insurance companies.
3. Say something about the famous insurance companies in China.
4. Select one type of NBFI (except for insurance companies) and explain it to your partner.
5. Try to compare the NBFIs in China and in the US.

NOTES

1	trust company	信托公司
2	financial leasing company	融资租赁公司
3	finance company	金融公司
4	Lloyd's of London	伦敦劳埃德海上保险协会，伦敦劳埃德商船协会
5	liability insurance	责任保险
6	reinsurance company	再保险公司，分保公司
7	captive insurance companies	附属保险公司
8	ceding reinsurance	分出保险
9	assuming reinsurance	分入保险
10	Bulge Bracket	华尔街投资银行领导集团
11	initial public offering (IPO)	首次公开募股（发行）
12	open-end management investment company	开放式管理投资公司
13	open-end fund	开放式基金
14	mutual fund	共同基金（美国的一种投资公司形式）
15	closed-end management investment company	封闭式管理投资公司
16	close-end fund	封闭式基金

17　UITs（unit investment trusts）　单位投资信托基金

18　aggressive growth fund　积极成长型基金

19　balanced fund　平衡基金

20　hedge fund　对冲基金

21　China International Capital Corporation Ltd.（CICC）　中国国际金融有限公司（简称"中金公司"）

22　China Investment Corporation Ltd.　中国投资有限责任公司（简称"中投公司"）

23　estate administration　遗产管理

24　corporate trust services　法人信托业务

25　trust and investment corporation　信托投资公司

26　China International Trust and Investment Corporation（CITIC）　中国国际信托投资公司（现称为"中国中信集团公司"，即 CITIC Group，简称"中信集团"）

27　China Leasing Company Ltd.　中国租赁有限公司

28　credit union（credit cooperative）　信用合作社，合会，信用合作机构，信贷联盟

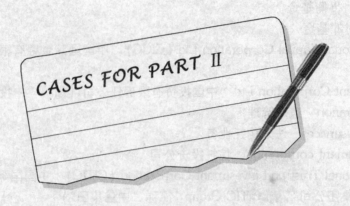

CASES FOR PART II

Bank of England
英格兰银行

About the Bank

The Bank of England is the central bank of the United Kingdom. Sometimes known as the "Old Lady" of Thread Needle Street, the Bank was founded in 1694, nationalized on 1 March 1946, and gained independence in 1997. Standing at the centre of the UK's financial system, the Bank is committed to promoting and maintaining monetary and financial stability as its contribution to a healthy economy.

Structure

In working towards its core purposes, the Bank is organized into four main operational areas — Monetary Analysis and Statistics, Markets, Financial Stability, Banking Services, which are supported by a Central Services area. This structure was introduced in June 1998 to reflect the Bank's new responsibilities in the light of the 1998 Bank of England Act. The Centre for Central Banking Studies offers teaching and technical assistance to other Central Banks.

Core Purposes

The Bank's roles and functions have evolved and changed over its three-hundred year history. Since its foundation, it has been the Government's banker and, since the late 18th century, it has been banker to the banking system more generally — the bankers' bank. As well as providing banking services to its customers, the Bank of England manages the UK's foreign exchange, gold reserves as well as other official reserve assets.

The Bank has two core purposes — monetary stability and financial stability. The Bank is perhaps most visible to the general public through its banknotes and, more recently, its interest rate decisions. The Bank has had a monopoly on the issue of banknotes (paper currency) in England and Wales since the early 20th century. But it is only since 1997 that the Bank has had statutory responsibility for setting the UK's official interest rate.

Interest rates decisions are taken by the Bank's Monetary Policy Committee. The MPC has to judge what interest rate is necessary to meet a target for overall inflation in the economy. The inflation target is set each year by the Chancellor of the Exchequer. The Bank implements its interest rate decisions through its financial market operations — it sets the interest rate at which the Bank lends to banks and other financial institutions. The Bank has close links with financial institutions and markets. This contact informs a great deal of its work, including its financial stability role and the collation and publication of monetary and banking statistics.

The Bank of England is committed to increasing awareness and understanding of its activities and responsibilities, across both general and specialist audiences alike. It produces a large number of regular and ad hoc publications on key aspects of its work and offers a range of educational materials. The Bank of England offers technical assistance and advice to other central banks through its Centre for Central Banking Studies, and has a museum at its premises in Thread Needle Street in the City of London, open to members of the public free of charge.

On-line Banking
网上银行

What Is On-line Banking?

On-line banking is a service provided by many thrifts, banks, and credit unions that allows their consumers to conduct banking transactions over the Internet using a mobile telephone, personal computer, or handheld computer. The consumers may be able to:

(1) access accounts round-the-clock, even on weekends;

(2) transfer funds between accounts;

(3) see balances on-line and find out whether checks or deposits have cleared;

(4) download information directly into personal finance software;

(5) receive and pay bills on-line (without check writing, envelopes, or stamps).

On-line banking can help the clients manage savings and checking accounts, apply for loans, or pay bills quickly and easily.

There are a growing number of so-called virtual banks that operate exclusively online. These on-line banks have low costs compared to traditional banks and so they may offer higher interest rates.

On-line Banking Security

Protection through single password authentication, as is the case in most secure Internet shopping sites, is not considered secure enough for personal on-line banking applications in some countries. On-line banking user interfaces are secure sites (generally employing the https protocol) and traffic of all information (including the password) is encrypted, making it next to impossible for a third party to obtain or modify information after it is sent. However, encryption alone does not rule out the possibility of hackers gaining access to vulnerable home PCs and intercepting the password as it is typed in (keystroke logging). There is also the danger of password divulgence and physical theft of passwords written down by careless users.

Many on-line banking services therefore impose a second layer of security. Strategies vary, but a common method is the use of transaction numbers (TANs) which are essentially single use passwords. Another strategy is the use of two passwords, only random parts of which are entered at the start of every on-line banking session. This is however slightly less secure than the TAN alternative and more inconvenient for the user. A third option, used in many European countries and currently in trial in the UK is providing customers with security token devices capable of generating single use passwords unique to the customer's token which is called two-factor authentication (2FA). Another option is using digital certificates, which digitally sign or authenticate the transactions, by linking them to the physical device (e. g. computer, mobile phone, etc.). While most on-line banking in the US still uses single password protection, the FFIEC (Federal Financial Institutions Examination Council) issued regulations requiring that banks implement more secure authentication mechanisms by the end of 2006. Most large US banks have responded not with security tokens or digital certificates, but by setting up a combination of controls that recognize a customer's computer, ask additional challenge questions for risky behavior, and monitor for fraudulent behavior.

Banks in many European countries (including the Scandinavian countries, the Netherlands, Austria and Belgium) are offering on-line banking for e-commerce payments directly from customer to merchants.

Internet Fraud

Some customers avoid on-line banking as they perceive it as being too vulnerable to fraud. The security measures employed by most banks can never guarantee the absolute safety, but in practice the number of fraud victims due to on-line banking is very small. This is probably due to the fact that a relatively small number of people use Internet banking compared with the total number of banking customers world wide. In fact, conventional banking practices may be more prone to abuse by fraudsters than on-line banking. Credit card fraud, signature forgery and identity theft are far more widespread "offline" crimes than malicious hacking. Bank transactions through Internet are generally traceable and criminal penalties for bank fraud are high. On-line banking becomes less secure if users are careless, gullible or computer illiterate.

The Illusions of Travel Insurance
旅游保险之幻象

Terrorism scares and hurricane warnings have spurred an increase in sales of travel insurance, but there's a catch: Most policies offer only very limited risk coverage, if any, should you want to cancel a trip because you're afraid to go.

Worried about liquid-explosive plots or subway bombings? That probably won't be covered. Thinking a hurricane 1,000 miles away could hit your favorite beach? It probably isn't covered, either. Sorry, but buying travel insurance now won't help.

The promise of travel insurance is that it will pay for the unreimbursable parts of a trip (such as airline tickets and hotel deposits) if a policyholder has to delay or cancel a trip, or help cover the cost of meals and hotel rooms if you get stranded. Policies often cover medical care if you get sick overseas and medical evacuation. That's potentially important since your medical insurance may not be accepted by hospitals overseas. But the travel insurance programs are filled with exclusions.

Many disasters that drive up the sales of policies aren't covered. Some policies exclude terrorism coverage altogether, forcing worried consumers to choose carefully. Only six of 24 Travel Guard International policies listed by Total Travel Insurance have any terrorism protection, for instance. The comprehensive policies that do have it account for 80% of sales, notes Travel Guard, one of the biggest travel insurers.

Even then, policies that include terrorism reimburse for canceled travel plans only if there's an attack in a city on your itinerary within 30 days of your departure. If a bombing in London makes you afraid to go to Paris, or even England, Manchester, your travel insurance won't help.

The reality is: there's no coverage for fear.

"It's the fear that drives up the sales, and that is something that these policies — the vast majority of them — don't protect," said Peter Evans, executive vice president of InsureMyTrip. com, which sells policies from 20 travel insurers.

One other catch: You may be out of luck, too, on issues like terrorism if you didn't buy the insurance within 15 days of when you booked the trip.

Like any insurance, the cost of a travel-insurance policy will vary depending on how expensive your trip is and what you want covered. You can buy a comprehensive policy with coverage for cancellations, delays that leave you stranded, flight accident, lost luggage, emergency medical and medical evacuations, or you can buy just the specific insurance pieces you want. "Trip Protector" insurance from Access America, which is sold through Orbitz, was priced yesterday at $194 for a $2,984 air and hotel package to Beijing. It offers reimbursement if you have to cancel for several specific reasons, including illness or injury (but it excludes pre-existing conditions), plus up to $500 for meals and hotels if you're delayed more than six hours, and some emergency medical benefits. It doesn't offer any terrorism coverage, Access America says.

Two travel-insurance companies, M. H. Ross and TravelSafe, do offer "cancel for any reason" policies that reimburse 75% of a trip's cost if you decide not to go. They typically cost 40% or more than standard insurance. Some companies have recently loosened restrictions. Last month, Travel Assist Network, which sells medical evacuation plans, said it eliminated its terrorism exclusion. The recent fighting between Israel and Hezbollah also showed the narrow limits of travel insurance. Travel Guard ruled it terrorism, but many insurers, including some of the biggest, such as Allianz AG's Access America, decided that the fighting was war rather than terrorism (even though Hezbollah is considered a terrorist organization). Claims weren't valid because all policies have a standard "act of war" exclusion, Access America spokeswoman Emily Porter noted.

Strict rules also limit the utility of travel insurance for hurricanes, consumer experts say. Once a tropical storm gets a name, even if it's 10 days or more from landfall, policies sold after the naming won't cover that storm because it's no longer an "unforeseen event". If you did buy travel insurance earlier, it will only cover you if the storm makes it impossible for you to get there, if there's a mandatory evacuation order, or if your destination is uninhabitable.

Just not wanting to go because of minor storm damage doesn't count. Or if you're simply worried that a hurricane might hit during your vacation and you cancel to avoid hassle, you'll get reimbursed only if the storm actually devastates your particular vacation spot, that is, the city of final destination, and of course exclude any spot you will just pass by.

"Travel insurance doesn't cover state of mind. A specific event has to happen," says Dan McGinnity, a spokesman for Travel Guard, a unit of American International Group Inc.

The US Travel Insurance Association says about 17 million travel insurance policies are sold each year, and annual sales have nearly doubled since Sept. 11, 2001. Cruise passengers and people traveling with tours and international vacations are most likely to purchase travel insurance. Many policies are sold by travel agents and tour companies, and on-line sales have been rising too.

Airline shutdowns, strikes and travel-company closures are other areas where policies sold after the first signs of trouble won't be valid. Once a strike date is set by an airline union, buyers are expected to be aware of possible trouble. If you buy travel insurance now for a coming trip on Northwest because you are worried about a possible flight attendants' strike beginning Friday, you won't be covered. And once an airline or tour company files for bankruptcy protection, a subsequent shutdown wouldn't be covered if the travel insurance was bought after the first court filing.

Some insurers post lists of financially troubled airlines whose tickets they won't cover. Total Travel Insurance, which sells policies from multiple insurers, says some insurers currently won't cover Delta Air Lines, UAL Corp.'s United Airlines, US Airways and Northwest Airlines.

It's the theory of the burning building, insurance companies say. If your house is on fire, you can't call up and buy fire insurance. Once terrorists attack, or tropical storms get names, or airlines run into financial trouble, or war breaks out, you can't insure yourself against those perils.

Insurance regulators say they don't get a lot of complaints about travel insurance, but when they do, the most frequent complaint is claim denial. So far this year, the Florida Department of Financial Services, which regulates insurers in Florida, has received 21 claim-denial complaints. It received 28 complaints during all of last year.

"It just seems to be that people are not reading the policy and understanding what they are buying," says Nina Banister, a spokeswoman for the agency.

PART III

Financial Market

金融市场

Chapter 5

Financial Markets and Financial Instruments

金融市场与金融工具

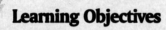

Learning Objectives

- ☑ To understand the definition and types of financial market
- ☑ To learn about the basics of financial instrument
- ☑ To grasp the four principal original financial instrument
- ☑ To learn the four major derivative financial instrument

Opening Vignette

Financial Instruments, Markets and Information

There are numerous financial instruments available to investors and financial managers. Each year new instruments arrive on the market and some leave. Many of the large investment houses have researchers developing new types of instruments. An example of one of the most recent innovations is the Caput. This instrument is an option on an option. Some investment houses have been selling call options (an option to buy at a pre-specified price) on put options (an option to sell at a pre-specified price).

The following is a short list of the major instruments available in the US. I have split the instruments into a number of broad categories according to my own opinions. The first is Money Market Instruments. These instruments are short-term cash substitutes. They usually have short maturities (one year or less), little or no default risk, and are highly liquid. The second category is Fixed-Income Capital Market Instruments. These instruments are characterized by longer term maturities (more than one year), their default risk is sometimes higher and they are generally less liquid. The third category is Equity Securities. These securities represent a residual claim on the assets of a corporation, i. e., all the fixed income obligations must be paid first. The fourth category consists of all the other types of instruments such as Futures and Options.

A. Money Market Instruments
1. Treasury bills[1]
2. Federal agency securities
3. Municipal notes
4. Certificates of deposit (CD)[2]
5. Commercial paper[3]
6. Repurchase agreements (repo)[4]
7. Bankers' acceptances (BA)[5]
8. Eurodollars
9. Federal funds
B. Fixed-Income Capital Market
1. US savings bonds
2. US treasury notes
3. US treasury bonds
4. US agency issues
5. Municipal issues
6. Corporate issues
7. Eurobonds
C. Equity Securities
1. Preferred stock[6]
2. Common stock[7]
D. Other Instruments
1. Investment company shares
2. Options
3. Warrants
4. Forwards and futures

There are two broad categories of financial markets: Primary and Secondary. The primary market is dominated by investment banking firms. New securities are usually sold in the primary market to these firms. The investment bank will then offer its part of the issue to the general investor. The secondary market is where securities are traded from investor to investor either on an organized exchange or over-the-counter (OTC)[8].

Organized Exchanges are centralized auction-like markets. The two largest stock markets in the US are the New York Stock Exchange (NYSE) and the American Stock Exchange (AMEX). Also, there are organized exchanges for options: the Chicago Board of Options Exchange (CBOE), the American Stock Exchange, the Philadelphia Stock Exchange and the Pacific Coast Stock Exchange. Futures contracts are traded on the Chicago Mercantile Exchange, the Chicago Board of Trade and the New York Futures Exchange.

The OTC market is a network of dealers in particular securities. Securities that are not traded on the organized exchanges but are traded on OTC. Prices are quoted through the National Association of Security Dealers Automated Quotation System (NASDAQ).

Information is critical to the operation of financial markets. Prices respond to the arrival of new information. There are two broad classifications of information: Public and Private.

Examples of public information are regularly scheduled macro-economic news announcements. A summary of the scheduled announcements for the week and the market forecasts appears on page 2 of the Wall Street Journal. Most of these announcements take place at 8:30am Eastern Time (before the US stock markets open but ten minutes after the many of the futures contracts have begun trading). Most in finance track these important macro-economic announcements. The surprises (actual minus forecast) move the market. For example, if inflation is higher than expected, the fixed income securities will almost always lose value (as investors demand a higher yield to compensate them for the higher inflation).

Private information is more difficult to pin down. It is usually revealed by trading activity. For example, an investor with negative information about a firm's prospects might sell a large block of stock. When the market observes the size of the block and the price drop, they will infer this negative news. However, the private information trader will act strategically. It is unlikely that it will dump all the stock in one block. Trades will probably be executed in smaller pieces (and might even be cloaked with some contradictory buy orders).

Timely information is the gold key to your success. The minimum condition is a daily read of the Wall Street Journal (WSJ). One should concentrate on the third section, "Money & Investing". You should also read the WSJ every day. The weekly Barron's also includes excellent financial coverage.

For an international perspective, I recommend the Financial Times. This is usually delivered one day late (however, same day delivery is possible in major cities). The Wall Street Journal Europe is also in the library.

Of course, for trading, these information sources are not enough. Most traders have access to the Reuters wire and most traders in the fixed income market use Telerate. Datastream is also an excellent service.

 Warm-up Questions

1. What do you think about the financial markets in US?
2. Do you think the financial instruments traded in US are all available in China at present?
3. Why the financial markets in US are much more developed than those in China?
4. Why the information is critical to trade successfully in financial markets?

5.1 An Overview of Financial Market
金融市场概述

5.1.1 The Definition of Financial Market 金融市场的定义

A financial market is a market in which financial assets (securities) such as stocks and bonds, commodities such as precious metals or agricultural goods, and other fungible items of value can be easily purchased or sold at low transaction costs and at prices that reflect efficient markets. Common examples of financial markets: credit markets, stock market, bond market, and foreign exchange market.

One party transfers funds in financial markets by purchasing financial assets previously held by another party. Financial markets facilitate the flow of funds from surplus units to deficit units and thereby facilitate financing and investing by household, firms, and government agencies. Typically a borrower issues a receipt to the lender promising to pay back the capital. These receipts are securities which may be freely bought or sold. In return for lending money to the borrower, the lender will expect some compensation in the form of interest or dividends[9].

In Finance, Financial markets facilitate the raising of capital (in the capital markets), the transfer of risk (in the derivatives markets), and international trade (in the currency markets).

Financial markets have evolved significantly over several hundred years and are undergoing constant innovation to improve liquidity.

5.1.2 The Elements of Financial Market 金融市场要素

1. The participants of financial market

In order to understand the financial market, it is important to identify those participating in it. At present in many countries, the participants can be roughly classified into the following four categories: central bank, lenders, borrowers and financial intermediaries.

1) Central bank

Central bank's primary responsibility of participating financial market is to maintain the stability of the national currency and money supply, but more active duties include controlling subsidized loan interest rates, and acting as a "bailout[10]" lender of last resort to the banking sector during times of financial crisis. It may also have supervisory powers, to ensure that banks and other financial institutions do not behave recklessly or fraudulently.

2) Lenders

Lenders are people who have available funds in excess of their desired expenditures that they are attempting to loan out.

Individuals often do not think of themselves as lenders but they lend to other parties in many ways. Lending activities may be: putting money in a savings account at a bank; contributing to a pension plan; paying premiums to an insurance company; investing in government bonds; or investing in company shares, etc.

Companies sometimes tend to be lenders of capital. When companies have surplus cash that is not needed for a short period of time, they may lend their cash surplus via money markets or other financial markets.

Households are the major lenders in financial markets. They lend their money via the savings of bank, or buying bond or stock, or others ways.

3) Borrowers

Borrowers are people who have a shortage of funds relative to their desired expenditures who are seeking to obtain loans. Borrowers attempt to obtain funds from lenders by selling to lenders newly issued claims against the borrowers' real assets.

Individuals borrow money via bank's loans for short term needs or longer term mortgages to help finance a house purchase.

Companies borrow money to aid short term or long term cash flows. They also borrow to fund future business expansion. They can borrow from banks, also can borrow by issuing bond or stock at financial market.

Governments often find their spending requirements exceed their tax revenues. To make up this difference, they need to borrow. Governments also borrow on behalf of nationalized industries, local authorities and other public sector bodies. Governments borrow by issuing bonds. In the UK, the government also borrows from individuals by offering bank accounts and premium bonds[11]. Government debt seemingly expands rather than being paid off. One strategy used by governments to reduce the value of the debt is to influence inflation. Local authorities may borrow in their own name as well as receiving funding from national governments.

Many borrowers needing large amount of fund may have difficulty in raising money within their own countries and they may turn to international financial markets to meet their demands.

4) Financial intermediaries

Financial intermediaries are financial institutions that engage in financial asset transformation. Financial intermediaries purchase one kind of financial asset from borrowers — generally some kind of long-term loan contract whose terms are adapted to the specific conditions of the borrower — and sell a different kind of financial asset to lenders, generally some kind of relatively liquid claim against the financial intermediary. In addition, financial intermediaries also hold financial assets as part of an investment portfolio rather than as an inventory for resale. In addition to making profits on their investment portfolios, financial intermediaries make profits by charging relatively high interest rates to borrowers and paying relatively low interest rates to savers.

Types of financial institutions are usually categorized into the two groups of banking institutions and non-bank institutions.

Table 5 – 1 illustrates where financial markets fit in the relationship between lenders and borrowers.

Table 5 – 1   Relationship between lenders and borrowers

Lenders	Financial Intermediaries	Financial Markets	Borrowers
Individuals Companies	Banks Insurance Companies Pension Funds Mutual Funds	Inter-bank Stock Exchange Money Market Bond Market Foreign Exchange	Individuals Companies Central Government Municipalities Public Corporations

2. Financial instrument

Financial instruments are instruments having monetary value or recording a monetary transaction, such as drafts, bills of exchange, checks and promissory notes. Financial markets provide their participants with the most favorable conditions for purchase/sale of financial instruments. There are many types of financial instruments, and they will be examined later.

3. The prices of financial instrument

The prices of financial instruments are the prices that well-informed and investors must pay for them in a free and competitive market. Financial markets provide vehicles by which prices are set both for newly issued financial assets and for the existing stock of financial assets.

4. The trading mechanisms of financial market

There are two general trading mechanisms of financial markets: floor trading markets[12] and over-the-counter (OTC) Markets.

Sometimes a market for a particular financial instrument has a specific geographic location such as the New York Stock Exchange or the Osaka Options and Future Exchange, which are institutions serving as financial marketplaces housed in buildings in New York City and Osaka (Japan) respectively. An exchange acts as an intermediary to all related transactions, and takes initial margin from both sides of the trade to act as a guarantee.

However, the market usually has no one specific location. This is the case for the over-the-counter market which enables the traders to make transactions through computer and telecommunication networks. For instance, many well-known common stocks are traded over-the-counter in the United States through NASDAQ (National Association of Securies Dealers' Automated Quotation System).

5.1.3　The Types of Financial Market　金融市场的类型

The financial markets can be divided into different types by different standards.

1. Money market & capital market

The financial market can be broadly divided into money markets and capital markets.

The money market is the market for shorter-term securities, generally those mature in one year, while the capital market is the market for longer-term securities, generally those with the maturity of more than one year.

Money markets match borrowers and lenders/investors of large short-term currency funds and capital markets match those of medium and long-term currency funds.

In practice, however, the distinction between short, medium and long-terms is not usually clear cut nor well-defined.

2. Primary market & secondary market

Primary markets are securities markets in which newly issued securities are offered for sale to buyers. Secondary markets are securities markets in which existing securities that have previously been issued are resold. The initial issuer raises funds only through the primary market.

3. Domestic financial market & international financial market

Domestic financial markets involve participants within a country and they operate in markets that are regulated by domestic rules and standards. Instead, international financial markets allow a number of traders who are not only across the country but also around the world to make transactions. There was a relative absence of uniform international standards to govern international transactions made by participants from jurisdictions at different stages of financial sophistication.

5.2 An Overview of Financial Instrument
金融工具概述

5.2.1 The Definition of Financial Instrument 金融工具的定义

Financial instrument is a legally enforceable agreement between two or more parties, certifying the amount, the maturity date and the price of a financial transaction.

Broadly speaking, all documents used in financial transactions may be regarded as financial instruments, such as bonds, stocks, checks, promissory notes, bills of exchange, and etc. Since most financial instruments have something to do with credit transactions, they may be also called credit instruments.

5.2.2 The Characteristics of Financial Instrument 金融工具的特点

Financial instruments commonly have three characteristics: liquidity, safety, and profitability.

Financial instruments can be traded on a market and turned into cash easily, which are described as being liquid, and having liquidity, if there are enough buyers and sellers to absorb sudden shifts in supply and demand without price distortions. Financial markets provide the holders of financial assets with a chance to resell or liquidate these assets.

Safety means that financial instruments should not be too risky or the risks could be controlled. Many financial instruments, such as derivatives, can be useful tools for corporations to manage risks. However, they may be very risky themselves. The risks of financial instruments include market risks and credit risks. Market risk refers to the risk of loss arising from movements in market variables such as interest rates, exchange rates, stock indices, and price levels. Credit risk is the risk that the counterparty does not fulfill his contractual obligation when it is due.

Financial instrument holders can make profit from hold financial instrument, which is the profitability of financial instrument. It is absolutely necessary to be profitable for any financial instrument, or else no one would like to buy or sell it.

5.2.3 The Types of Financial Instrument 金融工具的类型

Financial instruments can be divided into different categories as follows.

1. Original financial instrument vs. derivative financial instrument

Original financial instruments[13], such as paper currency, bonds and stocks, whose value are determined directly by markets. They can be divided into securities which are readily transferable, and other original instruments such as loans and deposits of which both borrower and lender have to agree on a transfer.

Derivative financial instruments[14] are financial instruments, whose value derives from the value of some other financial instruments, such as an underlying commodity, security, index, rate or event, which determine the prices of derivative instruments. For example, a stock option is a derivative instrument because its value derives from the value of a stock and an interest rate swap also a derivative because its value derives from one or more interest rate. Unlike stocks, bonds and bank loans, derivatives generally do not involve the transfer of a title or principle, and thus can be thought of as creating pure price exposure, by linking their value to a notional amount or principle of the underlying item. The assets from which a derivative derives its value is called underlying assets[15]. Some of the main uses of derivative instruments are to fix future prices in the present (forwards and futures), to exchange cash flows or modify asset characteristics (swaps) and to endow the holder with the right but not the obligation to engage in a transaction (options). It should be noted that the derivative instruments can either to decrease or increase the risks, depending on whether the trader was a hedger or a speculator.

The origin of derivatives can be traced back to the 12th century, but the modern financial derivatives emerged in the 1970s. Since then, with the development of economic and financial globalization, the financial derivative has been developing rapidly and playing a very important role in financial business in many countries and regions around the world.

There are various derivatives tradable in financial markets, but forward, future, option and swap are the ones most commonly used.

2. Debt instrument vs. equity instrument

Debt instruments are particular types of securities that require the issuer (the borrower) to repay the fund on the maturity date and generally pay the interest at regularly scheduled intervals until the maturity date to the holder (the lender), regardless of the success or failure of any investment projects for which the borrowed funds are used. A debt instrument holder will participate in the management of the issuer only when the issuer goes bankrupt. An example of a debt instrument is a 30-year mortgage. Debt instruments can be further categorized into short term (less than one year) and long term instruments (longer than one year).

In contrast, equity instruments are shares of ownership or stocks in a company, which confers on the holder an ownership interest of the issuer.

3. Money market instrument vs. capital market instrument

Money market instruments are those instruments which are traded in the money market and they usually mature in less than one year and have good liquidity. Examples are treasury bills, certificates of deposit, commercial paper, repurchase agreements, and banker's acceptance.

In contrast, capital market instruments are generally traded in capital market, and their maturity terms are longer than one year. Examples are stocks and bonds.

5.2.4　The Prices of Financial Instrument　金融工具的价格

1. The prices of financial instrument

The prices of financial instruments are the prices that investors must pay for them in financial markets. There are two major prices: issue price and trade price.

Issue price is the price at which new securities are sold in the primary market (issuing market) and it is set for newly issued financial assets; whereas trade price is the price at which the existing financial instruments are traded in the secondary market (trading market) and it is set by the market.

The new instruments can be issued at par or face value, or at a discount or premium. Issue at par means that a new financial instrument is firstly sold at a price that is equal to its face (or par) value, and issue at a discount is at a lower price than the face value while at a premium is at a higher price than the face value.

2. The pricing models of financial instrument

There are three famous pricing models of financial instruments: capital asset pricing model (CAPM), arbitrage pricing theory (APT), and option pricing theory (OPT).

1) CAPM

This model was originally developed in 1952 by Harry Markowitz and fine-tuned over a decade later by others, including William Sharpe. The CAPM describes the relationship between risk and expected return, and it serves as a model for the pricing of risky securities. CAPM manifests that the expected return of a security or a portfolio equals the rate on a risk-free security plus a risk premium[16]. If this expected return does not meet or beat the required return, the investment should not be undertaken.

Various assumptions must be defined in order to arrive at the CAPM equilibrium.

(1) Investors maximize expected utility of wealth.

(2) Investors have homogenous expectations and use the same input list.

(3) Markets are frictionless and the borrowing rate is equal to the lending rate.

(4) There are many investors, each with an endowment of wealth which is small compared to the total endowment of all investors (investors are price-takers).

(5) All investors plan for one identical holding period.

(6) There are no taxes or transaction costs.

With these assumptions we can build the CAPM model and arrive at the prevailing equilibrium. The commonly used formula to describe the CAPM relationship is as follows:

$$E(R_i) = R_f + \beta_{im}(E(R_m) - R_f)$$

Where: $E(R_i)$ is the expected return on the capital asset; R_f is the risk-free rate of interest[17]; β_{im} (the beta coefficient) is the sensitivity of the asset returns to market returns; $E(R_m)$ is the expected return of the market; $(E(R_m) - R_f)$ is sometimes known as the market premium or risk premium (the difference between the expected market rate of return and the risk-free rate of return).

Note that the expected market rate of return is usually measured by looking at the arithmetic average of the historical returns on a market portfolio and the risk free rate of return used for determining the risk premium is usually the arithmetic average of historical risk free rates of return and not the current risk free rate of return.

It is important to remember that high beta shares usually give the highest returns. Over a long period of time, however, high beta shares are the worst performers during market declines (bear markets). The investors might receive high returns from high beta shares, but there is no guarantee that the CAPM return will be realized.

2) APT

The Arbitrage Pricing Theory model, proposed by Stephen Ross in 1976, assumes that the risk premium is a function of several variables, not just one, i. e. macro-economic variables (V_1, V_2, $\cdots$, V_n), as well as a company "noise", etc.

APT holds that the expected return of a financial asset can be modeled as a linear function of various macro-economic factors or theoretical market indices, where sensitivity to changes in each factor is represented by a factor-specific beta coefficient. The model-derived rate of return will then be used to price the asset correctly, and the asset price should equal the expected end of period price discounted at the rate implied by model. If the price diverges, arbitrage should bring it back into line.

The APT, along with CAPM, is one of the two influential theories on asset pricing. The APT differs from the CAPM in that it is less restrictive in its assumptions. It allows for an explanatory (as opposed to statistical) model of asset returns. It assumes that each investor will hold a unique portfolio with its own particular array of betas, as opposed to the identical "market portfolio". In a sense, the CAPM can be considered a "special case" of the APT in that the security market line represents a single-factor model of the asset price, where beta is exposure to changes in value of the market.

In addition, the APT can be seen as a "supply side" model, since its beta coefficients reflect the sensitivity of the underlying asset to economic factors. Thus, factor shocks would cause structural changes in the asset's expected return, or in the case of stocks, in the firm's profitability. In contrast, the CAPM is considered a "demand side" model. Its results, although similar to those in the APT, arise from a maximization problem of each investor's utility function, and from the resulting market equilibrium (investors are considered to be the "consumers" of the assets).

3) OPT

Robert C. Merton was the first to publish a paper expanding the mathematical understanding of the options pricing model and coined the term "Black-Scholes" options pricing model, by enhancing work that was published by Fischer Black and Myron Scholes. The paper was first published in 1973. The foundation for their research relied on work developed by scholars such as Louis Bachelier, A. James Boness, Edward O. Thorp, and Paul Samuelson.

The fundamental insight of Black-Scholes model is that the option is implicitly priced if the stock is traded.

The key assumptions of the Black-Scholes model are as follows.

(1) The price of the underlying instrument S_t follows a geometric Brownian motion with constant drift μ and volatility σ:

$$dS_t = \mu S_t dt + \sigma S_t dW_t$$

(2) It is possible to short sell the underlying stock.

(3) There are no arbitrage opportunities.

(4) Trading in the stock is continuous.

(5) There are no transaction costs or taxes.

(6) All securities are perfectly divisible (e. g. it is possible to buy 1/100 of a share).

(7) It is possible to borrow and lend cash at a constant risk-free interest rate.

(8) The stock does not pay a dividend (see below for extensions to handle dividend payments).

The above assumptions lead to the following formula for the price of a European call option[18], with exercise price K on a stock currently trading at price S, i. e. the right to buy a share of the stock at price K after T years. The constant interest rate is r, and the constant stock volatility is σ. Thus, the price of the European call option P can be simplified to:

$$P = SN(d_1) - Ke^{-rT}N(d_2)$$

Where:

$$d_1 = \frac{\ln(S/K) + (r + \sigma^2/2)T}{\sigma\sqrt{T}}$$

$$d_2 = \frac{\ln(S/K) + (r - \sigma^2/2)T}{\sigma\sqrt{T}} = d_1 - \sigma\sqrt{T}$$

(Here N is the standard normal cumulative distribution function.)

On the contrary, the price of a put option[19] may be computed from this by put-call parity and simplified to:

$$P(S, T) = Ke^{-rT}\Phi(-d_2) - S\Phi(-d_1)$$

(Here Φ also refers to the standard normal cumulative distribution function.)

Option pricing model determines the fair market value of European options but may also be used to value American options.

Option pricing theory has been successfully applied in the valuation of both financial and real investments in the last two decades.

5.3 The Original Financial Instruments
原生金融工具

5.3.1 Note 票据

The term note (bill) is used to cover a security with a relatively short maturity, generally up to nine months. The yield is usually obtained, not through the regular payment of interest, but through discounting. Bills can be issued by local or national governments (when they are termed t-bills.); or by private bodies (bills of exchange, for example, are the traditional instruments to finance international trade).

The most important notes are the commercial bills/notes.

Commercial bill is a money market instrument issued by large banks and corporations. It is generally not used to finance long-term investments but rather for purchases of inventory or to manage working capital. It is commonly bought by money funds (the issuing amounts are often too high for individual investors), and is generally regarded as a very safe investment. With a relatively low risk level, commercial bill returns are not large. There are three basic types of commercial bill: promissory note[20], bill of exchange[21], and check.

1. Promissory note

A promissory note represents a promise by a borrower to repay a loan. Generally promissory notes are not known as securities. Failure to pay a promissory note renders the borrower immediately liable to be sued for payment.

The promissory note referred to as a note payable in accounting, is a contract detailing the terms of a promise by one party (the maker or drawer) to pay a sum of money to the other (the payee). The obligation may arise from the repayment of a loan or from another form of debt. For example, in the sale of a business, the purchase price might be a combination of an immediate cash payment and one or more promissory notes for the balance.

A company may issue promissory notes to raise money. Typically, an investor agrees to loan money to the company for a set period of time. In exchange, the company promises to pay the investor a fixed return on his/her investment, typically principal plus annual interest.

The term of a promissory note typically include the principal amount, the interest rate if any, and the maturity date. Sometimes there may be provisions concerning the payee's rights in the event of a default, which may include foreclosure of the maker's interest. Demand promissory notes are notes that do not carry a specific maturity date, but are due on demand of the lender. Usually the lender will give the borrower a notice a few days before the payment is due.

A promissory note differs from an I.O.U. in that the latter is a simple acknowledgement of the existence of a debt owed, whereas a promissory note, as its name implies, contains an affirmative undertaking to pay the amount stated.

A promissory note that meets certain conditions may be a negotiable instrument. Negotiable promissory notes are commonly used together with mortgages in the financing of real estate transactions. Other uses of promissory notes include the capitalization of corporate finances through the issuance and transfer of commercial papers.

The most welcome promissory note in the market is a bank note, which is defined as a promissory note made by a bank and payable to the bearer on demand.

2. Bill of exchange

A bill of exchange, also called a draft, is a written order by the drawer to the drawee to pay money to the payee. The bill of exchange is used widely in international trade, and is an unconditional order made by one person to his bank to pay the payee a specific sum on a specific date.

The bill of exchange involves three basic parties, the drawer—the one who issues the bill, and through which he instructs the drawee to pay a sum of money, the drawee—the one who is nominated to pay the sum of money at the due date, and he must have a liability towards the drawer and this liability constitutes the provision and the due amount, and the beneficiary or payee—the one to whom the drawee makes the payment. The beneficiary can be the drawer himself or a third party to whom he might owe money.

Bill of exchange can be divided into the following two categories by the differences between the issuers (drawers): bank bill and trade bill[22]. If the bill of exchange is issued by a bank it is a bank bill while a trade bill if drawn by a company. In general, a bank bill is more acceptable than a trade bill because the risk involved and therefore the discount rate is relatively low.

According to the time of payment, sight drafts and time drafts[23] could be defined respectively. The sight draft, sometimes also called demand draft, is a draft payable on demand or at sight or on presentation. Time draft, also called usance draft, is a draft payable at a fixed or determinable future time.

Acceptance is an engagement to pay money according to the terms and conditions on the bill, which usually made by writing the word "accepted" across the face of the bill. The time draft needs to be accepted. When accepted by a bank, a draft will be ranked as a banker's acceptance draft, which is one of the tradable instruments in money market.

3. Check

A check is a negotiable instrument instructing a commercial bank to pay a specific amount of a specific currency from a specific demand account held in the maker/depositor's name with this commercial bank. Both the maker and payee may be natural persons or legal entities. Checks are available to organizations and individuals that have checkable deposit accounts with commercial bank to make various payments.

The check had its origins in the ancient banking system, in which bankers would issue orders at the request of their customers, to pay money to identified payees. Such an order was referred to as a bill of exchange. So check also can be defined as a bill of exchange drawn on a bank and payable on demand.

Parties to a check normally include a maker or drawer—the depositor with a bank, a drawee—the bank with which the drawer has a checkable deposit account, and a payee—the party to whom the money is paid.

A check issued by a bank on its own account for a customer for payment to a third party is called a cashier's check[24] (or a treasurer's check, a bank check). A check issued by a bank but drawn on an account with another bank is a teller's check[25].

5.3.2 Stock 股票

1. The definition of stock

In financial markets, stock is the capital raised by a corporation or joint-stock company through the issuance and distribution of shares. A person or organization which holds at least a partial share of stocks is called a shareholder (stockholder). The aggregate value of a corporation's issued shares is its market capitalization.

Stocks can represent ownership in a corporation, and have been one of the best investments one can make. Every shareholder becomes a part owner of the company. If the company does well, shareholders may receive periodic dividends and/or be able to sell their stock at a profit. If the company does poorly, the stock price may fall and shareholders could lose some or all of the money their invested. The income received from shares is called a dividend. The potential for profit is much greater than with guaranteed investments or interest-paying investments. Shares can be voting or non-voting, which means that they respectively do or do not carry the right to vote on the board of directors and corporate policies.

The main benefits for corporations to issue shares of stock are: the owners (stockholders) are liable only for the amount invested; it can raise large amounts of fund through the sale of stocks; and complete control is vested in a board of directors, which the stockholders vote out. However, it can not be neglected that it is disadvantageous for the stock corporations to publish and distribute detailed financial reports periodically, as stipulated by law, to all stockholders and some supervisory government agencies.

2. The history of stock

During Roman times, the empire contracted out many of its services to private groups called "*publicani*". Shares in "*publicani*" were called "*socii*" (for large cooperatives) and "*particulae*" which were analogous to today's Over-the-Counter shares of small companies. Though the records available for this time are sketchy, there is some evidence that a speculation in these shares became increasingly widespread and that perhaps the first ever speculative bubble in "stocks" occurred.

The first company to issue shares of stock after the Middle Ages was the Dutch East India Company in 1606. The innovation of joint ownership made a great deal of Europe's economic growth possible following the Middle Ages. The technique of pooling capital to finance the building of ships, for example, made the Netherlands a maritime superpower. Before adoption of the joint-stock corporation, an expensive venture such as the building of a merchant ship could be undertaken only by governments or by very wealthy individuals or families.

Economic Historians find the Dutch stock market of the 1600 particularly interesting: there is clear documentation of the use of stock futures, stock options, short selling, the use of credit to purchase shares, a speculative bubble that crashed in 1695, and a change in fashion that unfolded and reverted in time with the market (in this case it was headdresses instead of hemlines). Dr. Edward Stringham also noted that the uses of practices such as short selling continued to occur during this time despite the government enacting laws against it. This is unusual because it shows individual parties fulfilling contracts that were not legally enforceable and where the parties involved could incur a loss. Stringham argues that this shows that contracts can be created and enforced without state sanction or, in this case, in spite of laws to the contrary.

3. The types of stock

Stocks can be broadly classified as common stock and preferred stock.

Common stock, also referred to as common or ordinary shares, as the name implies, are the most usual and commonly held form of stock in a corporation. The other type of shares that the public can hold in a corporation is known as preferred stock (preference share), which has priority over common stock in the distribution of dividends and assets.

Common stock typically has voting rights in corporate decision matters, though perhaps different rights from preferred stock. In order of priority in a liquidation of a corporation, the shareholders of common stock are near the last. Dividends paid to the stockholders must be paid to preference shareholders before common shareholders.

Common shareholders have the following legal rights: the right to receive stock certificates as evidence of ownership, to vote at stockholders meetings, to receive any declared dividends, to sell the stock, to information and to receive financial reports about the company and to buy newly issued shares of stock by the company before the shares are sold to the public so that current owners can maintain their proportionate interest in the company.

Although being called preferred stock, most preferred shares provide no voting rights in corporate decision matters. The dividend paid to the preferred share holders are generally fixed no matter how much the profit made by the corporation is.

5.3.3 Bond 债券

1. The definition of bond

A bond is a debt security, in the form of a written promise to pay a specific sum at a specified future date—typically 5 to 10 years—and to pay a specific annual rate of interest (the coupon) during its lifetime. It is the principal vehicle through which markets exist in assets representing public or corporate debt.

Bonds are long-term debt or funded debt, issued by corporations, and governments and their agencies to finance operations or special projects. Corporations pay back interest and principal from earnings, whereas governments pay from taxes, or revenues from special projects. Unlike preferred stock, a corporation must pay interest on its bonds, and if the corporation goes bankrupt, bondholders are paid before any stockholders.

The holder of a bond is paid interest until the date when the bond matures. Then the amount of the bond, its face value, is paid back. Investors can buy a new bond and keep it until it matures. Or they can buy and sell existing bonds. The return on a bond is called the yield. As an investable instrument, the bond is riskier, but paid a higher interest rate than money market fund or demand deposit, while it is safer than the stock, but usually less profitable because its yield is fixed and has no potential for growth.

A bond is simply a loan, but in the form of a security, although terminology used is rather different. The issuer is equivalent to the borrower, the bond holder to the lender, and the coupon to the interest. Bonds enable the issuer to finance long-term investments with external funds.

In some nations, both bonds and notes are used irrespective of the maturity. Market participants normally use bonds for large issues offered to a wide public, and notes for smaller issues originally sold to a limited number of investors. There are no clear demarcations. There are also "bills" which usually denote fixed income securities with three years or less, from the issue date, to maturity. Bonds have the highest risk, notes are the second highest risk, and bills have the least risk. This is due to a statistical measure called duration, where lower durations have less risk, and are associated with shorter term obligations.

2. The elements of bond

All bonds have a par (face) value[26], an interest rate, and a maturity date.

The interest rate is often called the coupon rate, because many bond certificates have coupons that the bondholder must present to receive the interest. In a primary offering, the investor buys the bond for par value. This money goes to the issuer. Periodically, the issuer pays interest to the investor, which is calculated by multiplying the par value by the interest rate divided by the number of payments in a year. Example: if the interest rate is 8% and the par value is $1,000, then the interest earned annually is $80. If the company pays interest semi-annually, then the bondholder will receive twice payments of $40 every year until maturity. When the bond matures, then the current owner gets back the par value of the bond. In other words, the loan is paid off. Because the amount of interest the bond pays is fixed, bonds are a type of fixed-income security.

Bond maturities vary widely. Generally speaking, long-term bonds mature in 10 to 30 years or more; medium-term bonds have maturity term longer than 1 year, but less than 10 years; short-term bonds mature in a year or less. Normally, the longer the maturity term, the greater the interest rate for a given risk ranking.

3. The types of bond

Bonds can be described as different types, including fixed rate bond, floating rate bond, zero-coupon bond, inflation linked bond, bearer bond, registered bond, book-entry bond, municipal bond, and international bond.

(1) Fixed rate bond has a coupon that remains constant throughout the life of the bond.

(2) Floating rate bond (FRN) has a coupon that is linked to a variable money market index. Such a coupon is then reset periodically, normally every three months.

(3) Zero coupon bond does not pay any interest. It is issued at a substantial discount from par value. The bond holder will receive the par value on the maturity date. An example of zero coupon bonds is Series E savings bonds issued by the US government.

(4) Inflation linked bond, in which the principal amount is indexed to inflation. The interest rate is lower than for fixed rate bonds with a comparable maturity. However, as the principal amount grows, the payments increase with inflation. The government of the UK was the first to issue inflation linked Gilts in the 1980s. Treasury Inflation-Protected Securities (TIPS) and I-bonds are examples of inflation linked bonds issued by the US government.

(5) Bearer bond is an official certificate issued without a named holder. In other words, the person who has the paper certificate can claim the value of the bond. Often they are registered by a number to prevent counterfeiting, but may be traded like cash. Bearer bonds are very risky because they can be lost or stolen. Especially after federal income tax began in the United States, bearer bonds were seen as an opportunity to conceal income or assets. US corporations stopped issuing bearer bonds in the 1960s, US Treasury stopped in 1982, and state and local tax-exempt bearer bonds were prohibited in 1983.

(6) Registered bond is a bond whose ownership (and any subsequent purchaser) is recorded by the issuer, or by a transfer agent. It is opposite to the bearer bond. Interest payments and the principal are paid directly to the registered owner on maturity date.

(7) Book-entry bond is a bond that does not have a paper certificate. As physically processed paper bonds and interest coupons became more expensive, issuers (and banks that used to collect coupon interest for depositors) have tried to discourage their use. Most book-entry bonds are issued without the option of a paper certificate, even to the investors who prefer them.

(8) Municipal bond is a bond issued by a local government or their agencies. Interest incomes received by holders of municipal bonds are often exempted from the income tax of the local government in which they are issued, although those municipal bonds issued for certain purposes may not be tax exempted.

(9) An international bond is a bond available to be sold outside the country of its issuer. There are two types of international bond: foreign bond and Eurobond. A foreign bond is an international bond issued by a country that is denominated in a foreign currency and that is for sale exclusively in the country of that foreign currency. A Eurobond is an international bond denominated in a currency other than that of the country in which it is sold. More precisely, it is issued by a borrower in one country, denominated in the borrower's currency, and sold outside the borrower's country.

5.3.4   Fund   基金

1. The definition of fund

Fund, is generally a professionally managed pool of money from a group of investors. A fund manager invests the funds in securities, including stocks and bonds, money market instruments or some combination of these, based upon the fund's investment objectives.

When investing in a fund, the investor buys shares (or portions) of the fund and become a shareholder of the fund. One can make money from a fund in three ways.

(1) Income is earned from dividends on stocks and interest on bonds. A fund pays out nearly all income it receives over the year to fund owners in the form of a distribution.

(2) If the fund sells securities that have increased in price, the fund has a capital gain. Most funds also pass on these gains to investors in a distribution.

(3) If fund holdings increase in price but are not sold by the fund manager, the fund's shares increase in price. The investor can then sell his fund shares for a profit.

Reading Material

Funds in China

For most investors hoping to play the Chinese market, owning funds is the easiest way to go. A sampling of funds with big positions in China is as follows:

JF Great China—Fund objective to provide long-term capital growth by investing primarily in companies in China (include the Mainland, Hong Kong, and Taiwan).

Fidelity Greater China Fund—The fund invests principally in equity securities quoted on stock exchanges in China.

Matthews China Fund—A single country fund that invests in the companies of the Chinese Mainland listed on the stock markets of Shanghai, Shenzhen and Hong Kong.

Aliance Bernstein Greater China '97 Fund—A non-diversified investment company that seeks long term capital appreciation through investment, under normal circumstances, of at least 80 percent of its net assets in equity securities issued by Greater China companies.

US Global Investors China Region Opportunity Fund—Fund's objective is to achieve capital appreciation by capitalizing on the economic growth in the Greater China Region, including China and Singapore.

Alger China-US Growth Fund—This new fund invests not only in China but also in US and other Asian or multinational companies that stand to benefit from China's economic expansion.

The advantages of fund investment are as follows:

(1) Professional management. The primary advantage of funds (at least theoretically) is the professional management of your money. Investors purchase funds because they do not have the time or the expertise to manage their own portfolio. A fund is a relatively inexpensive way for a small investor to get a full-time manager to make and monitor investments.

(2) Diversification. By owning shares in a fund instead of owning particular stocks or bonds, your risk is spread out. The idea behind diversification is to invest in a large number of assets so that a loss in any particular investment is minimized by gains in others. In other words, the more stocks and bonds you own, the less any one of them can hurt you. Large funds typically own hundreds of different stocks in many different industries. There is little chance for an individual investor to build this kind of a portfolio with a

small amount of money.

(3) Economies of Scale. Because a fund buys and sells large amounts of securities at a time, its transaction costs are much lower than an individual needs to pay.

(4) Liquidity. Just like the stock, the fund allows you to request that your shares be converted into cash at any time.

2. The history of fund

Massachusetts Investors Trust was founded on March 21, 1924, and, after one year, had 200 shareholders and $ 392, 000 in assets. The entire industry represented near $ 10 million in 1924.

The stock market crash of 1929 slowed the growth of funds. In response to the stock market crash, the US Congress passed the Securities Act of 1933 and the Securities Exchange Act of 1934. These laws require that a fund be registered with the Securities and Exchange Commission (SEC) and provide prospective investors with a prospectus that contains required disclosures about the fund, the securities themselves, and fund manager. The SEC helped draft the Investment Company Act of 1940, which sets forth the guidelines with which all SEC-registered funds today must comply.

With renewed confidence in the stock market, funds began to blossom. By the end of the 1960s, there were approximately 270 funds with $ 48 billion in assets. The first retail index fund, the First Index Investment Trust, was formed in 1976 and headed by John Bogle, who conceptualized many of the key tenets of the industry in his 1951 thesis at Princeton University. It is now called the Vanguard 500 Index Fund and is one of the largest funds ever with in excess of $ 100 billion in assets.

One of the largest contributors of fund growth was Individual Retirement Account (IRA) provisions added to the Internal Revenue Code in 1975, allowing individuals (including those already in corporate pension plans) to contribute $ 2, 000 a year. Funds are now popular in employer-sponsored defined contribution retirement plans and IRAs.

As of April 2006, there are 8, 606 funds that belong to the Investment Company Institute (ICI)—the national association of investment companies in the United States, with combined assets of $ 9. 207 trillion.

3. The types of fund

The major types of fund are as follows.

A closed-end fund has a predefined and fixed number of shares available to the public. The total number of shares cannot be increased, also cannot be redeemed. Fresh demand for investment in the fund will push up the price of existing shares, allowing the fund manager to issue more shares. The price of closed-end fund shares traded on a secondary market after their initial public offering is determined by the market and may be greater or less than the share's net asset value.

An open-end fund, (referred to as a mutual fund by some authors), is opposite to the closed-end fund and refers to the fund whose size is variable in accordance with the investor's free purchase and redemption. It is one of the major investment vehicles in developed countries and has been widely accepted by the public. An investor can purchase shares in such funds directly from the fund company, or through a brokerage house.

An index fund maintains investments in companies that are part of major stock (or bond) indices, such as the S&P 500[27]. The assets of an index fund are managed according to the performance of a particular published index. Since the composition of an index changes infrequently, an index fund manager makes fewer trades.

A fund of funds (FOF) is funds which invest in other underlying funds (i. e., they are funds comprised of other funds). The funds at the underlying level are typically funds which an investor can invest in individually. A fund of funds will typically charge a management fee which is smaller than that of a normal fund because it is considered as a fee charged for asset allocation services.

A hedge fund is a fund aiming to arbitrage, which can take both long and short positions, buy and sell undervalued securities, trade options or bonds, and invest in almost any opportunity in any market where it foresees impressive gains at reduced risk.

A stock fund, also known as equity fund, invests in stocks. While funds most often invest in the stock market, fund managers don't only buy any old stock they find attractive. Some funds specialize in investing in large-cap stocks, others in small-cap stocks, and still others invest in the left-mid-cap stocks.

On the contrary to the stock fund, a bond fund invests in various bonds. Bond funds account for 18% of fund assets. Types of bond funds include term funds, which have a fixed time period before they mature. Municipal bond funds generally have lower returns, but have tax advantages and lower risk. High-yield bond funds invest in corporate bonds, including high-yield bonds or junk bonds. With the potential for high yield, these bonds carry with high risk.

A money market fund is a fund that invests in money market ultra short-term securities. Money market funds hold 26% of fund assets in the US. They are often touted as the safest kind of fund, but that depends on your perspective. On the one hand, it's almost impossible to lose your principal by investing in such funds. On the other hand, their returns are so low (4% to 6% on average) that they can't beat inflation over time. In the long run, your money loses its buying power and therefore actually becomes less valuable.

5.4 The Derivative Financial Instruments
衍生金融工具

The most common derivatives are forwards, futures, options and swaps. They were all originally created as ways of hedging against risks in financial markets. But trading in futures or options can also be highly speculative, with large gains or losses to be made.

5.4.1 Forward 远期

The simplest and perhaps oldest form of a derivative is the forward contract. It is the obligation to buy (borrow) or sell (lend) a specified quantity of a specified item at a specified price or rate at a specified time in the future.

A forward contract on foreign currency might involve party A agreeing to buy (while party B to sell) 2,000,000 Euros for US dollars at $0.8615 on a determinable time in future. A forward agreement on interest rate might involve party A agreeing to borrow (while party B to lend) $2,000,000 for 3 months at a 2.90% annual rate on a determinable time in future. If an investor enters into a forward contract/agreement at a particular price/rate, the price/rate might either go up or come down, and therefore the investor might either make a profit or a loss.

The typical usage of a forward would be something under the following circumstances. A firm having its assets in a local currency has taken a loan repayable in a foreign currency after 3 months. There is an exchange rate risk for the business: if the local currency depreciates in relation to the foreign currency, the firm has to suffer a loss. To cover against this risk, the firm may choose to enter into a forward contract— that is, it agrees today to buy the foreign currency from the other party to the contract (the seller) after 3 months at prices prevailing today, against a pre-fixed premium. Obviously, only when the perceptions of the seller and the buyer as to future prices of the foreign currency differ, such a forward contract can be concluded and both parties will consider it as a win-win deal.

As one of the major derivative financial instruments, forwards can be used either for speculation or for hedging. The forward contracts may be entered into for transactions of commodities, securities, loans or others, and the terms and conditions of the contracts vary widely.

5.4.2 Futures 期货

Futures were originated to help minimize risk for both the buyers and sellers of commodity transactions, but eventually it evolved into a financial instrument that could be traded like stocks. The futures contract for each commodity was standardized in order to facilitate the futures business. Standard specifications in a futures contract include the amount of the commodity, the grade, and delivery dates. More recently, new futures were created on the basis of the items completely different from agricultural products, such as stock indexes, interest rates, and even the weather, and provided more investment choices for the investors. They have become great tools to hedge portfolios or to simply profit from buying and selling.

In short, the futures can be defined as a standardized futures contract, traded in a futures exchange, stipulating the parties to buy or sell a certain underlying item at a certain date and a set price in the future. The future date is called the delivery date or final settlement day. The pre-set price is called the futures price. The price of the underlying items on the delivery date is called the settlement price.

The buyers and sellers of futures can be classified as hedgers or speculators. Hedgers use futures to minimize risk, like the farmers who use futures to guarantee a price for their product when they will be sold after harvest, or a miller who wants an expectable price for grain that he will have to purchase in the harvest season. Futures can also be used to hedge investment portfolios. However, speculators use futures to make a profit, by buying low and selling high (not necessarily in that order). The speculator has no intention of making or taking delivery. A speculator is making a bet on the future.

A buyer of a futures contract has the long position, whereas the seller of the contract has a short position. The short position holder should deliver the commodity described in the futures contract to the long position holder at the final settlement date. The long position holder profits when the price of the commodity increases, whereas the short position holder profits when it decreases.

When the buyer and the seller agree to the price, quantity, delivery time, and the underlying item, the clearinghouse then assumes the obligation to buy the seller's contract and sell it to the buyer (as shown in Figure 5 – 1). Because the clearinghouse is the trader to both parties, they don't have to worry about the performance of the contract. Furthermore, the clearinghouse allows each trader to close out his position independently of the other party to the futures contract.

In practice, few futures contracts will be actually implemented by delivering the specified commodity and most positions will be closed out. The long position holder closes out his position by selling an identical futures contract and the short position could be offset by buying an identical contract before the delivery date.

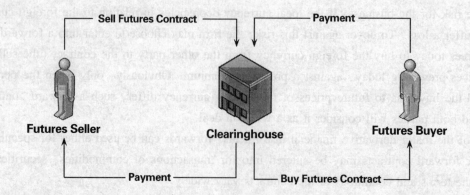

Figure 5 – 1   The trading of future

5.4.3   Option   期权

Options are contracts where one party agrees to pay a fee to another for the right (not the obligation) to buy something from or sell something to the other. The buyer of the option has the right to exercise the option in order to buy or sell at the more favorable strike price, the writer or seller of the option, who is in the short position, has the obligation to fulfill the contract if the buyer choose the exercise the option.

The fee paid to buy an option is known as the premium. What determines premium for an option is the length of time before the option expires, the volatility in the price of the underlying item, the current market price and the strike price.

The option-buyer will choose to exercise the option only when he is in-the-money, otherwise the only loss is the cost of buying and holding the option. On the other hand, the option-seller only makes returns by way of charging premium for selling the option, against which he takes the risk of being out-of-money. If the option is not exercised, he gains the premium, but if the option is exercised, he might lose substantially. Hence, the option has an asymmetric return profile.

Two basic types of options are call options and put options. A call option is an option to call, that is, the option-buyer has the right to buy the underlying asset at a specified price (known as the strike or exercise price) at a specified time in the future. A put option is just the reverse—the option-buyer has the right to sell the underlying item at a specified price at a specified time in the future.

For example, a person who worries the price of his ABC stock may go down before he plans to sell it may pay a fee to buy a put option from another person. Thus the former became the buyer of a put option while the latter is the seller. If the ABC stock price actually declines after a few days and the former will choose to exercise the put option by selling the ABC stock at the price specified in the option contract.

In sum, a call option gives the option-buyer the right to buy the underlying item at the strike price, and therefore the option will be profitable if the market price of the underlying item goes up. A put option gives the option-buyer the right to sell at the strike price, and will be profitable if the market price goes down. Here is a useful memory device: call up — put down.

The options can be divided into the two groups of European options and American options[28]. A European option can only be exercised on the expiration date. An American option may be exercised at any time during the life of the option.

In modern financial markets, the underlying items of the options include stock, stock index, interest rate, foreign currency and futures.

5.4.4 Swap 互换

Swap contracts, in comparison to forwards, futures and options, are one of the more recent innovations in financial derivative markets. The first currency swap contract, between the World Bank and IBM, dated in August of 1981.

The basic idea in a swap contract is that the counterparties agree to swap two different types of payments. Each payment is calculated by applying a specific interest rate, index, exchange rate, or the price of some underlying commodity or asset to a notional principal. The principal is considered notional because the swap generally does not require the transfer or exchange of principal (except for some foreign currency swaps). Payments are scheduled at regular intervals throughout the tenor or lifetime of the swap. When the both payments are denominated in the same currency, only the net balance of the two payments need be made actually.

Two major types of swaps are: interest rate swaps and currency swaps.

Interest rate swap refers to one party agrees to swap cash flows with another. A typical usage of interest rate swap is a swap of fixed interest rates with floating rates. For example, firm A may have a fixed-rate loan while another firm B may have a floating-rate loan; each of the firms would prefer to have the other type of loan. Rather than cancel their existing credit line (if this is possible, it may be expensive), the two firms can achieve the same effect by agreeing to "swap" cash flows: A pays B based on a floating-rate loan, and B pays A based on a fixed-rate loan. By swapping the cash flow, each converts his loan into another type. Interest rate swaps are derivative financial instruments used for hedging and speculation in interest rates.

A currency swap is a foreign exchange agreement between two parties to exchange a given amount of one currency for another, and after a specified period of time, to give back the original amounts swapped. Currency swaps fulfill the same function in spreading the risk of exchange-rate fluctuations. Typically, two banks with matching exposures (i.e. obligations to make similar payments), but in two different currencies, at some future date may choose to swap the risks. Without the swap, any movement in the exchange rate of one currency against the other in the future paying date would bring windfall profit to one bank, but substantive loss to the other. By making the swap, however, the future exchange rate of this currency pair is pre-set between the two banks and there will be no profit or loss for either bank to pay in the future.

Currency swaps are often combined with interest rate swaps. For example, a US corporation plans to acquire a French company may seek to swap a cash flow for their fixed rate debt denominated in US dollars for a floating-rate debt denominated in Euro. This is especially common in European financial markets where companies "shop" for the cheapest debt regardless of its denomination and then seek to swap it for the debt in desired currency.

Group Discussion ▶▶▶

1. Talk about the definition and elements of financial market.
2. Discuss the characteristics of financial instrument.
3. Compare the origin and derivative financial instruments.

4. Tell the difference between stock and bond.

5. Try to simulate a trade of futures or other derivative instruments with your partner.

NOTES ▶▶▶

1 treasury bill 国库券（也称"T-bill"）

2 certificate of deposit（CD） 存（款）单（通常指"negotiable CD"，即"可转让存单"）

3 commercial paper 商业票据（亦用"commercial note/bill"）

4 repurchase agreement（repo） 回购协议

5 bankers' acceptance（BA） 银行承兑（汇票）

6 preferred stock 优先股（亦用"preferred share"或"preference stock"）

7 common stock 普通股（亦用"common share"、"equity stock"、"ordinary stock/share"或"general stock"）

8 over-the-counter（OTC） 场外市场，店头市场

9 dividend 股息（口语中有时简称"divi."）

10 bailout 最后贷款人，拯救银行

11 premium bond 溢价债券，（英）政府有奖债券

12 floor trading market 场内市场

13 original financial instrument 原生金融工具（亦用"primary financial instrument"）

14 derivative financial instrument 衍生金融工具

15 underlying asset 基础资产，标的资产

16 risk premium 风险升水，风险补偿

17 risk-free rate of interest 无风险利率

18 call option 看涨期权，买权

19 put option 看跌期权，卖权

20 promissory note 本票，期票

21 bills of exchange 汇票

22 bank bill 银行汇票（亦用"banker's bill"）；trade bill 商业汇票（亦用"trader's draft"）

23 sight draft 即期汇票（亦用"demand draft"）；time draft 远期汇票（亦用"usance draft"）

24 cashier's check 银行支票

25 teller's check 出纳支票

26 par（face）value 面值（亦用"face value"）

27 S&P 500 标准普尔 500 股票指数（全称为"Standard & Poor's Composite 500 Index"）

28 European option 欧式期权；American option 美式期权

Chapter 6

Money Market
货币市场

Learning Objectives

- ☑ To understand the basics about money market
- ☑ To learn the inter-bank market and inter-bank rate
- ☑ To learn about the commercial notes and treasury bills
- ☑ To learn about the repos market and the CDs market

Opening Vignette

Money Market: What Is It?

Whenever a bear market comes along, investors realize that the stock market is a risky place for their savings. It's a fact we tend to forget while enjoying the returns of a bull market! Unfortunately, this is the truth of the risk-return tradeoff. To get higher returns, you have to take on a higher level of risk. For many investors, a volatile market like stock market is too much to stomach—then the money market offers an alternative to these higher-risk investments.

The money market is better known as a place for large institutions and governments to manage their short-term cash needs. However, individual investors have access to the market through a variety of different securities. In this article, we'll cover various types of money market securities and how they can work in your portfolio.

The money market is a subsection of the fixed income market. Many investors generally think of the term fixed income as being synonymous to bonds. In reality, a bond is just one type of fixed income security. The difference between the money market and the bond market is that the money market specializes in very short-term debt securities (debts that mature in less than one year). Money market investments are also called cash investments because of their short maturities.

Money market securities are essentially I.O.U.s issued by governments, financial institutions and large corporations. These instruments are very liquid and considered extraordinarily safe. Because they are extremely conservative, money market securities offer significantly lower returns than most other securities.

One of the main differences between the money market and the stock market is that most money market securities trade in very large denominations. This limits access for the individual investor. Furthermore, the money market is a dealer market, which means that firms buy and sell securities in their own accounts, at their own risk. Compare this to the stock market where a broker receives commission to acts as an agent, while the investor takes the risk of holding the stock. Another characteristic of a dealer market is the lack of a central trading floor or exchange. Deals are transacted over the phone or through electronic systems.

The easiest way for individual investors to gain access to the money market is with a money market fund, or sometimes through a money market bank account. These accounts and funds pool together the assets of thousands of investors in order to buy the money market securities on their behalf. However, some money market instruments, like treasury bills (T-bills), may be purchased directly. Failing that, they can be acquired through other large financial institutions with direct access to these markets.

There are several different instruments in the money market, offering different returns and different risks. In the following sections, we'll take a look at the major money market instruments.

T-bills are short-term government securities that mature in one year or less from their issue date. They are considered to be one of the safest investments and thereby they don't provide a great return.

A certificate of deposit (CD) is a time deposit with a bank. CDs are safe, but the returns aren't great, and your money is tied up for the length of the CD.

Commercial paper is an unsecured, short-term loan issued by a corporation. Returns are higher than T-bills because of the higher default risk.

Banker's acceptances (BA) are negotiable time draft for financing transactions in goods. BAs are used frequently in international trade and are generally only available to individuals through money market funds.

Eurodollars are US dollar-denominated deposit at banks outside of the United States. The average Eurodollar deposit is very large. The only way for individuals to invest in this market is indirectly through a money market fund.

Repurchase agreements (repos) are a form of overnight borrowing backed by government securities.

We hope this article has given you a basic idea of the securities in the money market. It's not exactly a sexy topic, but definitely worth knowing about, as there are times when even the most ambitious investor puts cash on the sidelines.

Warm-up Questions

1. What do you think about the money market?
2. Why money market has lower risk level than stock market?
3. What should he/she pay attention to when an individual investor accesses to money market?

6.1 An Overview of Money Market
货币市场概述

6.1.1 The Definition and Characteristics of Money Market
货币市场的定义及特点

Money market is financial market for borrowing and lending money for one year or less. The money market is not a physical place, but an informal network of banks and traders linked by telephones, fax machines, and computer networks.

The short-term debts and securities sold on the money markets—which are known as money market instruments—have maturities ranging from one day to one year, most often 30 days or even less. Money market instruments are considered one of the prime investment instruments in the market. They are safe, liquid and offer attractive returns to investors. Some examples of common money market instruments include treasury bills, certificates of deposit, commercial papers, and repos.

ECB Injects More Funds into Money Market

The European Central Bank (ECB) injected 61.05 billion Euros (around 83 billion US dollars) into the money market on Friday after pumping in huge funds on the previous day.

The move was aimed at maintaining short-term rate stability, according to the Frankfurt-based central bank of the Euro-zone.

Friday's cash injection came after the ECB had unexpectedly pumped 98.4 billion Euros (around 129.65 billion US dollars) into the market on Thursday.

Thursday's injection is the largest liquidity injection in the history of the ECB.

The average rate for Friday's operation came in at 4.08 percent, whereas the ECB had offered unlimited overnight funds Thursday at exactly 4 percent.

ECB spokesman Niels Buenemann said Thursday's overnight liquidity injection was unusual, but added that it had been motivated by the aim "to ensure orderly conditions in the money market."

The ECB wanted the money market rates close to their key refinancing rate of 4 percent, and when they spiked up well above that level, the bank had decided to act, he said.

The spokesman denied that this conflicted with repeated ECB indications that an interest rate hike was on the cards for the Sept. 6 Governing Council meeting.

Although aimed at settling markets, Thursday's ECB fine-tuning operation caused widespread anxiety on stock markets around the world. The US Federal Reserve also provided the money market with two smaller injections.

Investors believed that the central banks foresaw serious problems in the banking sector arising from the US subprime mortgage crisis.

Wall Street fell sharply with the news, and the decline spread to Asian markets on Friday and to Europe when markets opened, although European markets later recovered some lost ground.

Generally speaking, trading in the money market is a very safe investment coming with a relatively low return, which is most appropriate for temporary excess cash or short-term time deposits. Bid and ask spreads are comparatively small due to the large size and high liquidity of the market. The major traders in money market are financial institutions and individual corporations and governments who prefer the highest liquidity and the lowest risk.

Although securities traded on the money market carry less risk than long-term debt, they are still not entirely risk free. After all, banks do sometimes fail, and the fortunes of companies may change in unexpected rapidness. The range of possible outcomes is less for money market investments because of their relative low risks.

Nevertheless, even though the distant future may be clouded, the investors can usually be confident that a particular company will survive for at least the next month. Second, only well-established companies can borrow the desired fund in money markets. Because the lenders in money markets are going to lend money for only several days, and can't afford to spend too much time in evaluating the credit risk, therefore they will only lend to the blue-chip borrowers whose financial trustworthiness are considerably good.

6.1.2　The Functions of Money Market　货币市场的功能

The money market is important for promoting the liquidity of capital because it allows the companies with a temporary cash surplus to invest in short-term securities, and the companies with a temporary cash shortfall to borrow funds on a short-term basis. In essence, it acts as a repository for short-term funds.

Large corporations generally handle their own short-term financial transactions, participating in the money market through dealers. Small businesses, on the other hand, often choose to invest in money-market funds, which are professionally managed funds only investing in short-term securities.

6.1.3　The Participants of Money Market　货币市场的参与者

The core of money market consists of banks' borrowing and lending to each other, using certificates of deposit, repurchase agreements and other similar instruments.

Finance companies typically fund themselves through issuing large amounts of commercial paper secured by the pledge of eligible assets. Examples of eligible assets include auto loans, credit card receivables, residential/commercial mortgage loans, mortgage backed securities and other similar financial assets. Certain large corporations with strong credit ratings, issue commercial paper on their own credit. Other large corporations arrange for banks to issue commercial paper on their behalf via commercial paper lines.

Governments are involved in money markets through the trading activities by the treasury and the central bank. They interact with other players in the market such as the commercial banks, the funds and corporate companies.

Other financial institutions, such as insurers and trust companies, also play some parts to keep the money market vibrant and liquid.

Trading companies often purchase bankers acceptances in money markets to make payments to overseas suppliers.

Individuals play an important and integral part of the money market through deposits and lending, investments and borrowings at banks and funds. The easiest way for individual investors to gain access to the money market is with money market funds, or sometimes through a bank account. These accounts and funds pool together the assets of thousands of individual investors in order to trade the money market instruments on their behalf and consequently the out coming yields and risks will be shared by all these investors.

6.1.4   The Types of Money Market   货币市场的类型

Money market could be classified into the following submarkets by the different instruments traded: inter-bank market, commercial notes market, treasury bills market, repos market, and CDs market.

An inter-bank market is a market for banks to finance each other.

Commercial notes market is a market where commercial bills/papers are issued and traded.

Treasury bills market is a market for governments to raise fund by issuing treasury bills and investors to trade these bills for profit.

Repos market is a market in which a dealer or other holder of securities (usually T-bills) sells the securities to a lender and agrees to repurchase them at a specified future date at a specified price. Repo is the abbreviation for repurchase agreement. Repo is usually very short-term, mostly from overnight to 30 days. The very-short-term maturity and governmental backing make repos carry with extremely low risks.

CDs market is a market in which certificates of deposit are traded.

6.2   Inter-bank Market
银行同业市场

6.2.1   A Brief Introduction to Inter-bank Market   银行同业市场简介

An inter-bank market is a market in which only banks trade. It refers to the short-term money or foreign exchange markets which are only accessible to banks or financial institutions. There is no geographical or physical marketplace and the inter-bank transactions take place over communication networks such as Bloomberg or Reuters. So it is more appropriate to define inter-bank market as a financial system and trading of currencies among banks and financial institutions, excluding retail investors and smaller trading parties.

Inter-bank transactions are generally termed to be of "marketable size" over five million US dollars and approximately 50% of all foreign exchange transactions in the world are inter-bank trades. While some inter-bank trading is performed by banks on behalf of large customers, most inter-bank trading takes place from the banks' own accounts.

The inter-bank market is significant to banks because it allows their day-to-day liquidity positions to be adjusted, enabling banks' surplus funds to be used profitably, and marginal funds to be raised to support additional business. The existence of an efficient inter-bank market means that the banks' lending activities and therefore profitability are not limited by the amount of their customers' retail deposits. Apart from satisfying the official need for maintaining liquidity, the banks can cut the margin of their liquidity to a minimum and acquire profit-making assets. The inter-bank funds have always been a major source of funding for the banking system.

6.2.2 Inter-bank Rate 银行同业拆借利率

The lending rate in inter-bank market is the inter-bank offer rate, which is important as a determinant of the general interest rates banks charge and pay to borrowers and depositors respectively. Another important rate in inter-bank is the inter-bank bid rate which is quoted for deposits.

Given the key position of the inter-bank market in the financial process, inter-bank rate are also central to other financial transactions. For lenders in the inter-bank market, the inter-bank offer rate represents the rate of return on their funds. The higher the rate is, the greater the incentive that the banks have to offer higher interest to attract customers' deposits. For the borrowers, the inter-bank offer rate represents the cost of funds that they borrow to finance their business. Moreover, other marketable instruments such as the CDs are usually tied closely to the inter-bank offer rate as well.

Reading Material

China Opens Inter-bank Lending Market Wider

Non-banking financial organizations engaged in insurance, trust, financial or insurance assets management, financial leasing and auto financing have been allowed for the first time to borrow and lend money on China's inter-bank market as of Aug. 6.

Under a formal method on inter-bank lending market released Monday by the People's Bank of China, a total of 16 types of financial institutions have become eligible to apply for the access to the market, covering "all banking institutions and most non-banking financial institutions".

Analysts said that the new market players would help improve the transparency of financial market, break down the capital barriers among banks, securities, insurance and funds, and facilitate the interest rate reform. The regulations also extended the maximum term for inter-bank lending by commercial banks, urban and rural credit cooperatives and policy banks from the previous four months to one year.

New players such as financial assets management companies, financial leasing, insurance and auto financing are allowed to borrow or lend for three months at most while companies engaged in financing, securities, trust and the management of insurance assets, for only seven days.

The maximum borrowing limits for inter-bank lending also vary with the qualifications of financial institutions, with commercial banks, urban and rural credit cooperatives and policy banks allowed to borrow 8 percent of their major liabilities.

Inter-bank lending market is where financial institutions buy or sell funds needed to meet their reserve requirements in short term. Established in 1996, the market has seen 703 market participants by the end of 2006 with an annual trade volume of 2.15 trillion yuan, over 10 times of the original volume ten years ago.

The Shanghai Inter-bank Offered Rate was introduced in last September as a major inter-bank offered rate and has become one of the most important interest rate indexes for China's money market.

Zhou Rongfang, deputy director of the Financial Market Department of the Shanghai Headquarters of the People's Bank of China said in late June that financial institutions would gain more autonomy in participating in inter-bank market operation and managing risks control.

6.3   Note Market
票据市场

6.3.1   A Brief Introduction to Note Market   票据市场简介

The primary instrument traded in the note market is the commercial note/bill.

For many corporations, borrowing short-term money from banks is often a laborious and annoying task. The desire to avoid such tasks as much as possible has led to the widespread popularity of commercial notes/bills, which are also referred to as commercial papers by most western authors.

Commercial papers consist of unsecured notes issued for raising short-term funds by large non-bank institutions which have a very high credit rating. Interest on commercial paper is often incorporated in the price in terms of a discount to coupon value. One of the most significant aspects of commercial paper is that it is negotiable, which means that it can be freely transferred from one party to another, either through endorsement or delivery.

Commercial papers and other notes may be payable on demand or on a specified future date. The notes to be redeemed on a future date are called time bills and usually need to be accepted. The time bills drawn on and accepted by banks are known as banker's acceptances, which are also tradable instruments in money markets.

Various investors are involved in the note market and the commercial banks are always the biggest ones. They may accept or discount the notes and then resell or rediscount them before the maturity date in order to obtain financing or make a profit. Alternatively, they can also choose to hold and present the notes to the drawers for payment on the maturity date.

Note markets differ very much from one country to another. Undoubtedly, the note markets in the most developed countries are most developed, such as the US note market, which were originated in the early 19th century and have become considerably matured and sophisticated nowadays. Their market-sizes, the structure of investors and the types of tradable instruments are far more advanced than those of note markets in the developing countries.

6.3.2 The Types of Note Market 票据市场的类型

1. Commercial paper market

Commercial papers are generally used for purchases of inventory or to manage working capital rather than to finance long-term investments. They are commonly used in business transactions, since it is a reliable and expedient means of dealing with large sums of money and minimizes the risks inherent in using cash, such as the increased possibility of theft. Maturities on commercial paper are usually no longer than nine months, with maturities of between one and two months being the average.

Commercial paper is highly liquid. By its nature, it relates to transaction flows that usually involve days, sometimes months, and very rarely, years. Because these assets are considered very liquid, they tie very well with short-term lending programs. Ideally, a company who is trying to eliminate their cash flow gap will use short-term liquid assets to deal with the cash flow gap and support and sustain the long-term viability of the business with infrastructure related loans to lands, buildings and equipments that are focused on long-term objectives.

For the most part, commercial paper is a very safe investment because the financial situation of a company can easily be predicted over a few months. Furthermore, typically only companies with high credit ratings and credit worthiness issue commercial paper. Over the past 40 years, there have only been a handful of cases where corporations have defaulted on their commercial paper repayments. As a relatively low risk instrument, commercial papers' returns are moderate.

Commercial paper essentially can be compared as an alternative to lines of credit with a bank. Once a company becomes large enough, and maintains a high enough credit rating, then using commercial paper is always cheaper than using a bank line of credit. Nevertheless, many companies still maintain bank lines of credit to act as a "backup" to the commercial paper. In this situation, banks often charge fees for the amount of the line of credit that doesn't have a balance. While these fees may seem like pure profit, if the company ever actually needs to use the line of credit it would likely be in serious trouble and have difficulty paying it back.

Currently more than 1,700 companies in the United States issue commercial papers. Financial companies comprise the largest group of commercial paper issuers, accounting for nearly 75% of the commercial paper outstanding at mid-year 1990. The commercial paper is usually issued in denominations of $100,000 or more. Therefore, smaller investors can only invest in commercial paper indirectly through money market funds.

There are two methods of issuing commercial paper. The issuer can market the papers directly to a buyer or holder such as most money funds. Alternatively, it can sell the papers to a dealer, who then sells them in the market. The dealer market for commercial paper involves large securities firms and subsidiaries of bank holding companies.

Direct issuers of commercial paper usually are financial companies which have frequent and sizable borrowing needs, and find it more economical to sell papers without the use of an intermediary. In the United States, direct issuers save a dealer fee of approximately 3 basis points annualized, or $30,000 on every $100 million annualized outstanding. This saving compensates for the cost of maintaining a permanent sales staff to market the papers. Outside the United States, dealer fees are rather lower.

2. Banker's acceptance market

A bankers' acceptance (BA), is a time draft drawn on and accepted by a bank. Before acceptance, the draft is not an obligation of the bank; it is merely an order by the drawer to the bank to pay a specified sum of money on a specified date to a named person or to the bearer of the draft. Upon acceptance, which occurs when an authorized bank accepts and signs it, the draft becomes a primary and unconditional liability of the bank. If the bank is well known and enjoys a good reputation, the accepted draft may be readily sold in an active note market. A banker's acceptance is also a money market instrument—a short-term discount instrument that usually arises in the course of international trade.

A bankers' acceptance starts as an order to a bank by a bank's customer to pay a sum of money at a future date, typically within six months. At this stage, it is like a postdated check. When the bank endorses the order for payment as "accepted", it assumes the responsibility for ultimate payment to the holder of the accepted draft (acceptance). At this point, the acceptance may be traded in secondary markets much like any other claim on the bank.

Bankers' acceptances are considered as very safe assets, since they allow traders to substitute the bank's credit standing for their own. They are used widely in international trade where the creditworthiness of one trader is unknown to the trading partner. Acceptances sell at a discount from face value of the payment order, just as US Treasury bills are issued and traded at a discount from par value. Banker's acceptances trade at a spread over T-bills. The rates at which they trade are called banker's acceptance rates. The Fed publishes BA rates weekly. Those rates are a standard index used as an underlying item of various interest rate swaps and other derivatives.

Acceptances arise most often in connection with international trade. For example, an American importer may request acceptance financing from its bank when, as is frequently the case in international trade, it does not have a close relationship with and cannot obtain financing from the exporter it is dealing with. Once the importer and bank have completed an acceptance agreement, in which the bank agrees to accept drafts for the importer and the importer agrees to repay any drafts the bank accepts, the importer draws a time draft on the bank. The bank accepts the draft and discounts it; that is, it gives the importer cash for the draft but gives it an amount less than the face value of the draft. The importer uses the proceeds to pay the exporter.

The bank may hold the acceptance until it is redeemed by the importer on the maturity date, or it may sell or rediscount it in the secondary market. In the above case, the bank is in effect substituting its credit for that of the importer, enabling the importer to borrow in the money market. On or before the maturity date, the importer pays the bank the face value of the acceptance. If the bank rediscounted the acceptance in the market, the bank pays the holder of the acceptance the face value on the maturity date.

6.4 Treasury Bill Market
国库券市场

6.4.1 A Brief Introduction to Treasury Bill Market 国库券市场简介

1. Treasury bill and treasury bill market

Treasury bill is a short-term government (treasury) security issued and denominated in domestic currency, which matures in one year or less, and most commonly with three-month, six-month or one-year maturity.

The government issues treasury bills (T-bills) to meet its short-term financial requirements. Treasury bills are direct and unconditional obligations of the government and issued by the Treasury, the central bank or other government agency.

T-bills can be purchased directly through the auctions or indirectly through the secondary market. They can be traded in the secondary market before maturity. Purchasers of T-bills at auction can enter a competitive bid (although this method entails a risk that the bills may not be made available at the bid price) or a noncompetitive bid. T-bills for noncompetitive bids are supplied at the average price of all successful competitive bids.

Treasury bills are the most marketable securities in money market. Their popularity is mainly due to their simplicity. Essentially, T-bills are a way for the government to raise money from the public. Another reason is that they are one of the few money market instruments that are affordable to the individual investors. T-bills are usually issued in denominations of $1,000, $5,000, $10,000, $25,000, $50,000, $100,000 and $1 million in US. Other advantages are that T-bills are considered to be the safest investments because the government backs them. In international finance practice, those T-bills issued by the governments of developed nations or regions are considered risk-free. Furthermore, they are exempt from state and local taxes.

2. The characteristics of treasury bill

The following four characteristics distinguish the T-bills from other money market instruments: little possibility of default risk, high liquidity, favorable tax status, and a low minimum denomination.

1) Default risk

Treasury bills are generally considered to be free of default risk because they are obligations of the government. They are categorized as one of the safest investments, especially when they have three-month or even shorter maturities. If an investor would need the money before the T-bills mature, he/she can always sell them on the open market through an investment dealer. In contrast, even the highest grade ones of other money market instruments, such as commercial papers or certificates of deposit, are perceived to have some degree of default risk. Concerns over the default risk of securities other than treasury bills typically increase in times of weak economic conditions, and this tends to raise the differential between the rates on these securities and those on treasury bills of comparable maturity.

Because treasury bills are almost free of default risk, various regulations and institutional practices permit them to be used for the purposes that often cannot be served by other money market instruments. For example, banks use treasury bills to make repurchase agreements free of reserve requirements with firms and local governments, and to satisfy pledging requirements on government deposits. Treasury bills are widely accepted as collateral for selling short other various financial instruments and can be used instead of cash to satisfy initial margin requirements against futures market positions. Treasury bills are always a permissible investment for local governments, while many other types of money market instruments are not.

2) Liquidity

The second characteristic of T-bill is the high liquidity, which refers to the ability of investors to convert them into cash quickly at a low transactions cost. Investors in treasury bills have this ability because they are a homogeneous instrument and the T-bill market is highly organized and efficient in the international financial market. A measure of the liquidity of a financial asset is the spread between the price at which securities dealers buy it (the bid price) and the price at which they sell it (the asked price). In recent years the bid-asked spread on actively traded T-bills has been 2 basis points or less, which is lower than that on any other money market instrument.

3) Taxes

Unlike other money market instruments, the income earned on treasury bills is usually exempted from state and local income taxes. The relationship between, say, the CD rate (RCD) and the T-bill rate (RTB) that leaves an investor with state income tax rate (t) indifferent between the two, setting other considerations aside, is

$$RCD\ (1-t) = RTB$$

From this formula it can be seen that the advantage of the tax-exempt feature for a particular investor depends on the current level of interest rates and the investor's state and local tax rate. For an investor to remain indifferent between T-bills and CDs, the before-tax yield differential (RCD – RTB) must rise if the level of interest rates rises or if the investor's tax rate increases. For example, the interest rate differential at which an investor subject to a marginal state tax rate of 6% is indifferent between CDs and T-bills rises from 32 basis points when the T-bill rate is 5%, to 64 basis points when the T-bill rate is 10%. And with a fixed 5% T-bill rate, this interest rate differential rises from 32 basis points when the investor's tax rate is 6%, to 43 basis points when the tax rate is 8%.

However, this characteristic of T-bill only makes a difference to some investors. Other investors, such as local governments, are not subject to state income taxes. Still other investors, such as commercial banks in many states, pay a "franchise" or "excise" tax that in fact requires them to pay state taxes on interest income from T-bills.

4) Minimum denomination

The fourth characteristic of T-bills is their relatively low minimum denomination. Prior to 1970s, the minimum denomination of bills was $1,000 in the US. In early 1970s the Treasury raised the minimum denomination from $1,000 to $10,000. The Treasury made this change in order to discourage noncompetitive bids by small investors, reduce the costs of processing many small subscriptions yielding only a small volume of funds, and discourage the exodus of funds from financial intermediaries and the mortgage market.

Despite the increase in the minimum denomination of T-bills, investors continued to shift substantial amounts of funds out of depository institutions into the T-bill market in periods of high interest rates such as 1973 and 1974. Even at $10,000 the minimum denomination of T-bills is far below the minimum denomination required to purchase other short-term securities, with the exception of some government-sponsored enterprise and municipal securities. Generally speaking, it will take at least $100,000 to purchase any one of other money market instruments such as CDs or commercial paper.

3. The returns of treasury bill

T-bills are usually purchased for the price less than their par value; when they mature, the government pays the holder the full par value. Effectively, the interest gained by the investor is the difference between the purchase price of the security and what he gets at maturity. For instance, he might pay $970 for a $1,000 bill. When the bill matures, he would be paid $1,000. The difference between the purchase price and face value is the interest ($30 in this case). This differs from coupon bonds[1], which pay interest semi-annually.

T-bill yields are generally quoted on a discount basis using a 360-day year. The yield on a discount basis is calculated by dividing the discount interest (the difference between the face value of the bill and its purchase price) by the face value and expressing this percentage at an annual rate, using a 360-day year. For example, in the weekly auction of March 10, 2007, as discussed above, an average price of $98.992 per $100 of face amount for a three-month (91-day) bill produced an annual rate of return on a discount basis of $(100 - 98.992)/100 \times (360/91) = 3.99\%$.

The returns on T-bill are generally lower than those on longer term investments. However, they are ideal investments when an investor can't afford to risk his money. If he believes that the stock market or bond market is going to slump, T-bills can be a good place to park his money for a short while. In the US, big investors with lots of cash on hand might prefer to invest in T-bills rather than put the money in banks because bank account deposits are insured to a maximum of $60,000.

4. The investors in treasury bill market

Because of their unique characteristics, T-bills are held by a wide variety of investors. Available information suggests that individuals, commercial banks, central banks, money market funds, and foreigners are among the largest investors in T-bills. Banks and financial institutions, especially primary dealers[2], are the largest purchasers of T-Bills. Other investors in T-bill market are nonbank financial institutions, non-financial business firms, and state and local governments.

Because T-bills have a relatively low minimum denomination and can be purchased at banks without any service charge, the direct investment by individuals in T-bills has been greater than in any other money market instrument. (Since the late 1970s individuals have been heavily indirectly investing in all money market instruments through their investment in money market funds.) The percentage of T-bills awarded to noncompetitive bidders at the weekly T-bill auctions is a widely used barometer of individual investment activity in the market. In recent years the major reason for this appears to be that individuals as a group benefit most from the exemption of T-bill interest income from state and local income taxes. For a given spread between T-bill and other money market rates, this exemption makes T-bills more attractive—relative to other short-term investments—with a higher interest rate. Hence, investment in T-bills by individuals may rises along with the level of interest rates.

Commercial banks hold Treasury bills for the purpose to reverse the demand for commercial loans. When loan demand is slack, banks increase their holdings of T-bills as well as other treasury securities. Conversely, when loan demand is increasing, banks reduce their holdings of Treasury securities in order to expand loans. Of course, banks finance increases in commercial loans not only through the sale of securities but also through the issuance of liabilities such as CDs. Further, as mentioned above, banks also use Treasury bills to satisfy various collateral requirements and to make repurchase agreements with firms and state and local governments.

At the heart of this market is a group of security dealers designated by the central banks as primary dealers, who purchase the newly issued T-bills in the primary market and make an active secondary market for these bills. Primary dealers are expected by central banks to make markets in the full range of government securities, to participate meaningfully in treasury auctions, to be active participants in the open market operations, and to provide market information. In addition to the primary dealers, there are several hundred other banks and nonbank dealers investing in government securities. The dealers make markets by buying and selling securities for their own account through telecommunication and computer networks. They may also trade with each other, mostly through brokers who match buyers and sellers for a commission. Brokers quote bid and asked prices via electronic systems to the dealers, maintaining the anonymity of buying and selling dealers.

Central bank holds lots of Treasure bills which approximately account for the half of its total holdings of Treasury securities. Central bank changes the level of reserves available to commercial banks primarily through the purchase and sale of Treasury bills, either outright in the T-bill market or on a temporary basis in the market for repurchase agreements (repos). Repos have a temporary effect on the supply of bank reserves and are typically used to offset temporary fluctuations in reserves arising from other sources, such as changes in Treasury deposits at the central banks. On a day-to-day basis most reserve operations are repos. The increase in the central bank's outright holdings of T-bills over long periods of time reflects permanent increases in the level of reserves and the money supply.

Money market funds are another important type of investors in treasury bills. Some of them limit their assets to Treasury securities in order to appeal to the most risk-averse investors.

6.4.2   The Issue of Treasury Bill   国库券的发行

The Treasury issues bills at regularly scheduled auctions to refinance maturing issues and to help finance current treasury deficits. It also issue bills on an irregular basis to smooth out the uneven flow of revenues from corporate and individual tax receipts. Persistent treasury deficits have resulted in rapid growth in Treasury bills in recent years. Governments issue T-bills in very large denominations of $1 million or so. Banks and financial institutions, especially primary dealers, are the largest purchasers of T-bills. They purchase these large denominations in the primary market, and then break them up and resell to individual investors in the secondary market.

The issue and redemption of T-bills are handled by central bank on behalf of the government. Treasury bills are issued in bearer form, and the bearer or holder of the bill may present it for payment of the nominal amount at maturity. Central bank would normally pay this amount into the holder's current bank account on the maturity date.

In the US, regular weekly T-bills are commonly issued at discount of the par value and allocated on a tender (auction) basis, with maturity dates of 28 days (or 4 weeks, about 1 month), 91 days (or 13 weeks, about 3 months), and 182 days (or 26 weeks, about 6 months). Treasury Bills are firstly sold by single price auctions held weekly on Monday. Purchase orders at Treasury direct must be entered before 11:30 on the Monday of the auction. Mature T-bills are also redeemed on each Thursday. From time to time the government may issue treasury bills other than weekly treasury bills on a special tender basis to parties who regularly participate at weekly tenders.

Once the T-bills are sold (issued) on the formal issuing date in the primary market, then they can be traded in the secondary market by all the investors.

6.5 Repos Market
回购协议市场

6.5.1 A Brief Introduction to Repos Market 回购协议市场简介

Repurchase agreements (RPs or repos) are financial instruments commonly used in money markets (and sometimes in capital markets). A more accurate and descriptive term is "sale and repurchase agreement", since what occurs is that the cash receiver (seller) sells securities now, in return for cash, to the cash provider (buyer), and agrees to repurchase those securities from the buyer for a greater sum of cash at some later date, that greater sum being all of the cash lent and some extra cash (constituting interest, known as the repo rate). In essence, it is a way of borrowing or lending securities for cash, with the securities serving as collateral.

Although the underlying nature of the transaction is that of a loan, the terminology differs from that used when talking of loans due to the fact that the seller does actually repurchase the legal ownership of the securities from the buyer at the end of the agreement. So, although the actual effect of the whole transaction is identical to a cash loan, in using the "repurchase" terminology, the emphasis is placed upon the current legal ownership of the collateral securities by the respective parties. In common parlance, the seller does a repo and the lender of funds (buyer) does a reverse repo[3].

The repos are the most liquid instruments in money markets, ranging from 24 hours to several months, and even two years. In fact, they are very similar to bank deposit accounts, and many corporations arrange for their banks to transfer temporary excess cash to such funds automatically.

Repos can be of any duration but are most commonly overnight loans. Repos for longer than overnight are known as term repos[4]. There are also open repos that can be terminated by either side on a day's notice. Although legally defined as a sequential pair of sales, in fact, a repo is a short-term interest-bearing loan against collateral. The annualized rate of interest paid on such a loan is known as the repo rate.

The overnight repo rate normally runs slightly below the Fed funds rate in the US for two reasons: firstly, a repo transaction is a secured loan, whereas the sale of Fed funds is an unsecured loan; secondly, many who can invest in repos cannot sell Fed funds. Even though the return is modest, overnight lending in the repos market offers several advantages to investors. By rolling overnight repos, they can keep surplus funds invested without losing liquidity or incurring price risk. They also incur very little credit risk because the collateral is always high grade notes.

The over-the-counter repos market is now one of the largest and most active sectors in the US money market. Repos are widely used for investing surplus funds short term, or for borrowing short term against collateral. Dealers in securities use repos to manage their liquidity, finance their inventories, and speculate in various ways. The government uses repos to manage the aggregate reserves of the banking system.

Repos, however, are not designated for small investors. The largest investors of repos are the dealers in government securities. As of August 2006 there were 23 primary dealers in the US recognized by the Fed, which means they were authorized to bid on newly-issued treasury securities in the primary market for resale in the secondary market. Primary dealers must be well-capitalized, and often deal in hundred million dollar chunks. In the secondary market, there are several hundred dealers who trade treasury securities and do repos in at least one million dollar chunks.

As early mentioned, repos are popular because they can virtually eliminate credit problems. Unfortunately, a number of significant losses over the years from fraudulent dealers suggest that lenders in this market have not always checked their collateralization closely enough.

6.5.2 The Operations of Repos Market 回购协议市场的业务操作

Repos are made for a variety of reasons. Depending upon various circumstances, the transactions can be interpreted in different ways.

For example, many traders finance their long positions through repos. Rather than finance the purchase with their own capital, they purchase securities and make a repo. They receive cash by the repo which they use to finance the original purchase of the security. Hence, the repo is a source of leverage. The counterparty (buyer)'s role is to provide the leverage—they are extending a cash loan. The loan is secured by the repo security.

Now consider a very different circumstance. Suppose the counterparty of the above case is entering the repo transaction not only to provide a loan, but actually needs to borrow a certain security. Maybe they need to cover a short position on that particular security, or to deliver that particular security to settle a futures contract, or they need the particular security to avoid a failed trade.

In the first example, the security being repoed is just collateral. The specific security is not important so long as it is acceptable collateral. In such a transaction, the repo will be priced so that the counterparty earns the rate of interest for a collateralized loan. In the second example, the repoed security is more than collateral. It is the reason for performing the repo. In this case, the repo will be priced according to the supply and demand for the particular security being repoed. If the supply available of that security is limited in the market, the counterparty may accept a rate of interest from the repo below that of a collateralized loan.

Accordingly, the repos market is broadly divided into two segments. The "general collateral" market is one in which repos are priced as collateralized loans. The "special" market is one where specific securities are sought by counterparties. In such repos, the counterparty may accept a rate of interest below the general collateral rate if there is a limited supply of the desired security for lending and therefore any security which commands a below-general-collateral rate of interest in a repo is usually called a "special security."

There are various reasons for a particular security to be a special security. For example, it could be supply and demand relating to Treasury auctions, or the security might be the cheapest to deliver on a maturing futures contract.

To make a repo, security dealer must have an account at a clearing bank to settle his trades. For example, suppose X Company has $20 million to invest in the short term. After negotiating the terms with the dealer, X has its bank wire $20 million to the clearing bank. On receipt, the clearing bank recovers the funds it loaned the dealer to acquire the securities being sold, plus interest due on the loan. It then transfers the sold securities to a special custodial account in the name of X. Since treasury securities exist as book entries on a computer, this is a trivial operation.

The next morning the dealer repurchases the securities from X, pays the overnight interest on the repo, and regains possession of the securities. Assuming a 5% repo rate, the interest due on the $20 million overnight loan would be $2,777.78, which is based on a 360-day year. If both parties agree, the repo could be rolled over instead of paid off, through providing another day of funds for the dealer and another day of interest for X.

If the dealer is short on funds needed to repurchase the securities, the clearing bank will advance them with little or no interest if repaid on the same day. Otherwise the bank will charge the dealer interest on the loan and hold the securities as collateral until payment is made. Since dealer loans typically run at least 25 basis points above the Fed funds rate, dealers try to finance as much as they can by borrowing through repos. By rolling over repos day by day, the dealer can finance most of his inventory without resorting to dealer loans. It is sometimes advantageous to repo for a longer period, using a term repo to minimize transaction costs.

Clearing banks charge a fee for executing repo transactions. They prefer not to issue large dealer loans because it ties up the bank's own reserves at little profit. In fact, there is not enough capacity in all of the banks to provide dealer loans sufficient to cover the financing needs of the large securities dealers.

A dealer who holds a large position in securities takes a risk in the value of his portfolio from changes in interest rates. Position plays are where the largest profits can be made. However many dealers now run a nearly matched book to minimize market risk. This involves creating offsetting positions in repos and reverses by "reversing in" securities and at the same time "hanging out" identical securities with repos. The dealer earns a profit from the bid-ask spread. Profits can be improved by mismatching maturities between the asset and liability side, but at increasing risk.

As dealers move from simply using repos to finance their positions to using them in running matched books, they become de facto financial intermediaries. In borrowing funds at one rate and lending them at a higher rate, a dealer is operating like a finance company, doing for-profit intermediation.

6.6　CDs Market
可转让存单市场

6.6.1　A Brief Introduction to CDs Market　可转让存单市场简介

A certificate of deposit (CD) is a certificate issued by a bank for a deposit made at the bank. This deposit attracts a fixed rate of interest, which is normally payable to the holder of the instrument together with the nominal amount invested, at redemption (maturity) date.

CDs are bearer documents, which mean that the name of the owner (holder or depositor) does not appear on the certificate. Like all time deposits, the funds may not be withdrawn on demand like those in a checking account. The bearer or holder will receive the maturity value (the amount deposited plus interest) at maturity date.

In the US, large CDs are generally divided into four classes based on the type of issuer because the rates paid, risk, and depth of the market vary considerably among the four types. The oldest of the four groups consists of CDs issued by US banks domestically, they are called domestic CDs. Dollar-denominated CDs issued by banks abroad are known as Eurodollar CDs or Euro CDs. CDs issued by US branches of foreign banks are known as Yankee CDs. Finally, CDs issued by savings and loan associations and savings banks are referred to as thrift CDs.

A CD can be legally negotiable or nonnegotiable, depending on certain legal specifications of the CD. Negotiable CDs can be sold by depositors to other parties who can in turn resell them. Nonnegotiable CDs generally must be held by the depositor until maturity. Note that the CDs traded in the money markets are always negotiable in normal cases.

CDs offer a slightly higher yield than T-bills because of the slightly higher default risk for a bank but, overall, the likelihood that a large bank will go broke is pretty slim. Of course, the amount of interest earned depends on a number of other factors such as the current interest rate environment, how much money being invested, the length of time and the particular bank being chosen. While nearly every bank offers CDs, the rates are not always competitive, so it's important to shop around. A few general rules of thumb for interest rates are: the larger the principal, the higher the interest rate; the longer the term, the higher the interest rate (Unless the yield curve is inverted.); the smaller the bank, the higher the interest rate; personal CD accounts receive higher interest rates than business CD accounts.

A fundamental concept to understand when buying a CD is the difference between annual percentage yield (APY)[5] and annual percentage rate (APR)[6]. APY is the total amount of interest you earn in one year, taking compound interest into account. APR is simply the stated interest you earn in one year, without taking compounding into account.

The difference results from the different time when interest is paid. The more frequently interest is calculated, the greater the yield will be. When an investment pays interest annually, its rate and yield are the same. But when interest is paid more frequently, the yield gets higher. For example, say you purchase a one-year, $1,000 CD that pays 6% semi-annually. After six months, you'll receive an interest payment of $30 ($1,000×6%×0.5 years). Here's where the magic of compound rate starts. The $30 payment starts earning interest of its own, which over the next six months amounts to $0.90 ($30×5%×0.5 years). As a result, the rate on the CD is 6%, but its yield is $60.90 over the first year. It may not sound like a lot, but compounding yield adds up over time.

The main advantage of CDs is their relative safety and the ability to know the mature yield ahead of time. You'll generally earn more than in a savings account, and you won't be at the mercy of the stock market. Plus, in the US the Federal Deposit Insurance Corporation (FDIC) guarantees your investment up to $100,000.

Despite the benefits, there are still two main disadvantages to CDs. First of all, the returns are paltry compared to many other investments. Furthermore, if the CDs are nonnegotiable, your money will be tied up for the length of the CD's maturity and you won't be able to get it out in advance without paying a harsh penalty.

6.6.2 The Calculation of CDs' Maturity Value   可转让存单到期值的计算

The maturity value (MV) of a CD will be the nominal amount deposited (N) plus the interest for the period. Supposing a deposit of R1,000,000 is made on 1 March for 90 days, and interest paid on the amount is 10% (referred to as a 10% 90-day CD), the maturity value is calculated as follows:

Nominal amount = R1,000,000

Interest for period ($10\% \times$ R1,000,000 $\times 90/360$) = R25,000

MV = R1,000,000 + R25,000 = R1,025,000

The general formula would be：

$$MV = N \times (1 + (c \times d/360))$$

Where：

MV = maturity value；

N = nominal amount of the certificate (amount deposited)；

c = interest paid on the amount deposited, as indicated on the certificate (referred to as the coupon rate)；

d = period of the instrument in days referred to as the tenor.

In this case：

N = R1,000,000

c = 10%

d = 90

MV = R1,025,000

If the holder sells this instrument to another party before the redemption date, the proceeds can be calculated. Remember that financial instruments are traded between parties on a yield to maturity (expressed as an interest rate) basis, because interest is the price that is paid for money borrowed. The proceeds of the sale are calculated as follows：

$$Proceeds = MV/[1 + (d/360 \times i/100)]$$

Where：

MV = maturity value；

d = remaining tenor in days；

i = yield at which the instrument was traded expressed as a fixed amount.

If, in the above example, the CD is sold on 31 March at a yield of 9%, the proceeds to the seller (the amount the buyer will pay) is：

$$Proceeds = R1,025,000/[1 + (60/360 \times 9/100)] = R1,009,852$$

Where：

MV = R1,025,000；

d = 60；

i = 9.

The buyer will be the new holder, and he may present the CD to the bank on redemption date to receive the maturity value of R1,025,000 or sell it in the secondary market prior to maturity.

6.6.3　The Operations of CDs Market　可转让存单市场的业务操作

The consumer who opens a CD may receive a passbook or paper certificate, but now it is common for a CD to consist simply of a book entry and an item shown in the consumer's periodic bank statements; that is, there is usually no "certificate" as such.

At most institutions, the CD purchaser can arrange to have the interest periodically mailed as a check or transferred into a checking or savings account. This reduces total yield because there is no compounding.

Some institutions allow the customer to select this option only at the time the CD is opened (issued).

Commonly, institutions mail a notice to the CD holder shortly before the CD matures requesting directions. The notice usually offers the choice of withdrawing the principal and accumulated interest or "rolling it over" (depositing it into a new CD). Generally, a "window" is allowed after maturity where the CD holder can cash in the CD without penalty. In the absence of such directions, it is common for the institution to "roll over" the CD automatically, once again tying up the money for a period of time (though the CD holder may be able to specify at the time the CD is opened to not "roll over" the CD).

CDs typically require a minimum deposit, and may offer higher rates for larger deposits. In the US, the best rates are generally offered on "Jumbo CDs" with minimum deposits of $100,000 (though some, recognizing that some investors don't want more in the account than is covered by FDIC insurance, have lowered the minimum deposit to $95,000). However there are also institutions that do the opposite and offer lower rates for their "Jumbo CDs".

Withdrawals before maturity are usually subject to a substantial penalty. For a five-year CD, this is often the loss of six months' interest. These penalties ensure that it is generally not in a holder's best interest to withdraw the money before maturity—unless they have another investment with significantly higher return or have a serious need for the money.

CDs can be negotiated (sold) before the maturity date. They have built-in liquidity. Gathering of funds through the issuance of CDs to the public has become quite popular with the commercial banks, because the inter-bank market is quite thin in respect of funds that mature beyond one year.

The CDs market is dominated by investors who intended to hold the certificates till maturity, nearly 50% of all issues are held till maturity. This restricted liquidity of the market and reduced the activity in the secondary market.

Group Discussion ▶▶▶

1. Talk about the characteristics and functions of the money market.
2. Discuss the five major submarkets of the money market and their correlations.
3. Tell the operations of T-bills and repos in detail.
4. Say something about the Chinese money market.

NOTES ▶▶▶

1　coupon bonds　附息债（票面附有息票，定期或到期付利息的债券）
2　primary dealer　一级交易商
3　reverse repo　逆回购（协议）
4　term repo　定期回购（协议）
5　annual percentage yield (APY)　年收益
6　annual percentage rate (APR)　年收益率

Chapter 7

Capital Market
资本市场

Learning Objectives

- ☑ To understand the basics about capital market
- ☑ To learn the issue and trade of the stock
- ☑ To learn the issue and trade of the bond
- ☑ To know the differences between stock market and bond market

Opening Vignette

The Global Capital Market Has Grown Rapidly in Recent Decades

Dictionary of Business defines the capital market as a market in which long-term capital is raised by industry and commerce, the government, and local authorities. The money comes from private investors, insurance companies, pension funds, and banks and is usually arranged by issuing houses and merchant banks. Stock markets are also part of the capital market. It is the presence and sophistication of their capital markets that distinguishes the developed countries from the developing countries, in that this facility for raising industrial and commercial capital is either absent or immature in the latter.

However, with the progressing of the globalization in the past years, the capital markets around the world are increasingly integrate into a global market, and more and more countries, especially the developing countries, get involved in the global capital market. More and more governments and corporations in developing countries begin to raise capital in the global market. Furthermore, more and more new instruments are innovated and traded in the global capital market.

Capital market-based finance has in fact been increasing in importance, both absolutely and relative to financial intermediary-based finance, in both developed and developing countries over the past decades. Moreover, capital markets are in fact winning the present and seem likely to dominate the future of corporate finance in developed and developing countries alike.

Ordinary "relationship banking" appears to be (at best) holding its own as a source of corporate financing around the world, and is more likely in decline. The bits of banking that are growing rapidly are those parts that provide high value-added products (especially risk management tools) and provide large-scale syndicated credits to corporate borrowers. During the late-1980s and early-1990s, when Japan and Germany appeared to be outperforming major capital market-oriented countries such as the UK and the US, the academic literature often favored bank-based systems. More recently, however, the weight of opinion has swung strongly in favor of the idea that the capital market has decisive comparative advantages over banks and other financial intermediaries as optimal monitor and financier of a nation's corporate life. This reassessment has been driven in part by the observation, discussed at length above, that capital markets have been prospering relative to banks for many years. The repetitive nature (and massive costs) of banking crises in developed as well as developing countries alike has also convinced many observers that banks are inherently fragile institutions, whose role in corporate finance should be minimized as much and as quickly as possible.

In the period from 1983 to 2000, there was a long duration of very rapid growth in the capitalization of markets in every country except Japan. Total world market capitalization increased over ten-fold (to $35.0 trillion) between 1983 and 1999, and the total capitalization of the US market increased almost nine-fold (from $1.9 trillion to $16.6 trillion) over the same period.

Another way of measuring the rise of capital markets is to examine whether their share of annual corporate financing activity has grown relative to that of other sources of funding. Security offerings by US issuers accounted for two-thirds of the global total volume throughout 1990-1999, that implies that non-US securities issues in creased from $191 billion in 1990 to $750 billion in 1998, and then to $1.19 trillion in 1999. The surge in non-US issuance volume in 1999 was largely due to the popularity of Euro-denominated bond issues, which actually exceeded the dollar-denominated bond issues for much of 1999.

One highly specialized, but extremely important type of financing has also grown very rapidly over the past decades, and especially so since 1997. This is venture capital investment by US venture capital partnerships.

The almost incredible increase in the total volume of merger and acquisition activity has occurred since 1990. While takeovers have always played an important role in the United States, the rise in M&A (Merger and Acquisition) activity in Europe during the 1990s was even more dramatic. From less than $50 billion annually in the late-1980s, the total value of M&A involving a European target reached $592 billion in 1998, before more than doubling to $1.22 trillion in 1999—rivaling the US total. The global value of M&A activity in 1999 reached $3.4 trillion, an astounding 10% of world GDP.

The global capital market has grown so rapidly in recent decades. Why has this happened? In my opinion, the global capital market has grown so rapidly in recent decades because of the rise of privatizations mainly. With private capital flows rising from less than 5% of world GDP in 1975 to about 20% today, privatizations have significantly increased market liquidity. And also privatization takes a potential role in global capital market development.

It should be very careful in inferring causation regarding privatization's impact on the market growth, since a shift in ideology or some other exogenous political or economic change might have caused both the privatization and the overall boom.

It is clear that national governments have been among the biggest winners from privatization programs, since these have dramatically increased government revenues, which is clearly one important reason for the rapid spread of the policy to many developing countries. As mentioned above, Privatization International reports that the cumulative value of proceeds raised by privatizing governments exceeded $1 trillion sometime during the second half of 1999. As an added benefit, this revenue has come to governments without having to raise taxes or cut other public services.

All international investment banks compete fiercely for share issue privatization (SIP) mandates in those countries implementing large scale privatizations, for two principal reasons. First, because the offerings are so large and so visible—and are almost always designed to help promote the market's capacity to absorb subsequent stock offerings by private companies—these are very prestigious mandates. To date, the large brokerage houses in developed nations have had the most success in winning advisory and underwriting mandates, though all countries that launch large-scale SIP programs tend to favor local investment banks as "national champions" to handle the domestic share tranche. The second reason banks compete so fiercely for SIP mandates is because they can be extremely profitable. In spite of the fact that SIPs have significantly lower underwriting spreads than private sector offerings, their sheer size and lack of downside price risk make them very lucrative for underwriters.

Now we have already stepped into the 21st century. I believe that the growth of the global capital market is going to continue throughout the 2000s for the following reasons. First, most of the south-east Asia countries have recovered from the 1997 financial crisis. For these countries, they now need large amounts of capital to do businesses after they got back on the fast growing track. Second, by the end of 2001, China, the world's biggest developing country, has entered the World Trade Organization. This is real great news. As we all know, today's China takes a serious position in world's economy. Its policy of reformation and opening will make China keep achieving high GDP growth rate in the coming years and this is sure to contribute much to drive the global capital market keep growing.

Warm-up Questions

1. What do you think about the capital market?
2. What a role do you think China plays in the global capital market?
3. Why and how should China participate in the global capital market?

7.1 An Overview of Capital Market
资本市场概述

7.1.1 The Definition and Characteristics of Capital Market
资本市场的定义及特点

The capital market, in narrow sense, is the market for securities, where long-term capital is raised by industry and commerce, the government, and local authorities. The money comes from private investors, insurance companies, pension funds, and banks and is usually arranged by issuing houses and merchant banks. The financial regulator assigned by the government is responsible for supervision on the capital market in the country to ensure that investors are protected against fraud. The capital market consists of the primary market where new issues are distributed to particular investors, and the secondary market where existing securities are traded by various investors.

Unlike the money market, which functions basically to provide short term funds, the capital market provides funds to industries and governments to meet their long-term capital requirements, such as financing for fixed investments —plants, bridges, railways, airports and etc. And it is made up of corporations and institutions, which facilitate the issuance and secondary trading of long-term financial instruments. Stock exchanges are also part of the capital market in that they provide a market for the shares and loan stocks that represent the capital once it has been raised.

Financing a company through the sale of stock in a company is known as equity financing. Alternatively, debt financing (for example issuing bonds) can be done to avoid giving up shares of ownership of the company. Equity and debt financing are usually used for longer-term investment projects such as establishment of a new factory.

When a company or government wants to raise long-term funds in the capital market, it usually first consult an issuing house or stockbroker. These specialists provide the company/government with financial advisory services to facilitate the financing activity. It is their duty to study the company performance over the years in order to determine its financial needs. More so, they do not only advise on the best option, they undertake total financial restructuring of the company before introducing the facility to the company.

For individuals wishing to invest in capital market in form of buying shares, what they need do is to consult a Stock broking firm and register with the broking firm.

7.1.2　The Functions of Capital Market　资本市场的功能

The functions of capital market are as follows:

(1) The primary aim of the capital market is to mobilize long-term funds for investment.

(2) Provide an additional channel for engaging and mobilizing domestic savings for productive investment and represent an alternative to bank deposits, real estate investment and the financing of consumption loans.

(3) Provide depositors with better protection against inflation and currency depreciation.

(4) Foster the growth of the domestic financial services sector and the various forms of institutional savings such as life insurance and pension funds.

(5) Improve the gearing of the domestic corporate sector and helps reduce dependence on borrowing.

(6) Improve the efficiency of capital by providing market measure of returns on capital and a market mechanism for management changes as compared with the administrative or political mechanism of public sector corporations.

(7) To facilitate the transfer of enterprises from the public sector to the private sector.

(8) To encourage privatization by increasing the marketability of new issues.

(9) Provide access to finance for new and smaller companies and encourage institutional development in facilitating the setting up of domestic funds, foreign funds and venture capital funds.

In sum, the capital market helps to stimulate industrial as well as economic growth and development of the economy.

7.1.3　The Types of Capital Market　资本市场的类型

The capital markets can be divided into primary and secondary markets.

The distinct difference between the two markets is that in the primary market, the money for the securities is received by the issuer of those securities from investors, whereas in the secondary market, the money goes from one investor to the other.

In the primary markets, securities may be offered to the public in a public offer. Alternatively, they may be offered privately to a limited number of qualified persons in a private placement. Often a combination of the two is used. The distinction between the two is important to securities regulation and company law. Privately placed securities are often not publicly tradable and may only be bought and sold by sophisticated qualified investors. As a result, the secondary market is not as liquid.

Another category of securities, such as government bonds, is generally sold by auction to a specialized class of dealers.

In order for the primary market to thrive, there must be a secondary market, or aftermarket, where holders of securities can sell them to other investors for cash, hopefully at a profit. Otherwise, few people would purchase primary issues, and, thus, companies and governments would be unable to raise money for their operations. Organized exchanges constitute the main secondary markets. Many smaller issues and most debt securities trade in the decentralized, dealer-based over-the-counter markets.

The capital market can also be divided into the stock market and the bond market, which will be examined respectively in the next two sections.

7.2 Stock Market
股票市场

7.2.1 A Brief Introduction to Stock Market 股票市场简介

1. The definition of stock market

A stock market (sometimes called a equity market) is a market for the trading of company stock, and derivatives of same; both of these are securities listed on a stock exchange as well as those only traded privately.

Strictly speaking, the term 'the stock market' is a concept for the mechanism that enables the trading of company stocks (collective shares), other securities, and derivatives.

The stocks are listed and traded on stock exchanges which are entities (a corporation or mutual organization) specialized in the business of bringing buyers and sellers of stocks and securities together. The stock market in the United States includes the trading of all securities listed on the NYSE, the NASDAQ, the Amex, as well as on the many regional exchanges, the OTCBB, and Pink Sheets. European examples of stock exchanges include the Paris Bourse, the London Stock Exchange and the Deutsche Börse

2. Market participants

Many years ago, worldwide, buyers and sellers in stock markets were individual investors, such as wealthy businessmen, with long family histories (and emotional ties) to particular corporations. Over time, markets have become more "institutionalized"; buyers and sellers are largely institutions (e. g. , pension funds, insurance companies, funds, hedge funds, investor groups, and banks). The rise of the institutional investor has brought with it some improvements in market operations. Thus, the government was responsible for "fixed" (and exorbitant) fees being markedly reduced for the "small" investor, but only after the large institutions had managed to break the brokers' solid front on fees (they then went to "negotiated" fees, but only for large institutions). However, corporate governance (at least in the West) has been greatly affected by the rise of institutional "owners".

3. The importance of stock market

The stock market is one of the most important sources for companies to raise money. This allows businesses to go public, or raise additional capital for expansion. The liquidity that an exchange provides affords investors the ability to quickly and easily sell securities. This is an attractive feature of investing in stocks, compared to other less liquid investments such as real estate.

History has shown that the price of stocks and other assets is an important part of the dynamics of economic activity, and can influence or be an indicator of social mood. Rising stock prices, for instance, tend to be associated with increased business investment and vice versa. Stock prices also affect the wealth of households and their consumption. Therefore, central banks tend to keep an eye on the control and behavior of the stock market and, in general, on the smooth operation of financial system functions. Financial stability is a important target of central banks.

Exchanges also act as the clearinghouse for each transaction, meaning that they collect and deliver the shares, and guarantee payment to the seller of a security. This eliminates the risk to an individual buyer or seller that the counterparty could default on the transaction.

The smooth functioning of all these activities facilitates economic growth in that lower costs and enterprise risks promote the production of goods and services as well as employment. In this way the financial system contributes to increased prosperity.

The financial system in most western countries has undergone a remarkable transformation. One feature of this development is disintermediation. A portion of the funds involved in saving and financing flows directly to the financial markets instead of being routed via banks' traditional lending and deposit operations. The general public's heightened interest in investing in the stock market, either directly or through funds, has been an important component of this process. Statistics show that in recent decades shares have made up an increasingly large proportion of households' financial assets in many countries.

In the 1970s, in Sweden, deposit accounts and other very liquid assets with little risk made up almost 60% of households' financial wealth, compared to less than 20% in the 2000s. The major part of this adjustment in financial portfolios has gone directly to stocks but a good deal now takes the form of various kinds of institutional investment for groups of individuals, e. g. , pension funds, funds, hedge funds, insurance investment of premiums, etc. The trend towards forms of saving with a higher risk has been accentuated by new rules for most funds and insurance, permitting a higher proportion of stocks to bonds. Similar tendencies are to be found in other industrialized countries. In all developed economic systems, such as the European Union, the United States, Japan and others, and particular developing nations such as China and India, the trend has been the same: saving has moved away from traditional (government insured) bank deposits to more risky securities of one sort or another, especially the stock.

Riskier long-term saving requires that an individual possess the ability to manage the associated increased risks. Stock prices fluctuate widely, in marked contrast to the stability of (government insured) bank deposits or bonds. This is something that could affect not only the individual investor or household, but also the economy on a large scale. The following deals with some of the risks of the financial sector in general and the stock market in particular.

This is certainly more important now that so many newcomers have entered the stock market, or have acquired other 'risky' investments (such as 'investment' property, i. e. , real estate and collectables).

The following is a quote from the preface to a published biography about the well-known and long term value oriented stock investor Warren Buffett. Buffett began his career with only 100 US dollars and has over the years built himself a multibillion-dollar fortune. The quote illustrates some of what has been happening in the stock market during the end of the 20th century and the beginning of the 21st.

"With each passing year, the noise level in the stock market rises. Television commentators, financial writers, analysts, and market strategists are all over-talking each other to get investors' attention. At the same time, individual investors, immersed in chat rooms and message boards, are exchanging questionable and often misleading tips. Yet, despite all this available information, investors find it increasingly difficult to profit. Stock prices skyrocket with little reason, then plummet just as quickly, and people who have turned to investing for their children's education and their own retirement become frightened. Sometimes there appears to be no rhyme or reason to the market, only folly."

4. The behavior of the stock market

From experience we know that investors may temporarily pull stock prices away from their long term trend level. Over-reactions may occur—so that excessive optimism (euphoria) may drive prices unduly high or excessive pessimism may drive prices unduly low. New theoretical and empirical arguments have been put forward against the notion that financial markets are efficient.

According to the efficient market hypothesis (EMH), only changes in fundamental factors, such as profits or dividends, ought to affect stock prices. (But this largely theoretic academic viewpoint also predicts that little or no trading should take place— contrary to fact— since prices are already at or near equilibrium, having priced in all public knowledge.) But the efficient-market hypothesis is sorely tested by such events as the stock market crash in 1987, when the Dow Jones index plummeted 22.6 % —the largest-ever one-day fall in the US. This event demonstrated that share prices can fall dramatically even though, to this day, it is impossible to fix a definite cause: a thorough search failed to detect any specific or unexpected development that might account for the crash. It also seems to be the case more generally that many price movements are not occasioned by new information; a study of the fifty largest one-day share price movements in the US in the post-war period confirms this. Moreover, while the EMH predicts that all price movement (in the absence of change in fundamental information) is random (i.e., non-trending), many researches have shown a marked tendency for the stock market to trend over time periods of weeks or longer.

Various explanations for large price movements have been promulgated. For instance, some research has shown that changes in estimated risk, and the use of certain strategies, such as stop-loss limits and value at risk limits, theoretically could cause stock markets to overreact.

Other research has shown that psychological factors may result in exaggerated stock price movements. Psychological research has demonstrated that people are predisposed to 'seeing' patterns, and often will perceive a pattern in what is, in fact, just noise. In the present context this means that a succession of good news about a company may lead investors to overreact positively (unjustifiably driving the price up). A period of good returns also boosts the investor's self-confidence, reducing his (psychological) risk threshold.

Another phenomenon— also from psychology— that works against an objective assessment is group thinking. As social animals, it is not easy to stick to an opinion that differs markedly from that of a majority of the group. An example with which one may be familiar is the reluctance to enter a restaurant that is empty; people generally prefer to have their opinion validated by those of others in the group.

There are some authors who draw an analogy with gambling. In normal times the market behaves like a game of roulette; the probabilities are known and largely independent of the investment decisions of the different players. In times of market stress, however, the game becomes more like poker (herding behavior takes over). The players now must give heavy weight to the psychology of other investors and how they are likely to react psychologically.

The stock markets, as any other business, show little mercy to amateurs. Inexperienced investors rarely get the assistance and support they need. In the period running up to the recent NASDAQ crash, less than 1% of the analyst's recommendations had been to sell (and even during the 2000–2002 crash, the average did not rise above 5%). The media amplified the general euphoria, with reports of rapidly rising share prices and the notion that large sums of money could be quickly earned in the so-called new economy stock market. (And later amplified the gloom which descended during the 2000–2002 crash, so that by summer of 2002, predictions of a DOW average below 5000 were quite common.)

Sometimes the market tends to react irrationally to economic news, even if that news has no real effect on the technical value of stock itself. Therefore, the stock market can be swayed tremendously in either direction by press releases, rumors and mass panic.

Furthermore, the stock market comprises a large amount of speculative analysts, or pencil pushers, who have no excess money or financial interest in the market, but make market predictions and suggestions regardless. Over the short-term, stocks and other securities can be battered or buoyed by any number of fast market-changing events, making the stock market difficult to predict.

7.2.2　The Operations of Stock Market　股票市场的业务操作

When a company issues public stock for the first time, this is called Initial Public Offering (IPO). A company can later issue more new shares, or issue shares that have been previously registered in a shelf registration. These later new issues are also sold in the primary market, but they are not considered to be an IPO. Issuers usually retain investment banks to assist them in administering the IPO, getting the approval by the supervision authority, and selling the new issue. When the investment bank buys the entire new issue from the issuer at a discount to resell it at a markup, it is called an underwriting, or firm commitment. However, if the investment bank considers the risk too great for an underwriting, it may only assent to a best effort agreement, where the investment bank will simply do its best to sell the new issue.

Stocks are often listed in a stock exchange, an organized and officially recognized market on which securities can be bought and sold. Issuers may seek listings for their securities in order to attract investors, by ensuring that there is a liquid and regulated secondary market in which investors will be able to buy and sell securities.

Traders in the stock market range from small individual investors to large hedge fund traders, who can be based anywhere. Their orders usually end up with a professional at a stock exchange, who executes the order. Some exchanges are physical locations where transactions are carried out on a trading floor, by a method known as open outcry. This type of auction is used in stock exchanges and commodity exchanges where traders may enter "verbal" bids and offers simultaneously. The other type of exchange is a virtual kind, and is referred as over-the-counter (OTC) market, composed of a network of computers where trades are made electronically via traders at computer terminals. Large volumes of securities are now bought and sold "over the counter", which has challenged the traditional business of stock exchanges. OTC dealing involves buyers and sellers dealing with each other electronically on the basis of prices that are displayed electronically, usually by commercial information vendors such as Reuters and Bloomberg.

Actual trades are based on an auction market paradigm where a potential buyer bids a specific price for a stock and a potential seller asks a specific price for the stock. (Buying or selling at market means you will accept any bid price or ask price for the stock.) When the bid and ask prices match, a sale takes place on a "first come first served" basis if there are multiple bidders or askers at a given price.

The purpose of a stock exchange is to facilitate the exchange of securities between buyers and sellers, thus providing a marketplace (virtual or physical). The exchanges provide real-time trading information on the listed stocks, facilitating price discovery.

The New York Stock Exchange (NYSE) is a physical exchange. This is also referred to as a "listed" exchange (because only stocks listed with the exchange may be traded in the secondary market). Orders enter by way of brokerage firms that are members of the exchange and flow down to floor brokers who go to a specific spot on the floor where the stock trades. At this location, known as the trading post, there is a specific person known as the specialist whose job is to match buy orders and sell orders.

Prices are determined using an auction method known as "open outcry": the current bid price is the highest amount any buyer is willing to pay and the current ask price is the lowest price at which someone is willing to sell; if there is a spread, no trade takes place. For a trade to take place, there must be a matching bid and ask price. (If a spread exists, the specialist is supposed to use his own resources of money or stock to close the difference, after some time.) Once a trade has been made, the details are reported on the "tape" and sent back to the brokerage firm, who then notifies the investor who placed the order. Although there is a significant amount of direct human contact in this process, computers do play a great and critical role in the process, especially for so-called "program trading".

The NASDAQ is a virtual and listed exchange, where all of the trading is done over a computer network. The process is similar to the above, in that the seller provides an asking price and the buyer provides a bidding price. However, buyers and sellers are electronically matched. One or more NASDAQ market makers will always provide a bid and ask price at which they will always purchase or sell their stock.

The Paris Bourse is an order-driven, electronic stock exchange. It was automated in the late 1980s. Before, it consisted of an open outcry exchange. Stockbrokers met in the trading floor or the Palais Brongniart. In 1986, the CATS trading system was introduced, and the order matching process was fully automated.

From time to time, active trading (especially in large blocks of securities) moves away from the exchanges. Large securities firms, already steer 12 % of US security trades away from the exchanges to their internal systems. That share probably will increase to 18% by 2010 as more investment banks bypass the NYSE and NASDAQ and match buyers and sellers of securities themselves, according to data compiled by Boston-based Aite Group LLC, a brokerage-industry consultant.

Now that computers have eliminated the need for trading floors like the Big Board's[1], the balance of power in equity markets is shifting. By bringing more orders in-house, where clients can move big blocks of stock anonymously, brokers pay the exchanges less in fees and capture a bigger share of the $11 billion a year that institutional investors pay in trading commissions.

7.2.3 The Price of Stock   股票的价格

1. The types of stock price

The price at which the security is sold in the primary market is called "the issuing price". When the security is listed on the exchange it is traded among investors and the issuing company is not part of these transactions. This trading takes place with a price that differs from the issuing price and is called "the market price" or "the trading price".

It can be said that trading price is the most important price in the stock market. It is determined by the volume of offers and bids, that is, the supply and demand in the market, which is the reason why it is also called market price.

There are four important trading prices in the stock market: opening price, closing price, highest price, and lowest price.

Opening price is the price at which a stock first trades upon the opening of an exchange on a given trading day. Quite commonly, a stock's opening price will not be identical to its closing price on the previous day. This is due to after-hours trading and the changes in investors' valuations or expectations of the stock occurring outside of trading sessions. The opening price serves as a benchmark for a trading day: if the stock finishes trading at a higher price it is said to have closed up, and if it finishes trading below the opening price it is said to have closed down.

In case of capital increase, the opening price can not be determined until the day following the end of the subscription period and it will be determined according to the last trading price in addition to the specified value of subscription in each share.

Closing price is the price of the last transaction for a given stock at the end of a trading day. Many investors use closing prices reported in the newspapers to monitor their holdings. But not all closing prices are the same, and the differences may be important to be noted. For many market centers, including the New York Stock Exchange, the American Stock Exchange, and the NASDAQ Stock Market, regular trading sessions run from 9:30 a.m. to 4:00 p.m. Eastern Time. But a number of market centers offer after-hours trading. Some financial publications and market data vendors use the last trade in these after-hours markets as the closing price for the day. Others, however, publish the 4:00 p.m. price as the closing price and display prices for after-hours trading separately.

This discrepancy in the way the media and other institutions report closing prices can cause confusion—especially when a single, low volume after-hours trade occurs at a price that's substantially different from the 4:00 p.m. closing price. For example, an investor might read on a company's website that its stock closed at one price but then see a much different price on the consolidated tape flashing across the bottom of her/his television screen. Or, the next day, the investor might hear that the stock opened "up" when, in fact, it opened "down" compared with the price at the 4:00 p.m. close.

To help clear up this confusion, the central distributor of transaction prices for exchange traded securities—the Consolidated Tape Association (CTA)—implemented a system designed to make closing prices uniform. Under this system, the regular session closing price for stocks will be the 4:00 p.m. price. Sometimes orders come in before 4:00 p.m., but they can't be filled until after 4:00 p.m. Therefore, the CTA produces a 4:15 p.m. market summary for vendors and the media that includes regular session trades that are reported before 4:15 p.m. but should include in regular session 4:00 p.m. prices. Any trades that take place during after-hours trading sessions will be "tagged" with the letter "T" on the consolidated tape and will not affect the regular session closing price (or the regular session highest and lowest prices). The NASDAQ Stock Market, which operates a similar system for trades in its securities, uses similar conventions.

The highest price is the highest sales price the stock has achieved during the regular trading hours, while the lowest price is the lowest sales price the stock has fallen to during the regular trading hours in a trading day.

2. The factors affecting the stock price

There are many factors, such as the overall performance of the stock market, the long-term and short-term trends of the market price, affecting the demand for a particular stock. The investors usually examine these factors by using the methods of fundamental analysis[2] and technical analysis[3] to predict the future changes in the stock price. A recent study shows that customer satisfaction, as measured by the American Customer Satisfaction Index (ACSI), is significantly related to the stock market value. Stock price is also changed based on the forecast for the company's operation and whether their profits are expected to increase or decrease.

In economics and financial theory, analysts use random walk techniques to model behavior of asset prices, in particular share prices on stock markets, currency exchange rates and commodity prices. This practice has its basis in the presumption that investors act rationally and without bias, and that at any moment they estimate the value of an asset based on future expectations. Under these conditions, all existing information affects the price, which changes only when new information comes out. By definition, new information appears randomly and influences the asset price randomly.

The major determinants of stock prices are corporate earnings and interest rates. The stock market almost always falls before recessions. In the US, in fact, out of the forty one recessions from 1802 through 1990, thirty eight of them (93%) have been preceded or accompanied by declines in the stock returns index (the only exceptions were the 1829/30, 1945, and 1953 recessions). In the postwar period the peak of the stock market preceded the peak of the business cycle by between six and seven months.

The largest one day drop in the US stock market history occurred on Monday, October 19, 1987, when the Dow Jones industrial average fell 508 points (22.6%). No significant news event explains the decline, although rising interest rates and a falling dollar began to weigh on a market that had become tremendously overvalued after a five year bull run. Once the decline gained momentum, selling begat more selling and a panic developed. Since a recession did not follow and stock prices subsequently recovered to new highs, many pointed to Black Monday as a confirmation of the "irrationality" of the stock market.

Stock prices, however, are determined by expectations of the future, which must, by definition, be unknown. Shifts in sentiment and psychology can sometimes cause substantial changes in the valuation of the market. Despite false alarms, the stock market is still considered an important indicator of future economic conditions.

7.2.4 Stock Price Index 股票价格指数

A stock price index, also called stock market index, is a listing of stock and a statistic reflecting the composite value of its components. It is used as a tool to represent the characteristics of its component stocks, all of which bear some commonality such as trading on the same stock market exchange, belonging to the same industry, or having similar market capitalizations. Many indices compiled by news or financial services firms are used to benchmark the performance of portfolios such as funds. Famous examples of stock market index are Dow Jones Industrial Average (DJIA)[4] and S&P 500.

To accurately measure the growth of a stock market, an index must have a sufficient sample size of stocks which are representative of the particular market that the index seeks to measure. Weighting of each component of an index is an important consideration. There are three common index weightings: market capitalization, price, and equal weighting.

Market capitalization weighting (value weighting) easily accommodates stock splits and stock dividends, because they do not change the market capitalization of the company, and therefore, the weighting in the index. The market cap is computed by multiplying the share price times the number of shares outstanding. Market Capitalization Formula is as follows:

$$\text{Market Cap} = \text{Share Price} \times \text{Number of Shares Outstanding}$$

A portfolio based on market capitalization weighting would have more money invested in larger companies. For instance, the S&P 500 index, which is a market capitalization weighted index, is calculated by adding up the current market capitalization of each company, then dividing by the market capitalization of each company in the base years 1941 – 1943, then multiplying the result by 10. However, this weighting often leads to less diversification because a few large-cap stocks dominate the index. It can also lead to lesser returns because large companies generally have a lower growth potential than smaller companies.

Price weighting is based on the prices of each stock. A price-weighted portfolio would have the same number of shares of each stock. Price weighting is equal to the sum of the prices of each individual stock in the index divided by the number of stocks. When there are stock splits or dividends, the divisor must be adjusted; otherwise, the index would not measure actual growth. For instance, if there were 2 companies composing an index with the stock of each priced at $100, then the average price is their sum divided by 2, which is $100. However, if one company has a 2-for-1 stock split, then its stock will be priced at $50 per share (the number of shares will also double), then the average becomes $(100 + 50)/2 = 75$, even though the size of each company and its market value has not changed. In order to keep the average the same, the divisor must be changed so that the average stays the same. General Formula is:

$$New\ Divisor = New\ Sum\ of\ Share\ Prices/Previous\ Average$$

For instance, the Dow Jones Industrial Average first consisted of 30 stocks in 1928, and had a divisor of 30. In 1999, the divisor was 0.19740463—the divisor will continue to get smaller as there are more stock splits and stock dividends. (However, it could temporarily increase if there is a reverse stock split, where a number of shares are merged into one share, as sometimes happens when the stock price has fallen too much.) Because the DJIA consists of only 30 stocks, it is not representative of the stock market. However, it persists for historical reasons. Only a small number of stocks were considered because when the DJIA was started in 1884 with 12 stocks, it was time consuming to figure such averages every day without the aid of computers or calculators. The number of stocks was increased to 20 in 1916, then to its present 30 in 1928.

Equally weighted indexes simply gives each stock an equal weight, regardless of stock price or market capitalization, so, obviously, stock splits and stock dividends will not affect an equally weighted index. An equally weighted portfolio would have the same amount of money invested in each unique stock. Therefore, the number of shares of each stock would be different, with more shares of cheaper stocks. An equally weighted portfolio would have to be rebalanced more frequently to maintain equal weight, because stocks prices would diverge quickly.

An equally-weighted index will be more diversified than a value-weighted index, because it will not be dominated by large companies, so investments based on an equally weighted index may have higher returns, since small companies generally have a greater growth potential than large companies.

7.3 Bond Market
债券市场

7.3.1 A Brief Introduction to Bond Market　债券市场简介

1. The definition and structure of bond market

The bond market, also known as the debt, credit, or fixed income market, is a financial market where participants buy and sell debt securities usually in the form of bonds.

Bond markets in most countries remain decentralized and lack common exchanges like stock, future and commodity markets. This has occurred, in part, because no two bond issues are exactly alike, and the number of different securities outstanding is far larger.

In the US, nearly all of the average daily trading volume in the Bond Market takes place between broker-dealers and large institutions in a decentralized, over-the-counter (OTC) market. However, a small number of bonds, mainly corporate, are listed on exchanges.

The New York Stock Exchange (NYSE) is the largest centralized bond market, representing mostly corporate bonds. The NYSE migrated from the Automated Bond System (ABS) to the NYSE Bonds trading system in April 2007 and expects the number of traded issues to increase from 1,000 to 6,000.

While practically there are different types of bonds traded in the bond markets, such as corporate bond, government bond and municipal bond, references to the "bond market" usually refer to the government bond market because of its size, liquidity, lack of credit risk and therefore, sensitivity to interest rates. Because of the inverse relationship between bond valuation and interest rates, the bond market is often used to indicate changes in interest rates or the shape of the yield curve

Bond market participants are similar to participants in most financial markets and are essentially either buyers (debt issuer) of funds or sellers (institution) of funds and often both. There are different participants who buy and sell bonds in the market: institutional investors, governments, traders and individuals. Because of the specificity of individual bond issues, and the lack of liquidity in many smaller issues, the majority of outstanding bonds are held by institutions like pension funds, banks and funds. In the US, approximately 10% of the market is currently held by private individuals.

2. Bond market volatility and risks

Bonds are often called "fixed income" investments, but don't let that term fool you. Bonds are not riskless investments, although they are usually considered much safer than stocks.

First, the bond market is volatile to some extent. For the investors who own a bond, collect the coupon and hold it to maturity, market volatility is irrelevant; principal and interest are received according to a predetermined schedule. But the investors who buy and sell bonds before maturity are exposed to many risks, most importantly changes in interest rates.

When interest rates increase (decrease), the value of existing bonds fall (rise), since new issues pay a higher (lower) yield. This is the fundamental concept of bond market volatility: changes in bond prices are inverse to changes in interest rates. Fluctuating interest rates are part of a country's monetary policy and bond market volatility is a response to expected monetary policy and economic changes.

With few exceptions, the coupon rate on a bond is set when it is issued, as is the principal that will be returned at maturity. If there is significant inflation over the time the investor held the bond, the real value (buying power) of the investment will suffer loss. This may be called an inflation risk. In general, the longer the maturity of the bond, the higher its coupon rate while the greater the inflation risk. So the real yield of a bond may not absolutely depend on its coupon rate.

Credit risk is also to be considered. It is the risk that the investor may lose part or all of his investment because of the issuer's insolvency, or inability to pay the interest and principal. The greater the credit risk, the more interest the issuer has to pay to sell its bonds. Bonds issued by the federal government, for the most part, are immune from default (if the government needed money it could just print more). Bonds issued by corporations are more likely to be defaulted on companies often go bankrupt. Municipalities occasionally default as well, although it is much less common. The good news is that you are compensated for taking on the higher risks associated with corporate bonds and municipal bonds. The yield on corporate bonds is higher than that of municipal bonds, which is higher than that of treasury bonds. Moreover, there is a credit rating system that enables the investors to know the amount of risk each class of bond entails.

The expectations of the investors will contribute to the market volatility. For instance, if most investors expect the inflation rate will rise up to a new high, they will probably sell the various bonds held and bring the market prices down. If a corporation issuer is expected to go bankruptcy, its bonds will be sold by the holders which may cause the price to drop sharply.

Economist's consensus views of economic indicators versus actual released data also contribute to market volatility. A tight consensus is generally reflected in bond prices and there is little price movement in the market after the release of "in-line" data. If the economic release differs from the consensus view the market usually undergoes rapid price movement as participants interpret the data. Uncertainty (as measured by a wide consensus) generally brings more volatility before and after an economic release. Economic releases vary in importance and impact depending on where the economy is in the business cycle.

3. The yield of bond and its calculation

The yield of a bond is, roughly speaking, the return on the bond. The yield is expressed as an annual percentage of the face amount. However, yield is a little more complicated (and therefore more useful) than the coupon rate.

The return of a bond is largely determined by its interest rate. The interest that a bond pays depends on a number of factors, including the prevailing interest rate and the creditworthiness of the issuer, which, of course, is what is assessed by the credit rating companies, such as Standard & Poor's and Moody's. The prevailing interest rate—the cost of money—is determined by the supply and demand of money. Like virtually anything else, the greater the supply and the lower the demand, the lesser the interest rate, and vice versa. An often used basis of the prevailing interest rate is the prime rate charged by banks to their best customers.

Nominal yield[5], is equal to the coupon rate, that is, the return on the bond without accounting for any outside factors. If you purchase the bond at par value and hold to maturity, this will be the annual return you receive on the bond. This yield is the percentage of par value, which is generally $5,000 for municipal bonds, and $1,000 for all other bonds, that is usually paid twice a year. Thus, a bond that pays 10% interest pays $100 dollars per year, and in 2 semi annual payments of $50. The return of a bond is the return/investment, or in the example just cited, $100/$1,000 = 10%.

Because bonds trade in the secondary market, they may sell for less or more than par value, which will yield an interest rate that is different from the nominal yield, called the current yield[6], or current return. Current yield is a measure of the return on the bond in relation to the current price. The price of bonds moves in the opposite direction of interest rates. If rates go up, the price of bonds decrease; if the rates go down, then the bonds increase in value.

We can consider this simple example. You buy a bond when it is issued for $1,000 that pays 6% interest. Suppose you want to sell the bond, but since you bought it, the interest rate has risen to 8%. You will have to sell your bond for less than what you paid, because why is somebody going to pay you $1,000 for a bond that pays 6% when they can buy a similar bond of equal credit rating and get 8%. So to sell your bond, you would have to sell it so that the $60 that is received per year in interest will be 8% of the selling price. (Actually, the price probably wouldn't go this low, because the yield to maturity is greater in such a case, since if the bond holder keeps the bond until maturity, he will receive a price appreciation which is the difference between $1,000, the bond's par value and what he paid for it.) In such a case, the bond is said to be sold at a discount. If the interest rate of a new bond issue is lower than what you are getting, then you will be able to sell your bond at a higher price than what you paid—you are going to sell your bond at a premium.

The Current Yield = Annual Interest Payment/Current Price of Bond

For example, depending on how interest rates have changed, you could purchase a $1,000 par value bond that pays 4.5% coupon ($45) annually for $900. The current yield is the return on your interest payments based on your $900 investment, which would be 45/900 = 5%. As you can see, this can differ from the coupon rate.

Because current bond prices fluctuate, an investor can pay more or less than the par value for a bond. In the case of holding the bond to maturity, the investor will lose money if he paid a premium for the bond, and he will earn money if he paid for it at a discount. The yield-to-maturity[7] (true yield) of a bond that is held to maturity will have to account for the gain or loss that occurs when the par value is repaid. The formula for yield to maturity is complicated and difficult to solve, but it generally will yield an interest rate comparable to newly issued bonds with the same credit rating. If the interest rate is a simple rate, the formula is as follows:

Approximate Yield to Maturity =

$$\frac{\text{Annual Interest Payment} + (\text{Par Value} - \text{Current Bond Price})/\text{Number of Years to Maturity}}{(\text{Par Value} + \text{Current Bond Price})/2}$$

When a bond is bought at a discount, yield to maturity will always be greater than the current yield; when it is bought at a premium, the yield to maturity will always be less than the current yield.

Reading Material

Bond Market Index

A number of bond market indices exist for the purposes of managing portfolios and measuring performance, similar to the S&P 500 or DJIA Indexes for stocks.

The most common American benchmarks are the Lehman Aggregate, Citigroup BIG and Merrill Lynch Domestic Master.

Most indices are parts of families of broader indices that can be used to measure global bond portfolios, or may be further subdivided by maturity and/or sector for managing specialized portfolios.

7.3.2   The Operations of Bond Market   债券市场的业务操作

Similar to stock market, there are two markets for bonds: the primary market and the secondary market. The primary market is where the bond is first issued. In the primary market the bond is purchased directly from the issuer. The secondary market occurs later, where bonds are traded by various investors.

Bonds are issued by various issuers in the primary market. The range of issuers of bonds is very large. Almost any organization could issue bonds, but the underwriting and legal costs can be prohibitive. Regulations to issue bonds are very strict in most countries. Issuers are often classified as follows:

(1) Supranational agencies, such as the European Investment Bank or the Asian Development Bank issue supranational bonds.

(2) National governments issue government bonds in their own currency. They also issue sovereign bonds in foreign currencies.

(3) Sub-sovereign, provincial, state or local authorities (municipalities). In the US, state and local government bonds are known as municipal bonds.

(4) Government sponsored entities. In the US, examples include the Federal Home Loan Mortgage Corporation (Freddie Mac), the Federal National Mortgage Association (Fannie Mae), and the Federal Home Loan Banks. The bonds of these entities are known as agency bonds, or agencies.

(5) Companies (corporations) issue corporate bonds.

(6) Special purpose vehicles are companies set up for the sole purpose of containing assets against which bonds are issued, often called asset-backed securities.

The most common process of issuing bonds is through underwriting. In underwriting, one or more security firms or banks, forming a syndicate, buy an entire issue of bonds from an issuer and re-sell them to other investors in the secondary market. Government bonds are typically auctioned.

Issue price is the price at which the particular investors buy the bonds when they are first issued. The net proceeds that the issuer receives are calculated as the issue price, minus issuance fees, times the nominal amount.

The interest rate that the issuer of a bond must pay is influenced by a variety of factors, such as current market interest rates, the length of the maturity and the creditworthiness of the issuer. These factors are likely to change over time, so the market value of a bond can vary after it is issued. Because of these differences in market value, bonds are priced in terms of percentage of par value. Bonds are not necessarily issued at par (100% of face value), but all bond prices converge to par when they reach maturity. At other times, prices can either rise, which is called trading at a premium, or fall, which is called trading at a discount. Most government bonds are denominated in units of $1,000, if in the US, or in units of £100, if in the UK. For example, a deep discount US bond, sold at a price of 75.26, indicates a selling price of $752.60 per bond sold.

Bonds markets, unlike stock markets, often do not have a centralized exchange or trading system. Rather, in most developed bond markets such as the US, Japan and Western Europe, bonds trade in decentralized, dealer based over the counter markets. In such a market, market liquidity is provided by dealers and other market participants committing risk capital to trading activity. In the bond market, when an investor buys or sells a bond, the counterparty to the trade is almost always a bank or security firm acting as a dealer. In some cases, when a dealer buys a bond from an investor, the dealer carries the bond "in inventory". The dealer's position is then subject to risks of price fluctuation. In other cases, the dealer immediately resells the bond to another investor.

Bond markets also differ from stock markets in that investors generally do not pay brokerage commissions to dealers with whom they buy or sell bonds. Rather, dealers earn revenue for trading with their investor customers by means of the spread, or difference, between the price at which the dealer buys a bond from one investor (the bid price[8]) and the price at which he or she sells the same bond to another investor (the asked or offered price[9]). The bid/offer spread represents the total transaction cost associated with transferring a bond from one investor to another.

To execute the trading transactions, investors must open a trading account with one of the licensed members or brokerage firms to buy or sell bonds. This usually requires filling the sample contract with the broker, who in turn executes the investor's orders and signing a contract with a custodian who keeps accounts of securities balances and transactions executed. When a client makes a buy order both the custodian and the broker should make sure that the necessary funds are available before the execution of the trade. In case the client makes a sell order they should ensure that the bonds being sold are available before execution of the order.

The prices of bonds in the secondary market are set by supply and demand and are impacted by what is expected of interest rates and inflation, how many coupon payments are left to maturity, and how long it will be until the bond matures, and how the issuing corporation operates.

1. Talk about the importance of stock market in modern economy.
2. Compare the stock market and the bond market.
3. Discuss the difference between the stock market in China and that in the US.
4. Would you like to invest in the stock market directly if you have excess money?

1　Big Board　纽约证券交易所行情牌（亦指纽约证券交易所）
2　fundamental analysis　基本面分析
3　technical analysis　技术分析
4　Dow Jones Industrial Average (DJIA)　道·琼斯工业平均指数
5　nominal yield　名义收益率
6　current yield　现行收益率（亦用"current return"）
7　yield-to-maturity　到期收益率
8　bid price　买价
9　asked price　卖价（亦用"offered price"）

China's Financial Market after the WTO Entry
入世之后的中国金融市场

After China's entry into the WTO, it is quite possible that the competition as well as cooperation among local banks and foreign banks will be intensified simultaneously in financial market in China. Under such circumstances, what kind of role the large transnational banks will play is a matter of concern but their strategies remain unclear. It seems that there are some uncertainties for them to worry about the China's financial market.

The Handling of Non-performing Loans (NPL) and the Three Major Debts

The four assets management companies (AMCs) were set up by the Chinese government in 1999 to manage NPL of the four major state-owned banks. A total amount of 1.4 trillion yuan RMB NPL was transferred to the AMCs in 2000. According to the latest information, the review of nearly 600 major state enterprises' debt-equity swap possibility has already been completed.

Concerning the handling of NPL through AMCs, many researchers in Mainland as well as in HK expressed their difficulties in supporting this scheme. Some of them hint that the scheme is just a "dressing-up" policy which cannot solve the fundamental structural problem, or the scheme has already on the deadlock. But at the same time they all seem to admit that this scheme is a second best measure and there is no other way at this moment.

As to the size of NPL, basically nobody knows the exact amount. Although the government decided to introduce the international standard of five categories of loan classification two years ago, it appears that human resources are not sufficient enough to handle the new standard, eventually most of the NPL is still classified by the old standard.

It is a common view that the ultimate recovery rate of the NPL, which was transferred to the AMCs, can only reach up to 20% – 30%. Furthermore, it is also pointed out that new NPL will be created unless fundamental measures are taken at the earliest possible time. On the other hand, in order to suppress new NPL, it is indispensable to get the local governments out of the loan decision-making process, and it should be noted that some progress was recognized in this aspect.

Another development to be noted is that since most of the NPL debtors are either A-shares listed companies or the major owners of such shares in those companies, some international financial institutions are trying to penetrate into the A-share market in China by joining the NPL management scheme.

Still, since there is a great difference in Chinese and international ways of handling NPL assets, in terms of laws and regulations or tax system, it is necessary to observe more how these developments will be expanded in the future.

A variety of reasons account for the poor performance of this scheme. The fundamental reason seems to be that China's capital market is still immature. Most probably the key to address NPL problem lies in whether and when this condition will be fulfilled.

The three largest debts of China are NPL, public outstanding debt and the external debt. While almost everybody admits the difficulty in addressing the NPL problem, they do not regard the fiscal deficit and external debt as serious problems to tackle. For external debt, the main reason is that a roughly same amount of foreign reserves are prepared and also medium-and long-term debts, which are rather stable, account for about 80% of total external debt. Regarding the fiscal deficit, the underlying reason may be due to the fact that the budgetary balance to the GDP is still below the international safety/acceptable level of 3% and that the ratio of the public outstanding debt to GDP is still below 30%, which is again lower than the one in many developed countries. In fact, unless unexpected political problems should happen, external debt may not become a serious matter for the moment. However, the NPL itself can be regarded as "hidden fiscal deficits" in its nature. Furthermore, various measures being taken to promote social safety net are expected to put pressure on the future government spending. Therefore, perhaps we should not be too optimistic. If we simply add NPL to the public outstanding debt, the total amount will come to 6 to 7 trillion RMB, which is 67% – 78% of GDP. If the recovery rate of the entire amount of the NPL is assumed at 25%, the total debt will be 5 to 5.7 trillion RMB, which becomes 56% – 64% of GDP. This means that even if we do not assume new NPL for the coming years, the ratio of the outstanding debt to the GDP has already reached 60% – 70%. This is worth noticing if we recall that the various estimates carried out two to three years ago suggested such figure were in the range of 20% – 30%.

When we look at the fiscal reform, financial reform and state-owned enterprise reform independently, they appear to be manageable or we can recognize some progress. However, we should bear in mind that the three reforms are interrelated with each other. Without state-owned enterprise reform, new NPL will be created and the financial reform will be on deadlock, which in turn exerts additional burden to the national budget. In this sense, it seems that the state-owned enterprise reform will be the key to the success of the economic reform as a whole.

The Capital Market Reform and the Financial Reform

According to a source at the PBOC Shanghai Branch Office, who do not want the name to be identified, the capital market reform lags far behind compared with other reforms in the financial sector, because China faces relatively less "opening-up" pressure from the US in this area. The background seems to be that thanks to the Chinese companies' large scale IPOs, many American investment banks have been benefited from the joining into the syndicated-groups since 2000. This opinion is very honest and may tell some truth. However, although the external pressure may affect the speed of reform, the basic direction for pursuing the reform and building up the capital market will not be much affected by any political reasons.

According to *The Report on China's Capital Market*, the development stages of China's capital market are divided into three stages: foundation laying stage, marketization stage, and internationalization stage. Currently, China is in the marketization stage, which is a very important stage to link between the preceding and the following stages. At this stage, a lot of conflicts and contradictions have to be expected between the planned economy and the market economy. Having said so, the report lists a number of issues to be addressed during this stage. These include a build-up of the secondary markets, the improvement of the corporate governance, the increase in the market liquidity (more specifically, the reduction of state-owned share holding), and the withdrawal rule of the listed companies (reflecting the recognition of the poor functioning of the ST and PT which were being introduced in 1998). It is also predicted that both marketization and internationalization stages will last about ten years.

The above clearly shows the concern from academic circles that not only the acceleration of solving the NPL problem but also facilitating the build-up of the capital market is all the more important and pressing issue for China's economy. It should be noted that some measures have already been taken including the liberalization of the B-share market to domestic investors and the establishment of the withdrawal mechanism of listed companies.

Stock Market Bubble
股票市场泡沫

A stock market bubble is a type of economic bubble taking place in stock markets when prices of stocks continually rise up and become overvalued by any measure of stock valuation.

The existence of stock market bubbles is at odds with the efficient market hypothesis (EMH) which assumes rational investor behavior. Behavioral finance theory attributes stock market bubbles to cognitive biases that lead to groupthink and herd behavior. Bubbles occur not only in real-world markets, with their inherent uncertainty and noise, but also in highly predictable experimental markets. In the laboratory, uncertainty is eliminated and calculating the expected returns should be a simple mathematical exercise, because participants are endowed with assets that are defined to have a finite lifespan and a known distribution probability of dividends. Other theoretical explanations of stock market bubbles have suggested that they are rational, intrinsic, and contagious.

The most bitter and recent example is that the NASDAQ Composite Index soared up in the late 1990s and peaked to the historical highest point of 5048. 62 on March 10, 2000; but then fell sharply by near 80% in the following two years as a result of the Dot-com bubble. Till now, the NASDAQ has not been able to reach a new high.

Two famous early stock market bubbles were the Mississippi Scheme in France and the South Sea bubble in England. Both bubbles came to an abrupt end in 1720 bankrupting thousands of unfortunate investors.

The two most famous bubbles of the twentieth century, the bubble in American stocks in the 1920s and the Dot-com bubble of the late 1990s were based on speculative activity surrounding the development of new technologies. The 1920s saw the widespread introduction of an amazing range of technological innovations including radio, automobiles, aviation and the deployment of electrical power grids. The 1990s was the decade when Internet and e-commerce technologies emerged.

Stock market bubbles frequently produce hot markets in Initial Public Offerings (IPO) since investment banks and their clients see opportunities to float new stock issues at inflated prices. These hot IPO markets misallocate investment funds to areas dictated by speculative trends, rather than to enterprises generating longstanding economic value.

Emotional and cognitive biases seem to be the causes of bubbles. But, often, when the phenomenon appears, the pundits try to find a rationale, so as not to be against the crowd. Thus, sometimes, people will dismiss the concerns about overpriced markets by citing a new economy where the old stock valuation rules may no longer apply. This type of thinking helps to further propagate the bubble whereby everyone is investing with the intent of finding a greater fool. However, some analysts still cite the wisdom of crowds and say that price movements really do reflect rational expectations of fundamental returns.

To sort out the competing arguments between behavioral finance and efficient markets theorists, observers need to find bubbles that occur when a readily-available measure of fundamental value is also observable. The bubble in closed-end country funds in the late 1980s is instructive here, as are the bubbles that occur in experimental asset markets. For closed-end country funds, observers can compare the stock prices to the net asset value per share. For experimental asset markets, observers can compare the stock prices to the expected returns from holding the stock.

In the both cases, closed-end country funds and experimental markets, stock prices clearly diverge from fundamental values. Nobel laureate Dr. Vernon Smith has illustrated the closed-end country fund phenomenon with a chart showing prices and net asset values of the Spain Fund in 1989 and 1990 in his work on price bubbles. At its peak, the Spain Fund traded near $35, nearly triple its net asset value of about $12 per share. At the same time the Spain Fund and other closed-end country funds were trading at very substantial premiums, the number of closed-end country funds available exploded due to many issuers creating new country funds and selling the IPOs at high premiums.

It only took a few months for the premiums in closed-end country funds to fade back to the more typical discounts at which general closed-end funds trade. Those who had bought them at premiums had run out of "greater fools". For a while, though, the supply of "greater fools" had been outstanding.

A rising price on any share will attract the attention of investors. Not all of those investors are willing or interested in studying the intrinsic value of the share and for such people the rising price itself is the reason enough to invest. In turn, the additional investment will provide buoyancy to the price, thus completing the loop.

Like all dynamical systems, financial markets operate in an ever changing equilibrium, which translates into price volatility. However, this balance is born instable, a self-adjustment (negative feedback) takes place normally: when prices rise more people are encouraged to sell, while fewer are encouraged to buy. This puts a limit on volatility. However, once a positive feedback takes over, the market, like all systems with positive feedback, will enter a state of increasing disequilibrium. This can be seen in financial bubbles where asset prices rapidly spike upwards far beyond what could be considered the rational "economic value", only to fall rapidly afterwards.

Subprime Mortgage Crisis
次级贷危机

The subprime mortgage crisis is a current economic problem characterized by contracted liquidity in the global credit markets and banking system. An undervaluation of real risk in the subprime market ultimately resulted in cascades and ripple effects affecting finance and economy all over the world.

The crisis began with the bursting of the US housing bubble and high default rates on subprime and adjustable rate mortgages (ARM). Loan incentives, such as easy initial terms, in conjunction with an acceleration in rising housing prices encouraged borrowers to assume difficult mortgages on the belief they would be able to quickly refinance at more favorable terms. However, once housing prices started to drop moderately in 2006 – 2007 in many parts of the US, refinancing became more difficult. Defaults and foreclosure activity increased dramatically, as easy initial terms expired, home prices failed to go up as anticipated, and ARM interest rates reset higher. Foreclosures accelerated in the US in late 2006 and triggered a global financial crisis through 2007 and 2008. During 2007, nearly 1.3 million US housing properties were subject to foreclosure activity, up 79% from 2006.

The mortgage lenders that retained credit risk were the first to be affected, as borrowers became unable or unwilling to make payments. Major banks and other financial institutions around the world have reported losses of approximately US $ 435 billion as of July 17, 2008. Owing to a form of financial engineering called securitization, many mortgage lenders had passed the rights to the mortgage payments and related credit risk to third-party investors via mortgage-backed securities (MBS) and collateralized debt obligations (CDO). Corporate, individual and institutional investors holding MBS or CDO faced significant losses, as the value of the underlying mortgage assets declined. Stock markets in many countries declined significantly.

On July 19, 2007, the Dow Jones Industrial Average hit a record high, closing above 14,000 for the first time. By August 15, the Dow had dropped below 13,000 and the S&P 500 had crossed into negative territory year-to-date. Similar drops occurred in virtually every market in the world, with Brazil and Korea being hard-hit.

The crisis has caused panic in financial markets and encouraged investors to take their money out of risky mortgage bonds and shaky equities and put it into commodities as "stores of value". Financial speculation in commodity futures following the collapse of the financial derivatives markets has contributed to the world food price crisis and oil price increases due to a "commodities super-cycle." Financial speculators seeking quick returns have removed trillions of dollars from equities and mortgage bonds, some of which has been invested into food and raw materials.

The widespread dispersion of credit risk and the unclear effect on financial institutions caused reduced lending activity and increased spreads on higher interest rates. Similarly, the ability of corporations to obtain funds through the issuance of commercial paper was affected. This aspect of the crisis is consistent with a credit crunch. The liquidity concerns drove central banks around the world to take action to provide funds to member banks to encourage lending to worthy borrowers and to restore faith in the commercial paper markets.

With interest rates on a large number of subprime and other ARM due to adjust upward during the 2008 period, US legislators, the US Treasury Department, and financial institutions are taking action. A systematic program to limit or defer interest rate adjustments was implemented to reduce the effect. In addition, lenders and borrowers facing defaults have been encouraged to cooperate to enable borrowers to stay in their homes. Banks have sought and received over $250 billion in additional funds from investors to offset losses. The risks to the broader economy created by the financial market crisis and housing market downturn were primary factors in several decisions by the US.

Federal Reserve to cut interest rates and the economic stimulus package passed by Congress and signed by President George W. Bush on February 13, 2008. Both actions are designed to stimulate economic growth and inspire confidence in the financial markets.

However, these measures are seemed to be helpless to pull the Wall Street through the crisis. One of the leading investment banks, Bear Stearns, was found on the verge of insolvency and acquired at a low price in March 2008. Another two famous players in the Wall Street, Merrill Lynch and Lehman Brothers, both of which ever ranked beyond the Bear Stearns in the Bulge Bracket, was acquired and voluntarily bankrupted respectively in September 2008. Stock markets all over the world slumped drastically. This was said to be the most severe stocks tumble since the "9.11"terrorist attack and may be the beginning of a global financial storm.

PART IV

International Finance
国际金融

Chapter 8

Balance of Payments
国际收支

▼ **Learning Objectives**

- ☑ To grasp the concept and the structure of balance of payments
- ☑ To understand the disequilibrium of balance of payments
- ☑ To learn how to adjust the balance of payments
- ☑ To know about international reserve and international debt

 Opening Vignette

China Makes Efforts to Promote the Balance of International Payments

China will take a variety of measures to promote the balance of international payments, said sources with the State Administration of Foreign Exchange (SAFE) Thursday. He said China is aiming to strike a basic balance in international payments, before the negative impact of persistent surpluses comes into full play.

Achieving a balance of international payments is of great significance to the healthy development of the Chinese economy. However, problems such as bigger foreign trade surplus and an imbalance of international payments still exist in China's rapidly growing economy.

Trade and capital account surpluses in recent years brought China's foreign exchange reserves up to USD 1.0663 trillion at the end of last year, the largest amount in the world.

Forex (Foreign exchange) reserve hikes have been hefty in recent years as businesses and individuals opted to hold Renminbi and trim their forex assets in pursuit of the higher interest rate on Renminbi deposits and betting on an appreciation of the local currency.

Some foreign countries have been stepping up pressure on the Chinese government to revalue the Yuan, which they say is undervalued and has caused job losses in the United States.

In order to promote the balance of international payments, the SAFE will improve the management of foreign exchange in current accounts and facilitate trade and investment. The SAFE will make further progress in the foreign exchange market and improve the managed, floating exchange rate regime.

In this way, the SAFE will improve financial services for small deals of foreign exchange, encourage financial institutions to make innovations in commodities and services and enhance monitoring and management on market risks.

The SAFE will expand channels for capital to flow in and out and advance capital account convertibility step by step. It will abolish quotas for foreign exchange overseas investment and provide more favorable policies to enterprises going abroad to make investments. It will expand channels for overseas financial investment step by step and improve the Qualified Foreign Institutional Investor (QFII) system.

The SAFE will make more efforts to standardize capital inflows to safeguard the economic and financial security of the country and improve the management of foreign exchange reserves. It will explore more effective ways of using capital reserves by improving money and capital structures and expanding investment fields for foreign exchange reserves. It will enhance its supervision of foreign exchange fund inflows and outflows and crack down on illegal foreign exchange deals.

Experience from other countries indicated that, when dealing with international balance of payment surpluses, "one can either ignore the role of the exchange rate, or rely too much on the exchange rate," but coordinated actions from both domestic economy players and foreign exchange regulators are needed, said a senior official of SAFE.

Therefore, other policy options will be made by the central government, which include supporting high-tech and high value-added exports and slashing less competitive exports, encouraging imports on a selective basis, and tightening supervision of capital inflow, particularly short-term capital that may be used in transactions involving the local currency, the Renminbi, the official said.

Meanwhile, the SAFE will still closely control local importers' trade financing that lead to foreign liabilities. The Chinese currency, the Renminbi, is convertible under the current account, which typically covers trade, but only partially convertible under the capital account.

"Measures will be taken to prevent import payment funds under the current account from becoming short-term foreign debt under the capital account, and it is an important step to promote balanced international payments," SAFE said in a statement.

Growing numbers of postponed import payments and export advances in recent years have already caused a rapid rise in China's short-term debts, a trend SAFE has vowed to closely monitor. Chinese importers increasingly opted for late payments while exporters found advance payments more desirable, largely as a result of expectations that the Renminbi will appreciate, and interest rate differentials between local and foreign currency deposits.

China's outstanding foreign debts reversed a downward trend since 1999 in the first half of 2003, and the proportion of short-term liabilities rose rapidly. Regulators attributed the trend to statistical adjustments that included trade-related credit and foreign liabilities of foreign financial institutions operating in China as part of foreign debt.

A policy-triggered borrowing craze by foreign banks operating in China further pushed up growth in the nation's short-term foreign debts. Chinese regulators insist the increases in foreign debts pose no threat to the nation's financial security, thanks to its massive foreign exchange reserves. But the rapid increases in forex reserves, partly due to speculation-driven capital inflows, have also complicated the Chinese monetary authorities' efforts to contain the growth of bank credit.

 Warm-up Questions

> 1. What do you think about the balance of international payments?
> 2. Why does China want to promote the balance of international payments?
> 3. How will the international payments surplus affect the country's economy?

8.1　An Overview of Balance of Payments
国际收支平衡表概述

8.1.1　A Brief Introduction to Balance of Payments　国际收支简介

The balance of payments (BOP)[1] is a statistical statement that summarizes, for a specific time period, the economic transactions of the residents of a given country with the rest of the world. In other words, it is a list, or accounting, of all of a country's international transactions for a given time period, usually one year. Payments into the country (receipts) are entered as positive numbers, called credits; payments out of the country (payments) are entered as negative numbers called debits. Therefore, this terminology of balance of payments has identical meaning with the balance of international payments[2]. If payments due in exceed those due out, a country is said to be in overall surplus; and when payments due out exceed payments due in, it is in overall deficit. And, if possible, it is in overall equilibrium when the two flows of payments are equal.

BOP transactions occur between residents and non-residents. The term "resident" covers (1) individuals, including foreign nationals, living in the given country for at least one year as well as the country's embassy staff and military staff located abroad, (2) the country's government enclaves located abroad (embassies, consulates, etc.), and (3) corporate bodies who have a centre of economic interest located here, including branches of foreign-registered companies. It is important to note that transactions in foreign assets and liabilities can occur between residents and should be recorded.

The double-entry bookkeeping[3] used in accounting for the balance of payments is similar to that used by business firms in accounting for their transactions. That is, the amount of each transaction is recorded both as a debit and a credit, and the sum of all debit entries must, therefore, equal the sum of all credit entries. This means that in the given time period the receipts gained by the country from the rest of the world are equal to the payments it makes. This is defined as the balance of payments equilibrium which is represented by the zero balance in the BOP statement.

Here is a simple example of the recording of transactions in balance of payments. Consider the US, when a foreigner gives up an asset to a resident of US in return for a promise of future payment, a debit entry is made to show the increase in the stock of assets held by US residents, and a credit entry is made to show the increase in US liabilities to foreigners (that is, in foreign claims on US residents). Or when a US resident transfers a good to a foreigner, with payment to be made in the future, a debit entry is made to record the increase in one category of US assets (US financial claims on foreigners, that is, US holdings of foreign IOUs), and a credit entry is made to record the decrease in another category.

BOP transactions, in principle, should be recorded on an accruals basis[4] using market valuation. In practice, the data collection system is designed to adhere to this approach and, for the most part, the valuations reported are either market values or a close approximation. In certain cases, income (interest) flows on debt securities may be reported on a cash rather than an accruals basis.

8.1.2 The Structure of Balance of Payments 国际收支平衡表的结构

The balance of payments accounts are commonly grouped into three major categories: the current account, the capital account, and the reserves assets.

There may be some discrepancies in names of accounts and recording details in different countries. For example, the name of the "capital account" was changed into "financial account" in the US in 1999. In China it is now referred to as the "capital and financial account". Here we will concentrate on the structure of Chinese BOP.

1. Current account

The current account is composed of there sub-accounts: goods and services, income, current transfers.

Goods (also called merchandise and specially referring to tangible goods) exports and imports are valued FOB (Free On Board) for BOP purposes. While imports are valued CIF (Cost, Insurance and Freight) in the official external trade statistics, adjustments are made to reflect an estimated FOB valuation. Some adjustments are also made to the official merchandise trade statistics to conform to the BOP change of ownership and market valuation principles. In addition, certain exports sales of software licenses are included in BOP service exports and not in BOP goods exports.

Services exports and imports are presented to show 13 categories of service types: transportation, travel, communications, construction services, insurance services, financial services, computer and information services, royalties and license fees, research and development, advertising and public opinion polling, audio-visual and related services, other business services, government service not elsewhere classified.

Income or factor income, a sub-account of the current account, covers (1) compensation of employees, which relates to the earnings of persons working outside China of residence for less than one year (i.e. students and other short-term cross-border workers) and earnings of local staff working in embassies and consulates, and (2) investment income, which covers earnings arising from foreign investors' investments in China and domestic investors' investment abroad, including interest on bonds and loans, dividends and other claims on profits.

Current transfers sub-account covers unrequited receipts and payments, which is the reason why it is called unilateral transfers formerly. Important components are aids and contributions from or to abroad and membership fees to the international organizations such as the UN and the WTO, and transfers related to non-life insurance business and income taxes receivable or payable on the earnings of cross-border workers.

The current account balance is the total of all current account credits less the total of all current account debits. If it is positive, it is called a current account surplus[5] while a deficit if negative.

The following equation could be used to show how to calculate the balance of current account.

$$\text{Current Account} = \text{Net Exports of Goods} + \text{Net Exports of Services} + \text{Net Income from Abroad} + \text{Net Current Transfers from Abroad}$$

2. Capital and financial account

The capital and financial account is formerly known as capital account. This section usually includes special debt transactions between nations and migrants' goods as they cross a country's borders. This account consists of two sub-accounts: capital account and financial account.

The capital sub-account comprises capital transfers and the acquisition and disposal of non-produced, non-financial assets (such as patents, copyrights, etc.). Estimates of migrants' transfers (i. e. the transfer of the net worth of immigrants and emigrants) are included but they are not well based.

The financial sub-account covers direct investment, portfolio investment and other investment. The direct investment includes the Chinese direct investment abroad and foreign direct investment[6] in China. The portfolio investment refers to the international transactions of the various kinds of equity and debt securities. Other investment involves those international transactions relating to trade credits, loans, currency and deposits.

3. Reserve assets

The account of reserve assets (it is included in the capital account formerly and this is still the case with some countries), also called official reserves, comprises monetary gold, special drawing rights (SDRs)[7] and reserve position[8] in the IMF, foreign exchange, and other claims.

4. Net errors and omissions

As mentioned in the previous section, the sum of debits and credits from all these three accounts should equal zero, because of the double entry accounting principle. Nevertheless, in practice, because some transactions may not be captured or because of differences in coverage, valuation and timing of transactions, exact symmetry does not occur.

Therefore, in order to make the balance of payments accounts always balance, a balancing item of net errors and omissions is inserted to balance the overall account. Ideally, the magnitude of this item should be relatively small in relation to the combined value of all credit and debit transactions expressed in absolute terms over all three accounts. It should also fluctuate frequently from positive to negative values.

8.2 Balance of Payments Disequilibrium
国际收支不平衡

8.2.1 What Is the Balance of Payments Disequilibrium
什么是国际收支不平衡

Theoretically, the balance of payments equilibrium (BPE)[9] is defined as a condition where the sum of debits and credits from the current account and the capital & financial account equal zero; in other words, equilibrium is where: current account + capital & financial account = 0.

Conversely, there will be the balance of payments disequilibrium[10], if this sum is not zero.

In practice, the balance of payments equilibrium rarely, even never happens to any country. No economy is self-contained. All countries must therefore develop trading and financial relationships with other countries, and make international payments to as well as receive payments from other countries. However, there is no necessary reason why, especially in the short-term, the international payments should balance. In normal cases, sometimes there is a surplus of receipt and sometimes a surplus of payout.

Short-term disequilibrium is not usually significant, but it is important that there will be a tendency to balance in the long term. Therefore, generally, the countries will make efforts to achieve a basic equilibrium of BOP which means allowing a small balance of payments surplus (or deficit)[11] in the short term.

8.2.2 The Balances of International Payments   国际收支差额

The following three important balances relative to international payments are frequently taken into consideration by the policymakers to measure the situation of their counties' international payments and make corresponding adjustment.

1. The balance of trade

The balance of trade[12] is the net exports of goods and services which is the sum of the exports of goods and services less the imports of goods and services. It is a trade surplus when positive while a trade deficit when negative.

2. The balance of current account

As stated previously, the balance of current account[13] is the total of all current account credits less the total of all current account debits. If it is positive, it is called a current account surplus while a deficit if negative.

3. The overall balance of payments

The overall balance of payments[14] covers the current account, the capital & financial account and the net errors & omissions and equals to the total sum of the balances of the former two accounts plus the net errors & omissions. Consequently, the numerical value of it is identical with that of net reserve assets but their signs are in opposition to each other.

Similarly, if the number of the overall balance is positive, it is a surplus while a deficit if negative.

The surplus or deficit must be balanced by a monetary movement in the opposite direction, generally through the changes in reserve assets, and this is the reason why the overall balance must always be equal to the changes in reserve assets.

The Imbalance of Payments Again

For half a century, the US hasn't had to worry about its huge (more than $2 billion a day!) balance of payments deficit. Those decades are over because of two basic changes in the world's economy, Professor Paul Nadler says.

Up till recently, foreigners simply took the dollars they earned from doing business with us and invested them right back in the US, thus financing our budget deficit. In other words, we bought stuff from them and they lent us the money to pay for it. They had to do so. There wasn't anybody else big and strong enough to lend their money to. Therein lies one of the changes. The upstart Euro, the joint currency of twelve nations, is now both big enough and strong enough to handle those dollars that have been floating around the globe, and furthermore the considerably higher interest rates in Europe make investment over there more attractive. The dollars we spend have stopped coming back to us. So much for the guaranteed financing of our budget deficit. We aren't the only game in town anymore. While we weren't looking, somebody started up a new game, with better odds, over on the other side of the creek.

The other change has similarly sneaked up on us. Used to be, we had a so much better trained workforce than any other country, and technology that was so much more advanced, we could get away with paying the world's highest wages. We were, after all, the only one who could do the work. Now, alas, the levels of both education and technology in many other countries have caught up with or surpassed ours. And since broadband enables information to be zapped around the world effortlessly and without cost, even highly technical work like reading x-rays can be performed in lower-wage countries. Our excuse for paying workers more doesn't hold up anymore.

These are just the beginning. What we have to do is to recognize that our days of indiscriminately spending without hurting our jobs, our dollar, and our living standard are over. We've got to change.

There must be something that we must to do to fight the huge balance of payments deficit right now.

8.2.3 The Reasons for Balance of Payments Disequilibrium
国际收支不平衡的原因

International experience has shown that there can be many reasons for the imbalance of international payments of a country. There are external reasons, like the cyclical changes of demand on international commodity markets and structural changes in international division of labor, changes in the interest rate on international capital markets, the international flow of capital or hot money, etc.

There are also two types of internal reasons. The first is the choice of development model. In an open economy, if domestic savings fall short of investment needs (either in quantity or type), the country can borrow from abroad to cover the gap. This makes obvious economic sense, especially for a country in the early stages of development. But the adoption of this model usually means that the country will show a rather large deficit on its current account for a number of years. The second type is the influence of abnormal economic or policy factors, such as cyclical economic developments, problems in the country's economic operations or structure, the inappropriate money supply (inflation or deflation) and foreign exchange rate, distorted prices in domestic markets, great fluctuations in national revenue, inconsistency between macroeconomic policy and managerial practices, etc.

Some temporary factors, such as war, natural disaster and international financial crisis, may also cause balance of payments disequilibrium. For example, a great extra increase in grain imports due to natural disaster may cause a considerable current account deficit resulting in the overall deficit. Once the temporary factors disappear, the balance can be quickly restored. Therefore, the imbalances of international payments resulted from such temporary factors are generally negligible.

8.2.4   The Effects of Balance of Payments Disequilibrium
国际收支不平衡的影响

As mentioned earlier, a small balance of international payments in short term, whether it is a surplus or deficit, will not do harm to the country's economy and it can be regarded as a normal case. However, a persistent and substantive balance of international payments (surplus or deficit), will do affect the economy adversely.

1. The effect on economy of a persistent and substantive BOP surplus

Persistent surplus of international payments will increase the foreign money capital held by the country, and the domestic currency[15] will tend to appreciate which may hamper the export of domestic products. If there is a persistent and substantive trade surplus which resulted from huge volume of exports, this may followed by the shortage of commodity and inflation in domestic market. In addition, a persistent surplus may cause discontentment among other countries. Especially, a persistent bilateral trade surplus with a major trade partner will inevitably discontent the partner who will consequently demand the surplus country to take measures to resolve the problem. If the problem can not be solved to both parties' satisfactions, there are chances that the friendly relationship between the two partners will be ruined.

2. The effect on economy of a persistent and substantive BOP deficit

Persistent deficit of international payments will increase the country's demand for foreign exchange. This will drive the foreign exchange rates up while press the domestic currency to depreciate, which may cause capital flight. A persistent and substantive deficit will also decrease the country's reserve assets, weaken its financial power and depress its debt paying ability, which will lower its international credit rating, and even worse, may result in an international debt crisis.

8.3   Balance of Payments Adjustment
国际收支调节

As mentioned above, it will be unfavorable to the national economy if there is a persistent and substantial imbalance of international payments. Therefore, the governments always pay much attention to the balance-of-payment adjustment for the purpose of achieving a basic balance of international payments in long term.

The adjustment mechanism of international payments could be categorized into the two types of automatic adjustment and policy adjustment. [16]

8.3.1 Automatic Adjustment 自动调节

Theoretically, the automatic adjustment of international payments refers to that, in an open and free economy which has a complete market mechanism, the imbalance of international payments will be automatically adjusted to be equilibrium by specific mechanisms of market, such as the price mechanism, the national income mechanism, the interest rate mechanism and the exchange rate mechanism.

1. The price mechanism

The BOP surplus will increase the foreign exchange earnings in the country which may cause credit inflation, lower the interest rates and boost the investment and consumption. Thereby the aggregate demand will accordingly expand, driving the prices up. With the rising prices of exports, the export will decrease while import increase. Thus the surplus will gradually diminish and may finally disappear.

On the contrary, a BOP deficit will decrease the foreign exchange reserves in the country which may result in credit contraction, raise the interest rates and depress the investment and consumption. This will restrain the aggregate demand and therefore bring the prices down. With the lowering prices of exports, the export will increase while import decrease. Thus the deficit will gradually diminish and the balance of international payments may be restored.

2. The national income mechanism

The foreign exchange earnings of the country will increase when there is a BOP surplus. This will probably result in credit inflation and the falling of interest rates, which may cause the aggregate demand to expand and the national income to increase. Thus the demand for imports will increase accordingly and the trade surplus will gradually diminish and then the balance-of-payments equilibrium is to be restored.

When there is a BOP deficit, just the reverse, the country's foreign exchange earnings will decrease. This will lead to credit contraction and the rising of interest rates, which may cause the aggregate demand to reduce and the national income to drop. Thus the demand for imports will drop accordingly, which is supposed to gradually eliminate the trade deficit and finally restore the balance-of-payments equilibrium.

3. The interest rate mechanism

The foreign assets held by the banks of the country increase while the liabilities decrease when there is a surplus of international payments in a country. This will then lead to the bank credit expansion and an easy money market in the country, and consequently make the interest rates go down. On the one hand, the drop of interest rates means that the yield of domestic financial assets reduces which will depress the demand for domestic financial assets whereas that of foreign financial assets rises which will stimulate the demand for the latter. Thus the capital outflow increases while the inflow relatively decreases, which will lessen the capital account surplus. On the other hand, the lower interest rates will bring down the cost (or opportunity cost) of domestic investments and consumption, which will certainly promote the both. Consequently the aggregate demand in the country rises up and the demand for imports goes up too, and therefore the import will increase and the export relatively decrease, and this will then reduce the current account surplus. Thus, the overall balance of payments tends to be equilibrium.

Contrariwise, a deficit of a country's international payments will cause the interest rates to rise. The higher interest rates will attract more capital inflow and stimulate more import of goods and services, which will respectively relieve the capital account deficit and the current account deficit. Thus the overall balance of international payments may be restored.

4. The exchange rate mechanism

A country has a surplus of international payments means that the foreign exchanges held by the country exceed the domestic demand for that. Therefore, the foreign exchange falls in value in relation to local currency which leads to the relative appreciation of local currency. Appreciation means that the local currency becomes more valuable in terms of the foreign currency and exports consequently become more expensive for the foreigners while imports cheaper for domestic consumers. Thus the export will decrease whereas the import will increase and then the current account surplus will reduce and the imbalance of international payments will be moderated

Conversely, a deficit of international payments in a country means that the foreign exchanges held by the country can not meet the domestic demand for that. Therefore, the values of foreign exchange in relation to local currency go up which leads to the depreciation of local currency. Depreciation involves devaluation of the local currency thus lowering the price of exports in the world's markets and raising the price of imports in the domestic market. Then the export will increase whereas the import will decrease and the current account deficit will mitigate and the overall deficit of international payments will be relieved.

However, depreciation of home currency may not cause the balance of payments to improve immediately. There is likely to be a time lag between the depreciation of any currency and its effects on domestic demand. In the short term, therefore, the deficit might actually get worse, as exporters are receiving a lower price for each item sold previously and importers are paying more for each item purchased previously. This effect is well known as the J curve which is illustrated in Figure 8 – 1.

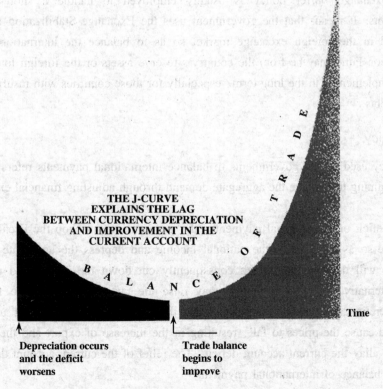

Figure 8 – 1   The J curve

8.3.2　Policy Adjustment　政策调节

As stated above, there are some automatic adjustment market mechanisms of international payments. However, in reality, these market adjustments do not work perfectly even in the developed market economies. Therefore, the automatic adjustment of imbalanced international payments by the market is very much limited in practice and the policy adjustment by governments is employed widely to balance the persistent disequilibrium of international payments.

The policy adjustment of international payments means the process by which the economic decision making and administrative departments in the government use macro-economic levers to eliminate the root causes of instability in social and economic development and thereby improve the international payments.

There are two types of policy adjusting method available to the government. One is the so-called indirect means, by which the government controls aggregate demand by adjusting macro-economic policy. The other is the so-called direct administrative regulation, by which the government forcefully adjusts the international payments by reinforcing the administrative control or legislation, such as the tightening of central planning, foreign exchange and foreign trade administrative laws and regulations, etc. Both methods have their own strong points. The former has an obvious advantage in an open economy and a sound and relatively complete market mechanism; whereas the latter has a quick and definite effect.

The indirect means could be used by the policymakers to adjust balance of payments include foreign exchange buffer policy[17], fiscal policy, monetary policy, international financial cooperation. The direct regulation methods usually involve foreign exchange control and trade control[18].

1. Foreign exchange buffer policy

The foreign exchange buffer policy is usually employed to handle a short-term imbalance of international payments. It means that the government uses the Exchange Stabilization Fund[19] to adjust the supply and demand in the foreign exchange market so as to balance the international payments. Such Exchange Stabilization Fund may be from the country's reserve assets or the foreign loans. Therefore, this policy can not be implemented in the long term, especially for those countries with insufficient reserve assets or excess foreign debts.

2. Fiscal policy

The fiscal policy used by the governments to balance international payments refers to an expansionary or deflation policy aiming to regulate the aggregate demand through adjusting financial expenditure or the tax rates.

To balance a deficit of international payments, the government can chop the fiscal budget and reduce financial expenditure so as to decrease the national income and depress the aggregate demand. Thus the demand for imports will decrease too which consequently cut down the import and mitigate the current account deficit. Alternatively, the government may raise the tax rates in order to make the return of investment and discretionary income drop. This will then restrain the investment and consumption in domestic market and cause the prices to fall, resulting in the increase of export and the decrease of import which will certainly allay the current account deficit. The relief of the current account deficit is sure to help improve the overall balance of international payments.

Vice versa, the surplus of international payments can also be adjusted by the fiscal policy.

3. Monetary policy

The balance of the international payments can also be achieved by the monetary policy which means that the governments generally use the interest rate lever to adjust the demand.

When there is a deficit of international payments, the government can raise the central bank's rediscount rate to tighten credit and money supply. Thereby, the interest rates will rise up and consequently the aggregate demand in domestic market will decrease while the capital inflow will increase. The reduced demand in domestic market will then decrease the import so that the current account deficit will be mitigated. Meanwhile, the increased capital inflow will mitigate the capital account deficit. Thus the overall balance of payments is improved.

Vice versa, the surplus of international payments can also be adjusted by the monetary policy.

4. International financial cooperation

Sometimes, the country may turn to abroad to get help to deal with the imbalance of international payments, if it can not achieve the balance by its own efforts. This may be called international financial cooperation.

There are some international organizations in the world, one of whose tenets is to help those less-developed countries to improve the balance of payments, such as the famous IMF. During the Asian Financial Crisis in 1998, the IMF offered some conditional financial aid to those suffering Asian countries.

In addition, those developing countries involved in the international debt crisis have been making struggles to ask the developed country to relive their debts and some progresses have been achieved.

5. Foreign exchange control

Some countries established a foreign exchange authority department to regulate the foreign exchange market and the exchange rates directly. Therefore, the domestic currencies of these countries are generally not convertible completely.

In China, the SAFE (State Administration of Foreign Exchange)[20] is responsible for the regulation of foreign exchange. It may use foreign exchange control measures to help to improve the balance of international payments.

For example, when there is a deficit, the SAFE may make strict restrictions on foreign exchange purchase, such as raising the buying rate or directly limit the purchase quantity of foreign exchange. These measures will increase the importers' cost and consequently decrease the import. Thus, the deficit of current account will be relived.

However, there are few countries which still have foreign exchange control system in the present world. The completely convertibility of currencies is an inevitable tendency in the long term with the development of the globalization. Therefore, the foreign exchange control can not be regarded as a normal and available method at any time to balance the international payments.

6. Trade control

A country can also restore the balance of international payments by controlling trade directly.

For example, in order to deal with a deficit, the government could use the export credits or subsidies to promote export and the importing licenses or other non-tariff barriers to restrict import so as to improve the balance of international payments.

However, since free trade is considered as the normal case in the present world, such trade control measures will tend to discontent the country's trading partners and may be prohibited by the WTO. So, the direct trade control measures should be used very cautiously in order to handle the imbalance of international payments.

8.4   International Reserve
国际储备

8.4.1   The Definition of International Reserve   国际储备的定义

The international reserves, which are referred to as reserve assets in the balance of payments, includes monetary gold and foreign exchange, IMF reserve position and SDRs held by the monetary authority, for the purpose of intervening in the exchange market to influence or peg the exchange rate when there is a international payments deficit. These are assets of the central banks which are held in different reserve currencies such as the US dollar, Euro and Yen, and which are used to back its liabilities, e. g. the home currency issued, and the various bank reserves deposited with the central bank, by the government or financial institutions.

International reserves were formerly held only in gold, as official gold reserves. But under the Bretton Woods System[21], the United States pegged the dollar to gold, and allowed convertibility of dollars to gold. This effectively made dollars appear as good as gold. The US later abandoned the gold standard, but the US dollar has remained relatively stable as a fiat currency, and it is still the most significant reserve currency. Nevertheless, the central banks of most countries today typically hold large amounts of multiple currencies in reserve.

It should be noted that there is another term international liquidity similar to international reserves. Sometimes they can replace each other. However, strictly speaking, international liquidity refers to the adequacy of a country's international reserves, which is more often expressed not as an absolute level, but as a percentage of short-term foreign debt, money supply, or average monthly imports.

It can be said that a country has a good international liquidity when it is able to borrow needed money from abroad even if it has few self-owned reserves. The most typical example is, the biggest one in the today's world — the US, it has few foreign exchange and gold reserves which can only cover a small portion of its foreign debt. However, no another country is going to say that the US has a bad international liquidity and not going to lend to it. Of course, this mainly because of the strongest positions of the US and its dollar in the present world. So, such a miracle can hardly take place in another country.

8.4.2   The Composition of International Reserve   国际储备的构成

1. Monetary gold

The gold held by the monetary authorities as one part of the reserve assets is particularly called monetary gold.

For most of the 19th century and the early part of the 20th century, the value of the major world currencies had been fixed in terms of gold. This is known as the Gold Standard. Each country holds the gold reserves prepare to exchange its currency for given quantity of gold. The gold is the major international reserve assets at that time.

Under the Bretton Woods system, both the gold and the US dollar were the base of the international monetary system so the gold still play an important role in international reserves.

After the collapse of the Bretton Woods system, no country's currencies is pegged to gold any longer, the role of gold declined substantially. However, as a sort of noble metal with good stability, gold is still held by most countries to be one part of their reserves. Nevertheless, it only constitutes a small percentage of the total amount of international reserves. Considering all IMF members, the gold reserves account for less 5% of the total reserve assets.

2. Foreign exchange

Foreign exchange (Forex, FX) reserves in a strict sense are only the convertible foreign currencies and other foreign financial assets held by monetary authorities, which mainly take the forms of foreign currency deposits and foreign government bonds.

However, the term foreign exchange reserves in popular usage commonly refers to the whole of international reserves, because foreign exchanges take the largest parts of most countries' reserve assets, and their percentages of the total international reserves are usually on top of 90%.

3. IMF reserve position

The IMF reserve position refers to the claimable assets owned by a member on the IMF.

A member must pay its quota subscription in full upon joining the IMF: up to 25 percent must be paid in SDRs or widely accepted convertible currencies (such as the US dollar, the Euro, the Yen, or the Pound Sterling), while the rest is paid in the member's own currency. Then its reserve position will include the 25% of its subscription paid in SDRs or widely accepted convertible currencies, the percentage of which has been used by the IMF out of the rest 75% subscription, and if any, the loans it lent to the IMF.

4. SDRs

SDRs basically were created by the IMF in 1969, which operates as a supplement to the existing reserves of member countries. Being that under a strict gold standard, the quantity of gold worldwide is relatively fixed, a need arose to increase the supply of the basic unit or standard proportionately. Thus SDRs, or "paper gold", are credits that nations with balance of trade surpluses can 'draw' upon nations with balance of trade deficits.

Reading Material

SDR Valuation

The value of one SDR is determined in terms of a basket of major currencies used in international trade and finance. At present, the currencies in the basket are the Euro, the Pound Sterling, the Yen and the US dollar. Before the introduction of the Euro in 1999, the Deutsche mark and the French franc were included in the basket. The amounts of each currency making up one SDR are chosen in accordance with the relative importance of the currency in international trade and finance. The determination of the currencies in the SDR basket and their amounts is made by the IMF Executive Board every five years. The weights of the currencies in the basket in the past were and currently are:

1991 – 1995: USD 40%, DEM 21%, JPY 17%, GBP 11%, FRF 11%

1996 – 2000: USD 39%, DEM 21%, JPY 18%, GBP 11%, FRF 11%

2001 – 2005: USD 45%, EUR 29%, JPY 15%, GBP 11%

2006 – 2010: USD 44%, EUR 34%, JPY 11%, GBP 11%

The value of one SDR in terms of United States dollars is determined daily by the IMF, based on the exchange rates of the currencies making up the basket, as quoted at noon at the London market. (If the London market is closed, New York market rates are used; if both markets are closed, European Central Bank reference rates are used.)

Special Drawing Rights (SDRs or SDR) is a potential claim on the freely usable currencies of IMF members. Holders of SDRs can obtain these currencies in exchange for their SDRs in two ways: first, through the arrangement of voluntary exchanges between members; and second, by the IMF designating members with strong external positions to purchase SDRs from members with weak external positions.

The SDR has only limited use as a reserve asset, and its main function is to serve as the unit of account of the IMF and some other international organizations. The SDR is neither a currency, nor a claim on the IMF, but only a potential claim.

The IMF allocates SDRs to members in proportion to their IMF quotas. Such an allocation provides each member with a costless asset on which interest is neither earned nor paid. However, if a member's SDR holdings rise above its allocation, it earns interest on the excess; conversely, if it holds fewer SDRs than allocated, it pays interest on the shortfall.

A few countries peg their currencies against SDRs, and it is also used to denominate some private international financial instruments. For example, SDRs are used to limit carrier liability on international flights under Warsaw Convention, and also used to transfer roaming charge files between international mobile telecoms operators.

8.4.3　The Functions of International Reserve　国际储备的作用

In a non-fixed exchange rate system, international reserves allow a central bank to purchase the domestic currency, exchanging its assets to reduce its liability. The purpose of reserves is to allow central banks an additional means to stabilize the domestic currency from excessive volatility, and protect the monetary system from shock, such as from currency traders engaged in flipping. Large reserves are often seen as a source of economic power, as it indicates the backing a currency has. Low or falling reserves may be indicative of an imminent bank run on the currency or default, such as in a currency crisis.

Central banks sometimes claim that holding large reserves is a security measure. This is true to the extent that a central bank can prop up its own currency by spending reserves. But often, very large reserves are not a hedge against inflation but rather a direct consequence of the opposite policy: the central bank has purchased large amounts of foreign currency in order to keep its own currency relatively cheap.

On one hand, if a country desires to have a government-influenced exchange rate, then holding bigger reserves gives the country a bigger ability to manipulate the currency market. On the other hand, holding reserves does induce opportunity cost. In addition, many governments have suffered huge losses on the management of the reserves portfolio — all of which is ultimately fiscal.

When there is a currency crisis and all reserves vanish, this is ultimately a fiscal cost. Even when there is no currency crisis, there can be a fiscal cost, as is taking place in 2005 and 2006 with China, which holds huge USD assets but the Renminbi has been continually appreciating.

8.4.4 International Reserve Management 国际储备管理

International reserve management is a process that ensures that adequate official public sector reserve assets are readily available to and controlled by the authorities for meeting a defined range of objectives for a country. Typically, official reserves assets are held in support of a range of objectives including to:

(1) support and maintain confidence in the policies for monetary and exchange rate management including the capacity to intervene in support of the national or union currency;

(2) limit external vulnerability by maintaining foreign currency liquidity to absorb shocks during times of crisis or when access to borrowing is curtailed and in doing so;

(3) provide a level of confidence to markets that a country can meet its external obligations;

(4) demonstrate the backing of domestic currency by external assets;

(5) assist the government in meeting its foreign exchange needs and external debt obligations;

(6) maintain a reserve for national disasters or emergencies.

Sound reserve management practices are important because they can increase a country's or region's overall resilience to financial shock. Through their interaction with financial markets, reserve managers gain access to valuable information that keeps policy-makers informed of market developments and views on potential threats. The importance of sound practices has also been highlighted by experiences where weak or risky reserve management practices have restricted the ability of the authorities to respond effectively to financial crises, which may have accentuated the severity of these crises. Moreover, weak or risky reserve management practices can also have significant financial and reputational costs. Several countries, for example, have incurred large losses that have had direct, or indirect, fiscal consequences during the Asian Financial Crisis in 1997/1998. Accordingly, appropriate portfolio management policies concerning the currency composition, choice of investment instruments, and acceptable duration of the reserves portfolio, and which reflect a country's specific policy settings and circumstances, serve to ensure that assets are safeguarded, readily available and support market confidence.

It should be stressed that, sound reserve management policies and practices can support, but not substitute for, sound macro-economic management. Moreover, inappropriate economic policies (fiscal or monetary) can pose serious risks to the ability to manage reserves.

8.5 International Debt
国际债务

8.5.1 The Definition of International Debt 国际债务的定义

From the viewpoint of an individual country, the term international debt means the foreign debt, also referred to as external debt, which is that part of the total debt in a country that is owed to creditors outside the country. The debtors can be the government, corporations or private households. The debt includes money owed to private commercial banks, other governments, or international financial institutions such as the IMF and World Bank.

Strictly defined, foreign debt is the outstanding amount of those actual current, and not contingent, liabilities that require repayment(s) of principal and/or interest by the debtor at some point(s) in the future and that are owed to non-residents by residents of an economy at any given time. There are four key elements in this definition as follows:

(1) Outstanding and actual current liabilities. For this purpose, the decisive consideration is whether a creditor owns a claim on the debtor. Here debt liabilities include arrears of both principal and interest.

(2) Principal and interest. When this cost is paid periodically, as commonly occurs, it is known as an interest payment. All other payments of economic value by the debtor to the creditor that reduce the principal amount outstanding are known as principal payments. However, the definition of foreign debt does not distinguish between whether the payments that are required are principal or interest, or both. Also, the definition does not specify that the timing of the future payments of principal and/or interest need be known for a liability to be classified as debt.

(3) Residence. To qualify as foreign debt, the debt liabilities must be owed by a resident to a non-resident. Residence is determined by where the debtor and creditor have their centers of economic interest — typically, where they are ordinarily located — and not by their nationality.

(4) Current and not contingent. Contingent liabilities are not included in the definition of foreign debt. These are defined as arrangements under which one or more conditions must be fulfilled before a financial transaction takes place. However, from the viewpoint of understanding vulnerability, there is analytical interest in the potential impact of contingent liabilities on an economy and on particular institutional sectors, such as government.

8.5.2　The Measurement of Foreign Debt of a Country　国家外债的衡量

There are various indicators for measuring the foreign debt of a country in order to determine a sustainable level of foreign debt. While each has its own advantage and peculiarity to deal with particular situations, there is no unanimous opinion amongst economists as to one sole indicator. These indicators are primarily in the nature of ratios. These indicators can be thought of as measures of the country's "solvency" in that they consider the stock of debt at certain time in relation to the country's ability to generate resources to repay the outstanding balance.

Examples of debt burden indicators include the debt to GDP ratio, the foreign debt to exports ratio, the government debt to current fiscal revenue ratio, etc. This set of indicators also covers the structure of the outstanding debt including the share of foreign debt, the short-term debt ratio.

A second set of indicators focuses on the short-term liquidity requirements of the country with respect to its debt service obligations. These indicators are not only useful early-warning signs of debt service problems, but also highlight the impact of the inter-temporal trade-offs arising from past borrowing decisions. Examples of liquidity monitoring indicators include the (1) debt service to GDP ratio, (2) foreign debt service to exports ratio, (3) government debt service to current fiscal revenue ratio and etc. The final indicators are more forward looking as they point out how the debt burden will evolve over time, given the current stock of data and average interest rate. The dynamic ratios show how the debt burden ratios would change in the absence of repayments or new disbursements, indicating the stability of the debt burden. An example of a dynamic ratio is the ratio of the average interest rate on outstanding debt to the growth rate of nominal GDP.

Four of these indicators will be stated in more details as follows.

The key index is the debt service ratio, which is represented by the debt service payments during the given year as percentage of the exports of goods and services during the same year. It is wise for government to keep this index under 20%.

The ratio of the outstanding foreign debt balance at the end of the given year to the year's exports is another important indicator. The government should see to it that this ratio will never exceed 100%.

Generally speaking, the debt to GDP ratio is considered to be normal when it ranges from 10% to 20%, and the ratio of short-term debt to total amount of debt is believed to be appropriate when it is less than 25%.

8.5.3　The Problem of International Debt　国际债务问题

1. Developing countries' debt

In the 1980s, much attention focused on the foreign debt problem that confronts many developing countries, especially those poorest countries.

Most present-day states in Africa and the majority of Asia did not have an independent financial existence as recently as World War II. However, not all external debts of these countries was acquired after independence. Indonesia was required to assume the Dutch colonial government's debt (much of which had been acquired fighting the pro-independence rebels the previous four years) as a condition of independence in 1949. This pattern was repeated elsewhere. In order to gain recognition from France as an independent nation, Haiti was required to pay France 150 million francs (modern equivalent of $21 billion) in exchange for its loss as a slave colony. Egypt, which had not been formally colonized, but had been effectively governed as first an Anglo-French and later British protectorate, did not have control over the lucrative Suez Canal, which links the Mediterranean Sea with the Red Sea (and therefore the Indian Ocean). Denied credit to build the Aswan Dam, Egypt's government moved to nationalize the canal, formally owned by a European corporation but built (at tremendous human cost) by Egyptian labor, in 1956, sparking the Suez Crisis.

In the first decades following decolonization, the rich countries and multilateral creditors such as the World Bank and IMF lent massively to the developing countries. Money was frequently directed towards massive infrastructure projects such as dams and highways. Additional funds focused on an import substitution model of development, creating a capacity to replace imports from industrialized countries in order to achieve the industrial modernization.

Additionally, a number of dictatorships and neocolonial governments imposed and/or backed by foreign powers received extensive debt-based financing to conduct civil wars or repression against their own population. In Central and South America, civil wars accumulated substantial debts in Guatemala, El Salvador, Colombia and Haiti. Foreign military operations, such as the invasions of East Timor by Indonesia; of Angola and Namibia by South Africa; and of Iran and Kuwait by Iraq also led to massive indebtedness.

Much of the current levels of debt were amassed following the 1973 oil crisis when the western members of OPEC pushed the price of oil up making the Arab nations very wealthy. They decided to deposit this money in large Western banks. The banks didn't want all of this money lying around so it was lent to the Third World countries. Banks lent large amounts of money to developing countries without much attention to where the money would be spent or whether countries would be capable of repaying the amount. While some of this money went towards trying to improve the living standards for those in the countries, most of the loans never reached the poor of the country either going towards large-scale development projects, some of which proved of little value, or to the private bank accounts of dictators. Overall, about one-fifth of loans went to arms.

2. International debt crisis

Massive lending was followed by the threat of major defaults, such as that of Mexico, in the early 1980s, precipitating what became known as an international debt crisis in Latin America.

A recent and telling example of international debt crises was the Argentine economic crisis. Argentina's debt grew continuously during the 1990s, climbing above $120 billion. Creditors continued to lend money, while the IMF suggested less state spending, as recession deepened. The crisis exploded in December 2001. In 2002, a default on about $93 billion of the debt was declared. Investment fled the country, and capital flow towards Argentina ceased almost completely.

The Argentine government met severe challenges trying to refinance the debt. The IMF became wholly uncooperative. Other creditors denounced the default as sheer robbery. Vulture funds who had acquired debt bonds during the crisis, at very low prices, asked to be repaid immediately. The state was broke and the foreign currency reserves were almost depleted. For four years, Argentina was effectively shut out of the international financial markets.

Argentina finally got a deal by which 76% of the defaulted bonds were exchanged by others, of a much lower nominal value and at longer terms. The exchange was not accepted by the rest of the private debt holders, who will continue to present a challenge to the country in years to come. However, in January 2006, President Kirchner announced the liquidation of all the remaining $9.81 billion debt to the IMF, along with Brazilian President Lula's similar decision. This move was seen as a means to end IMF's control of Argentinian and Brazilian economy.

3. International debt relief

Debt relief is the partial or total forgiveness of debt, or the slowing or stopping of debt growth, owed by individuals, corporations, or nations. International debt relief concerns in particular the Third World debt, which started exploding with the Latin American debt crisis.

Debt relief for heavily indebted and underdeveloped developing countries was the subject in the 1990s of a campaign by a broad coalition of development NGOs, Christian organizations and others, under the banner of Jubilee 2000. This campaign, involving, for example, demonstrations at the 1998 G8 meeting in Birmingham, was successful in pushing debt relief onto the agenda of Western governments and international organizations such as the IMF and World Bank. Ultimately the Heavily Indebted Poor Countries (HIPC) initiative was launched to provide systematic debt relief for the poorest countries, whilst trying to ensure the money would be spent on poverty reduction.

The HIPC programme has been subject to conditionalities similar to those often attached to IMF and World Bank loans, requiring structural adjustment reforms, sometimes including the privatization of public utilities, including water and electricity. To qualify for irrevocable debt relief, countries must also maintain macro-economic stability and implement a Poverty Reduction Strategy satisfactorily for at least one year. Under the goal of reducing inflation, some countries have been pressured to reduce spending in the health and education sectors.

The Multilateral Debt Relief Initiative (MDRI) is an extension of HIPC. The MDRI was agreed following the G8's Gleneagles meeting in July 2005. It offers 100% cancellation of multilateral debts owed by HIPC countries to the World Bank, IMF and African Development Bank.

However, opponents of debt relief argue that it is a blank check to governments, and fear savings will not reach the poor in countries plagued by corruption. Others argue that countries will go out and contract further debts, under the belief that these debts will also be forgiven in some future date. They use the money to enhance the wealth and spending ability of the rich, many of whom will spend or invest this money in the rich countries. They argue that the money would be far better spent in specific aid projects which actually help the poor. They further argue that it would be unfair to Third World countries that managed their credit successfully, or don't go into debt in the first place, that is, it actively encourages Third World governments to overspend in order to receive debt relief in the future. Others argue against the conditionalities attached to debt relief. These conditions of structural adjustment have a history, especially in Latin America, of widening the gap between the rich and the poor, as well as increasing economic dependence on the developed countries.

Group Discussion

1. Analyze the structure of the balance of payments.
2. Discuss the imbalance of international payments.
3. Compare the automatic and the policy adjustment of international payments.
4. Talk about the international reserves with your partner.
5. Tell your opinions on the international debt problems.

NOTES

1   balance of payments (BOP)   国际收支、国际收支平衡表
2   balance of international payments   国际收支，国际收支平衡（表）
3   double-entry bookkeeping   复式记账
4   accruals basis   权责发生制（基础）
5   current account surplus (deficit)   经常账户盈余（赤字），经常账户顺差（逆差）
6   foreign direct investment   外国直接投资（缩写为"FDI"）
7   special drawing rights (SDRs)   特别提款权
8   reserve position   储备头寸，准备金头寸
9   balance of payments equilibrium (BPE)   国际收支平衡
10   balance of payments disequilibrium   国际收支不平衡（也可用"imbalance of payments"）

11 balance of payments surplus（deficit）　国际收支盈余（赤字），国际收支顺差（逆差）

12 balance of trade　贸易差额（亦可用"trade balance"）

13 balance of current account　经常账户差额（亦可用"current account balance"）

14 overall balance of payments　国际收支总差额

15 domestic currency　本币（也可用"home currency"或"local currency"）

16 automatic adjustment　自主性调节；policy adjustment　政策性调节

17 foreign exchange buffer policy　外汇缓冲政策

18 foreign exchange control　外汇管制；trade control　贸易管制

19 Exchange Stabilization Fund　外汇平准基金

20 SAFE（State Administration of Foreign Exchange）　国家外汇管理局

21 Bretton Woods System　布雷顿森林体系

Chapter 9

International Financial Market

国际金融市场

Learning Objectives

☑ To know the definition and types of international financial markets
☑ To learn about foreign exchange and international exchange market
☑ To learn about international money market and international capital market
☑ To understand the basics about the Eurocurrency market

Opening Vignette

The Future of Global Financial Markets

Forecasting is always difficult, especially when it involves the future. More than the usual degree of difficulty is involved when the task is forecasting the future of global financial markets. In the mid-1970s, when I was a student in Yale, global financial markets and private capital flows to developing countries were just beginning to awaken from a long period of somnolence.

Those who anticipated that World Bank loans and official development assistance would remain the predominant sources of external finance for developing countries were surprised by the rapid growth of bank lending to Latin America and Eastern Europe by money-center banks recycling the surpluses of oil exporters and selected industrial economies. But no sooner had observers assimilated these facts than lending to emerging markets collapsed in 1982 in response to rising interest rates in the US and UK and debt crises in the developing world. The result was the lost decade of the 1980s, when resources flowed upstream from developing to developed economies and growth stagnated in Latin America. The inability of governments to credibly commit to repay their borrowings, it was argued, constituted a fundamental obstacle to sovereign lending to emerging markets, and efforts by the IMF to paper over the cracks were dismissed as creating more problems than they solved.

But no sooner had observers accustomed themselves to this brave new world than non-performing bank loans were converted into bearer bonds. The Brady Plan, which was announced by US Treasury Secretary Nicholas Brady in March 1989 and encouraged bank creditors to grant debt relief in return for greater collectability and liquidity of their remaining claims, linked that relief to policy reform, and provided for the conversion of non-performing bank loans into more liquid claims (Brady bonds), jump-started the market in fixed income securities, which quickly became the vehicle for renewed lending to emerging markets. Typically a country would issue both "par bonds" (equal to the full value of a tranche of loans but at a concessionary interest rate) and "discount bonds" (which bore market rates of interest but whose face value equaled only a fraction of the corresponding tranche of loans). Both classes of bonds were of a 30 year maturity. Bond markets transferred an impressive quantity of resources to developing countries in the course of the 1990s, but the decade was also punctuated by a series of emerging-market crises that repeatedly interrupted the flow of finance, sent spreads skyrocketing, and prompted emergency intervention by the IMF. This period drew to a close with Argentina's default at the end of 2001. Borrowers and lenders drew back from the market as if they had finally taken the lessons of the 1990s to heart. Developing countries shifted from external deficit to surplus, accumulating unprecedented quantities of international reserves. They repaid foreign debt to their private creditors and the IMF.

By early 2006 no major Latin American or Asian country was in debt to the IMF, and virtually the entire stock of Brady bonds had been retired from the market. The United States emerged as the world's principal deficit country and capital importer, absorbing some two-thirds of the net savings of the rest of the world. But the idea, which gained currency following the Argentine crisis, that international investors had learned that the returns from lending to emerging markets did not justify the risks was again dissolved by the subsequent resurgence of flows into local markets and the decline in emerging market spreads to unprecedented lows (below 200 basis points in the spring of 2006).

If one thing is sure, it is that the future will bring more surprises. Any effort to forecast by mechanically projecting recent events is certain to be wrong. This uncertainty creates a dilemma for an author whose assigned topic is the future of global financial markets.

 Warm-up Questions

1. **What do you think about the future of global financial markets?**
2. **Why are there so many uncertainties in the future of global financial markets?**
3. **Do you think of global financial markets the same as international financial markets?**

9.1 An Overview of International Financial Market 国际金融市场概述

9.1.1 The Definition of International Financial Market 国际金融市场的定义

The term financial market has been defined in Chapter 5, and it is no doubt that financial markets can be domestic or international. In this chapter, international financial markets will be focused on, which can be defined as the financial markets involving international trade of financial product. This "international" means that the buyers and the sellers of the financial market are from different countries, or the financial products traded are from foreign countries.

Since the "international" has so many meanings, there are various classifications of international financial markets by different criterion.

9.1.2 The Classifications of International Financial Market 国际金融市场的分类

1. By the terms of the financial products traded

International financial markets can be divided into international money markets and international capital market by the terms of financing. International money markets refer to those financial markets which provide international short term (up to 1 year) debt financing and investment, whereas international capital markets provide medium and long term international financing.

2. By the nature of the financial products traded

As mentioned in chapter 5, the financial instruments traded in financial markets can be categorized into original and derivative instruments. Correspondingly, international financial markets include international spot markets for the trading of original instruments and international derivative market for derivative instruments.

In addition, there is another special kind of financial products traded in international financial markets — foreign exchanges. Accordingly, international financial markets also include foreign exchange markets. Strictly speaking, foreign exchange markets can not be domestic but only international, and can be replaced by the term international exchange market. It should also be noted that the foreign exchange instruments can be original or derivative.

Reading Material

International Monetary Market

The International Monetary Market (IMM), largely the creation of Leo Melamed, is part of the Chicago Mercantile Exchange (CME), the largest futures exchange in the United States and the second largest in the world after Eurex (Europe's Global Financial Marketplace, based in Frankfort), for the trading of futures contracts and options on futures.

> The IMM was started on May 16, 1972. Two of the more prevalent contracts traded are currency futures and interest rate futures.

3. By the locations and the traders of the financial markets

So far, we have been discussing the financial markets without considering their geographic locations and indeed they do not mean geographic marketplaces but certain financial mechanisms.

However, we have to take their locations into account when looking at international financial markets. In today's world, there are some offshore financial centers (OFCs)[1] located in particular countries or regions, providing offshore financial services which refer to the financial services provided by banks and other institutions to non-residents. These offshore financial centers can be called offshore financial markets[2], whereas those financial markets which do not provide offshore financial services may be called onshore financial markets[3] contrastingly.

9.2 International Exchange Market
国际外汇市场

9.2.1 Foreign Exchange and Exchange Rate 外汇与汇率

1. Foreign exchange

Foreign exchange, commonly abbreviated as Forex or FX, means the buying of one unit of currency with that of another country. Although it is called foreign exchange, this is just a relative term. The term domestic or foreign is relative to the person using the term. What is foreign to one person is domestic to another. So currency exchange would be the more proper term.

Virtually every economy, with some few exceptions, has its own currency, and most of them can be traded. However, the currencies of a few countries or regions are the most actively traded, and constitute, by far, the largest volume of trades. The big 5 are the United States dollar (USD), Euro (EUR), Japanese yen (JPY), the British pound (GBP), and the Swiss franc (CHF).

Each currency is symbolized using 3-letter ISO[4] codes: the first two letters designate the country, the third designates the currency. The most famous illustration of this is for the United States dollar—USD. However, sometimes the country name or currency that is symbolized is not the most common name. Thus, the symbol for the Swiss franc is CHF, where CH stands for Confederation Helvetica, which refers to Switzerland, and MXN stands for the Mexican Nuevo Peso, even though the most common name for Mexico's currency is simply the peso.

The main reasons to exchange foreign currency for domestic currency is to pay for goods and services in the foreign country, to invest in foreign financial assets, to hedge against unfavorable rates of exchange in the future, or to profit from those changes. Foreign currency holders need to convert it back to their domestic currency to take profits, or to use the money at home.

2. Foreign exchange rate

Foreign exchange rate[5] is the amount of the foreign currency that is equal in value to a unit of domestic currency, or, more generally, it is the amount of currency received for each unit of the currency tendered. In fact, it is the price of domestic currency in terms of the foreign currency.

One currency can not be exchange for another without an exchange rate[6] and exchange rates are also known as currency rates.

Exchange rates are always listed as pairs, such as EUR/USD, and generally the first component (EUR in this case) will be called the base currency. The second is called the counter currency. For example: EUR/USD = 1.3387, means that EUR is the base and USD the counter, so 1 EUR = 1.3387 USD, which means that 1 euro can exchange for 1.3387 US dollars. Note that, it is a direct quotation[7] if it is quoted by US banks while an indirect quotation by European banks.

Definitely, direct quotation is where the cost of one unit of foreign currency is given in units of local currency, whereas indirect quotation is where the cost of one unit of local currency is given in units of foreign currency. Direct quotation (also called price quotation) are used by most countries and indirect quotation (or quantity quotation) are used in British newspapers and also common in Australia, New Zealand and Canada.

When using direct quotation, if the home currency is strengthening (i.e., appreciating) then the exchange rate number decreases. Conversely if the foreign currency is strengthening, the exchange rate number increases and the home currency is depreciating.

3. Major types of exchange rates

1) Basic exchange rate & cross exchange rate[8]

Basic exchange rates are the exchange rates of the local currency for several basic foreign currencies which play important roles in the country's foreign economic relations. Then cross exchange rates refer to those rates of the local currency for other foreign currencies. In China, there are four kind of basic exchange rates: CNY/USD, CNY/EUR, CNY/JPY, CNY/HKD[9].

2) Nominal exchange rate & real exchange rate[10]

The nominal exchange rate is the rate at which an organization can trade the currency of one country for the currency of another. The real exchange rate (RER) is an important concept in economics, though it is quite difficult to grasp concretely. It is defined by the model: $RER = e(P^*/P)$, where "e" is the nominal exchange rate, as the number of home currency units per foreign currency unit; where "P" is the price level of the home country; and where "P^*" is the foreign price level.

Unfortunately, this compact and simple model for RER calculations is only a theoretical ideal. In practical usage, there are many foreign currencies and price level values to take into consideration. Correspondingly, the model calculations become increasingly more complex.

3) Spot exchange rate & forward exchange rate[11]

The spot exchange rate refers to the current exchange rate. The forward exchange rate refers to an exchange rate that is quoted and traded today but for delivery and payment on a specific future date.

4) Official exchange rate & market exchange rate[12]

The official exchange rate means the exchange rate determined by the monetary authority in those countries which still have strict foreign exchange control. In contrast, the market exchange rate, of course, determined by the supply and demand in foreign exchange market.

9.2.2　International Exchange Rate Regime　国际汇率制度

1. Fixed exchange rates

A fixed exchange rate[13], sometimes (less commonly) also called a pegged exchange rate, is a type of exchange rate regime wherein a currency's value is matched to the value of another single currency or to a basket of other currencies, or to another measure of value, such as gold. As the reference value rises and falls, so does the currency pegged to it. A currency that uses a fixed exchange rate is known as a fixed currency. The opposite of a fixed exchange rate is a floating exchange rate[14].

There have been two distinct international monetary systems of fixed exchange rates in modern history and each of them will be examined in turn as follows.

1) The Gold Standard

For most of the 19th and the early decades of the 20th century, the value of the major world currencies has been fixed in terms of gold. Each country was prepared to exchange its currency for this given quantity of gold, thereby effectively determining the value of one currency in terms of another. So in 1900, the UK would have exchanged about 1/4 oz. gold for one pound sterling and the US would have exchanged 1/20 oz. gold for one dollar. Therefore, 1 pound was worth around 5 US dollars. If the exchange rate moved from this value, gold would be shipped from one country to another to reestablish the equilibrium rate.

The outbreak of World War I brought an abrupt halt to the Gold Standard. The need for larger and larger engines of war, including battleships and munitions, created inflation. Nations responded by printing more money than could be redeemed in gold, effectively betting on winning the war and redeeming out of reparations. Therefore, the major countries such as the UK, the US, Germany were forced to suspend use of the gold standard by the costs of the war.

In the UK the pound was returned to the gold standard in 1925, by the somewhat reluctant Chancellor of the Exchequer Winston Churchill, on the advice of conservative economists at the time. Although a higher gold price and significant inflation had followed the World War I ending of the gold standard, Churchill returned to the standard at the pre-war gold price. For five years prior to 1925 the gold price was managed downward to the pre-war level, meaning a significant deflation was forced onto the economy.

Keynes was one economist who argued against the adoption of the pre-war gold price believing that the rate of conversion was far too high and that the monetary basis would collapse. He called the gold standard "that barbarous relic." This deflation reached across the remnants of the British Empire everywhere the pound sterling was still used as the primary unit of account.

The Gold Standard collapsed in the early 1930s. In the UK the standard was again abandoned in 1931. Sweden abandoned the gold standard in 1929, the US in 1933, and other nations were, to one degree or another, forced off the gold standard.

2) The Bretton Woods System

In 1944, as World War II was still raging, the allied nations gathered met at Bretton Woods in New Hampshire, USA, for the United Nations Monetary and Financial Conference, trying to rebuild the international economic system. They entered into the Bretton Woods Agreement, setting up a system of rules, institutions, and procedures to regulate the international monetary system, the planners at Bretton Woods established the International Bank for Reconstruction and Development (IBRD) (now one of the five institutions in the World Bank Group) and the International Monetary Fund (IMF). These organizations became operational in 1946 after a sufficient number of countries had ratified the agreement.

The chief features of the Bretton Woods system were an obligation for each country to adopt a monetary policy that maintained the exchange rate of its currency within a fixed value — plus or minus one percent — in relation to the US dollar, which in turn was fixed in terms of gold, with the authorities in the USA willing to exchange gold for its dollars. So the US dollar was "as good as gold" and as a result it became well acceptable in international trade and finance.

The Bretton Woods system established the rules for commercial and financial relations among the world's major industrial states. It was the first example of a fully negotiated monetary order intended to govern monetary relations among independent nation-states.

Such an "adjustable peg" system of international exchange rate worked very well in the next twenty year. However, it began to show signs of strain in the late 1960s, and finally collapsed in 1971, following the United States' suspension of convertibility from dollars to gold.

2. Floating exchange rates

Floating rates are the most common exchange rate regime today. For example, the US dollar, Euro, Yen, and British Pound all float.

A floating exchange rate or a flexible exchange rate is a type of exchange rate regime wherein a currency's value is allowed to fluctuate according to the foreign exchange market. A currency that uses a floating exchange rate is known as a floating currency.

Many economists think that, in most circumstances, floating exchange rates are preferable to fixed exchange rates. They allow the dampening of shocks and foreign business cycles. However, in certain situations, fixed exchange rates may be preferable for their greater stability and certainty. This may not necessarily be true, considering the results of countries that attempt to keep the prices of their currency "strong" or "high" relative to others, such as the UK or the Southeast Asia countries before the Asian currency crisis.

There is no currency in the world whose value is absolutely and entirely determined by the foreign exchange market, except for Canada or possibly the United States; in cases of extreme appreciation or depreciation, a central bank will normally intervene to stabilize the currency. Thus, the exchange rate regimes of floating currencies may be known as managed floating rates, and sometimes even called dirty floating rates.

A central bank might, for instance, allow a currency price to float freely between an upper and lower bound, a price "ceiling" and "floor". Management by the central bank may take the form of buying or selling large lots of home currency in order to provide price support or resistance.

After the collapse of the Bretton Woods system, the IMF members reached the Jamaica Agreement in 1976, admitting the floating exchange rates and the demonetization of gold, allowing different exchange rate regimes employed by different countries. Therefore, there are a few countries still use somewhat fixed exchange rates, or "pegged floating" rates wherein the currency is pegged to some band or value, either fixed or periodically adjusted.

For the reasons mentioned above, some authors referred to the current international monetary system as Jamaica system.

9.2.3　International Exchange Market　国际外汇市场

The international exchange (currency) market exists wherever one currency is traded for another. It is by far the largest financial market in the world, and includes trading between large banks, central banks, currency speculators, multinational corporations, governments, and other financial institutions, and for various instruments (such as spot exchanges, forward exchanges, futures, options and swaps) similar to other financial markets. The average daily trade in the global foreign exchange markets currently exceeds 1.9 trillion US dollars.

1. The participants of international exchange market

The major participants in international exchange market are examined as follows.

1) Commercial banks

The inter-bank market caters for both the majority of commercial turnover and large amounts of speculative trading every day. A large bank may trade billions of dollars daily. Some of this trading is undertaken on behalf of customers, but much is conducted by proprietary desks, trading for the bank's own account. Until recently, foreign exchange brokers did large amounts of business, facilitating inter-bank trading and matching anonymous counterparts for small fees.

2) Commercial companies

An important part of this market comes from the financial activities of companies seeking foreign exchange to pay for goods or services. Commercial companies often trade fairly small amounts compared to those of banks or speculators, and their trades often have little short term impact on market rates. Nevertheless, trade flows are an important factor in the long-term direction of a currency's exchange rate. Some multinational corporations can have an unpredictable impact when very large positions are covered due to exposures that are not widely known by other market participants.

3) Central banks

The central banks play an important role in the foreign exchange markets. They try to control the money supply, inflation, and often have official or unofficial target rates for their currencies. They can use their often substantial foreign exchange reserves to stabilize the market. Friedman argued that the best stabilization strategy would be for central banks to buy when the exchange rate is too low, and to sell when the rate is too high — that is, to trade for a profit based on their more precise information. Nevertheless, the effectiveness of central bank "stabilizing speculation" is doubtful because central banks do not go bankrupt if they make large losses, like other traders would, and there is no convincing evidence that they do make a profit trading. The mere expectation or rumor of central bank intervention might be enough to stabilize a currency, but aggressive intervention might be used several times each year in countries with a dirty floating exchange regime. Central banks do not always achieve their objectives, however. The combined resources of the market can easily overwhelm any central bank. Several scenarios of this nature were seen in Southeast Asia ten years ago.

4) Investment management firms

Investment management firms use the foreign exchange market to facilitate transactions in foreign securities. For example, an investment manager with an international equity portfolio will need to buy and sell foreign currencies in the spot market in order to pay for purchases of foreign equities. Since the foreign exchange transactions are secondary to the actual investment decision, they are not seen as speculative or aimed at profit-maximization. Some investment management firms also have more speculative specialist currency overlay operations, which manage clients' currency exposures with the aim of generating profits as well as limiting risk. Whilst the number of this type of specialist firms is quite small, many have a large value of assets under management and hence can generate large trades.

5) Hedge funds

Hedge funds, such as the famous George Soros's Quantum fund[15] have gained a reputation for aggressive currency speculation since 1990. They control billions of dollars of equity and may borrow billions more, and thus may overwhelm intervention by central banks to support almost any currency, if the economic fundamentals are in the hedge funds' favor.

6) Retail forex brokers

Retail forex brokers or market makers handle a minute fraction of the total volume of the foreign exchange market. According to CNN, one retail broker estimates retail volume at $25 – 50 billion daily, which is about 2% of the whole market and it has been reported that inexperienced investors may become targets of forex scams.

2. The characteristics of the trading on international exchange market

There is no single unified foreign exchange market. Due to the over-the-counter (OTC) nature of currency markets, there are rather a number of inter-connected marketplaces, where different currency instruments are traded. This implies that there is no such thing as a single dollar rate — but rather a number of different rates (prices), depending on what bank or market maker is trading. In practice the rates are often very close, otherwise they could be exploited by arbitrageurs.

The main trading centers are in London, New York, Tokyo, Singapore, and Hong Kong, but banks throughout the world participate. As the Asian trading session ends, the European session begins, then the US session, and then the Asian begin in their turns. Traders can react to news when it breaks, rather than waiting for the market to open.

There is little or no "inside information" in the foreign exchange markets. Exchange rate fluctuations are usually caused by actual monetary flows as well as by expectations of changes in monetary flows caused by changes in GDP growth, inflation, interest rates, budget and trade deficits or surpluses, large cross-border mergers and acquisition deals and other macro-economic conditions.

Major news is released publicly, often on scheduled dates, so many people have access to the same news at the same time. However, the large banks have an important advantage; they can see their customers' order flow.

Currencies are traded against one another. For instance, EUR/USD is the price of the euro expressed in US dollars. Out of convention, the first currency in the pair, the base currency, was the stronger currency at the creation of the pair. The second currency, counter currency, was the weaker currency at the creation of the pair.

On the spot market, according to the BIS[16] study, the most heavily traded products were: EUR/USD — 28%, USD/JPY — 18%, GBP/USD — 14%, and the US dollar was involved in 89% of transactions, followed by the euro (37%), the yen (20%) and sterling (17%). (Note that volume percentages should add up to 200%, 100% for all the sellers and 100% for all the buyers).

Although trading in the euro has grown considerably since the currency's creation in January 1999, the foreign exchange market is thus far still largely USD-centered. For instance, trading the euro versus a non-European currency XXX will usually involve two trades: EUR/USD and USD/XXX. The only exception to this is EUR/JPY, which is an established traded currency pair in the inter-bank spot market.

Nowadays, electronic trading is growing in the FX market, and algorithmic trading is becoming much more common, although there is much confusion about the technique. As estimated, by 2008 up to 25% of all trades by volume will be executed using algorithm, up from about 18% in 2005.

3. The factors affecting currency trading

Although exchange rates are affected by many factors, in the end, currency prices are a result of supply and demand forces. The world's currency markets can be viewed as a huge melting pot: in a large and ever-changing mix of current events, supply and demand factors are constantly shifting, and the price of one currency in relation to another shifts accordingly. No other market encompasses (and distills) as much of what is going on in the world at any given time as foreign exchange.

Supply and demand for any particular currency, and thus its value, are not influenced by any single element, but rather by several. These elements generally fall into three categories: economic factors, political conditions and market psychology.

1) Economic factors

The economic factors include economic policy, enacted by government departments or central banks, and economic conditions, generally revealed through economic reports, and other economic indicators.

Economic policy, as known to all, comprises government fiscal policy and monetary policy. Generally speaking, the economic policies will make significant sense in the long run and may not have immediate effects on the market. However, the market always reacts to the economic conditions quickly.

Such economic conditions include the follow aspects.

(1) Government budget deficits or surpluses. The market usually reacts negatively to widening government budget deficits, and positively to narrowing budget deficits. The impact is reflected in the value of a country's home currency.

(2) Balance of trade levels and trends. The trade flow between countries illustrates the demand for goods and services, which in turn indicates demand for a country's home currency to conduct trade. Surpluses and deficits in trade of goods and services reflect the competitiveness of a nation's economy. Therefore trade deficits may have a negative impact on a nation's home currency.

(3) Inflation levels and trends. Typically, a currency will lose value if there is a high level of inflation in the country or if inflation levels are perceived to be rising. This is because inflation erodes purchasing power, thus demand, for that particular currency.

(4) Economic growth and health. Reports such as GDP, employment levels, retail sales, capacity utilization and others, detail the levels of a country's economic growth and health. Generally, the more

healthy and robust a country's economy, the better its currency will perform, and the more demand for it there will be.

2) Political conditions

Internal, regional, and international political conditions and events can have a profound effect on international exchange markets.

For instance, political upheaval and instability can have a negative impact on a nation's economy. Also, events in one country may spur positive or negative interest in a neighboring country and, in the process, affect its currency. The effects on the market of wars need not be dwelt on here and every one can see it with his (or her) own eyes.

3) Market psychology

Although it is difficult to define the term market psychology, we can conclude that market psychology influences the foreign exchange market in a variety of ways.

(1) Flights to quality. Unsettling international economic and political events can lead to a "flight to quality" — with investors seeking a "safe haven" to secure the quality of their investments. There will be a greater demand, thus a higher price, for currencies perceived as stronger over their relatively weaker counterparts.

(2) Long-term trends. Very often, foreign exchange markets move in long, pronounced trends. Although currencies do not have an annual growing season like tangible commodities, business cycles do make themselves felt. Cycle analysis looks at longer-term price trends that may rise from economic or political trends.

(3) "Buy the rumor, sell the fact". This market truism can apply to many currency situations. It is the tendency for the price of a currency to reflect the impact of a particular action before it occurs and, when the anticipated event comes to pass, react in exactly the opposite direction. This may also be referred to as a market being "oversold" or "overbought".

(4) Economic indexes. While economic indexes can certainly reflect economic policy, some reports and numbers take on a talisman—like effect — the indexes themselves becomes important to market psychology and may have an immediate impact on short-term market moves. "What to watch" can change over time. In recent years, for example, money supply, employment, trade balance figures and inflation numbers have all taken turns in the spotlight.

(5) Technical trading considerations. As in other markets, the accumulated price movements in a currency pair (such as EUR/USD) can form patterns that may be recognized and utilized by traders for the purpose of entering and exiting the market, leading to short-term fluctuations in price. Many traders study price charts in order to identify such patterns.

9.3 International Money Market
国际货币市场

9.3.1 A Brief Introduction to International Money Market 国际货币市场简介

The international money markets are the financial markets for short-term international financing, including investments, borrowing and lending. It provides short term liquid funding for the large institutions (such as international bank groups and multinational corporations) and national governments.

The financial instruments traded in international money markets commonly called "paper". This contrasts with the international capital market for longer-term funding, which is supplied by bonds and equity.

The international money markets consist of international banks borrowing and lending to each other, using commercial paper, repurchase agreements and other instruments similar to domestic money market. The operations in international money markets are also similar to those in domestic markets.

In the international money markets, participants from different parts of the globe borrow and lend internationally for short periods of time, typically up to 13 months.

The participants in international money markets are trading companies, retail and institutional money market funds, hedge funds, commercial banks, central banks and other financial institutions. They are usually the investors, the borrowers and the lenders at the same time.

It should be noted that, the international money markets around the world are now integrating into a global money market with the development of globalization. So the term global money market (or world money market) may be used more commonly.

Another point to be noted is that, currency exchange inevitably gets involved in international financing and therefore the international money markets do have some relations with international exchange markets. Some authors even regard the latter as a sub-market of the former.

9.3.2 Short-term Credit Market 短期信贷市场

International short-term credit markets generally refer to the international inter-bank markets, although it also theoretically includes the cases of banks' short-term credits to companies.

The international inter-bank markets provide short term liquid funding for banks and other financial institutions. There are specific interest rates for inter-bank short term financing, among which the most famous one may be the LIBOR (London Inter-Bank Offered Rate)[17].

The LIBOR is an interest rate at which banks can borrow funds, in marketable size, from other banks in the London inter-bank market. The LIBOR is fixed on a daily basis by the British Bankers' Association. The LIBOR is derived from a filtered average of the world's most creditworthy banks' inter-bank deposit rates for larger loans with maturities between overnight and one full year. It is the world's most widely used benchmark for short-term interest rates. It's important because it is the rate at which the world's most preferred borrowers are able to borrow money. It is also the rate upon which rates for less preferred borrowers are based. For example, a multinational corporation with a very good credit rating may be able to borrow money for one year at LIBOR plus 4 or 5 points. Countries that rely on the LIBOR for a reference rate include the United States, Canada, Switzerland and, of course, England.

Another inter-bank rate is the LIBID (London Inter-bank Bid Rate)[18], which is the opposite of the LIBOR (an asked rate) and therefore a bid rate. This is the rate bid by banks on deposits. It is normally one eighth of a percentage point lower than the LIBOR. The LIBID would be the international benchmark rate that banks lend to other banks.

The LIMEAN (London Inter-bank Mean Rate)[19] is also often used as base rate in international financial markets. It is the mid-market rate in the London inter-bank market, which is calculated by averaging the offer rate (LIBOR) and the bid rate (LIBID). The LIMEAN rate can be used by institutions borrowing and lending money in the inter-bank market, instead of using the LIBID or LIBOR rates, in any lending agreements. It can also be used to gain insight into the average rate at which money is being borrowed and lent in the inter-bank market.

9.3.3　Short-term Security Market　短期证券市场

Here, so-called "short-term security" includes all short-term "papers" such as treasury bills, certificates of deposit, bank acceptances, commercial papers and etc. Investors can trade foreign short-term securities in international money markets.

The trading operations of these short-term papers in international money markets are similar to those in domestic money markets, which have been expatiated in Chapter 6.

9.3.4　Discount Market　贴现市场

Discounting is the process of finding the present value of an amount of cash at some future date, and along with compounding cash forms the basis of time value of money calculations. Here, the discount means a financial operation that the holder of a usance note sells it to the bank or other financial institution before its maturity date for the discounted value. The discounted value equals the maturity value minus the discount interest and charges.

The discount bank or other financial institution may present the note to its drawer for payment on its maturity date, or choose to rediscount it to the central bank before the date.

The financial market providing international discount services are called international discount markets. There are various financial instruments could be discounted and various institutions making discount operations (such as banks and discount houses) in international discount markets.

9.4　International Capital Market
国际资本市场

9.4.1　A Brief Introduction to International Capital Market　国际资本市场简介

The international capital markets are those financial markets for governments and corporation to raise long-term funds internationally. Here the "long-term" means the time period longer than 1 year.

Many developing countries do not have sufficient resources to finance their domestic economic development and they may turn to international capital markets, either from official sources or from private capital sources. Governments in developed countries and the international financial institutions (such as World Bank and IMF) are examples of official capital sources for developing countries. Examples of private sources are commercial banks and other private financial institutions.

Besides the developing countries, those large multinational corporations would also depend on international capital markets to finance their global operations. They obtain the financing funds from private sources. The long-term financings for large corporations from private sources play the major roles in international capital markets.

With the development of globalization, the international capital markets around the world are now integrating into a global capital market. Therefore, the term global capital market (or world capital market) may be used sometimes.

9.4.2 International Medium and Long-term Credit Market
国际中长期信贷市场

When a multinational corporation needs capital to expand its business, it may choose to borrow medium or long term loans from banks. Generally, a loan with the term from 1 to 5 years is called a medium term loan and that with the term exceeding 5 years is a long term loan. However, in some western countries, the denomination of medium term loan is seldom used and all loans scheduled to repay after 1 or more years are referred to as long term loans.

Long term loans are normally secured, first, by the new assets purchased (up to 65%) and then by other unencumbered physical assets of the corporation (for the remaining 35%), or failing that, from additional funds from shareholders or personal guarantees from the principals. On the balance sheet, the equipment purchased shows up in the long term assets section, while the counterpart loan information is shown in the current and long term liabilities portions. The useful life of the assets is directly reflected in their depreciation schedules.

Debt lenders (creditors) make long-term loans to corporations that exhibit strong management ability and steady growth potential. A written business plan, including a cash flow demonstrating the business ability to repay the loan principal and interest over the term of the repayment schedule, is mandatory.

A long-term loan carries both interest and principal repayment provisions in a pre-set repayment schedule. Early repayment may entail a penalty because the lender had not planned an alternate investment for that money.

The percentage interest rate normally remains constant for the term of the loan. Each payment of principal reduces the balance of principal remaining and the subsequent interest is calculated on this reducing balance.

Different lenders make different types of loans. The interest rates may differ to different borrowers; in general, the shorter the term, the smaller the amount, and the more creditworthy the borrower, the lower the rate. Conversely, to the same borrower, different lenders may provide different interest rates and conditions for loan. Therefore, the borrowers often spend some time in seeking for the appropriate lenders in capital markets.

It will be international loans if the borrowers get them from foreign banks. Compared to domestic loans, international medium and long-term loans are always with much greater amounts, higher interest rates, more strict conditions, and less or even no restrictions on the uses of the loans.

9.4.3 International Security Market 国际证券市场

Governments and corporation can also raise long-term funds through issuing securities in international capital markets. Such securities are always with long terms exceeding 1 year and broadly categorized into debt and equity securities such as bonds and stocks respectively.

1. International bond market

An international bond is a bond issued by a foreign government or corporation. The most popular and liquid international bonds are those issued by high credit rated governments such as Japan, Switzerland, Germany, the UK and the US.

International bonds can be divided into foreign bonds and Eurobonds. Foreign bonds are issued on a local market by a foreign borrower and are usually denominated in the local currency. For example, a foreign corporation issues bonds in the US for placement in the US market alone. The issue is underwritten by a syndicate of US securities houses and denominated in the currency of the intended investors, i. e., USD. Foreign bond issues and trading are under the supervision of local market authorities.

Foreign bonds issued in national markets have a long history. They often have colorful names: Yankee Bonds (in the US), samurai bonds (in Japan), Rembrandt bonds (in the Netherlands) and bulldog bonds (in the UK), and panda bonds (in the PRC).

Eurobonds are underwritten by a multinational syndicate of banks and placed mainly countries other than the one in whose currency the bond is denominated. These bonds are not traded in a specific national bond market. The details about Eurobond will be examined in the next section.

2. International equity market

An equity security is a share in the capital stock of a company (typically common stock, although preferred stock is also a form of capital stock). So the term equity may be replace with the term stock.

An international equity (stock) market refers to the mechanism that enables the trading of foreign stocks. Theoretically, it is a complex mechanism including primary (issuing) and secondary (trading) market. However, in practice, when the international stock markets are referred, people always think of those famous stock exchanges such as the NYSE, the NASDAQ, Euronext[20], the London Stock Exchange, the HKEX[21], etc.

The various stocks and derivatives traded in international stock market are of similar types and similar trading operations to the domestic stocks. But their issuing are more complicated than in domestic markets.

There are some famous stock indexes in international stock markets and they are acting as important economic indicators of the world economy, such as the Dow Jones Industrial Index (USA), Hang Seng[22] (Hong Kong), Nikkei[23] (Japan), etc.

9.5 Eurocurrency Market
欧洲货币市场

9.5.1 A Brief Introduction to Eurocurrency Market 欧洲货币市场简介

Eurocurrency is the term used to describe deposits residing in banks that are located outside the borders of the country that issues the currency the deposit is denominated in. For example a deposit denominated in US dollars residing in a Japanese bank is a Eurocurrency deposit, or more specifically a Eurodollar deposit.

Key points are the location of the bank and the denomination of the currency, not the nationality of the bank, nor the owner of the deposit.

As the example identifies, it is important to note that despite its name, Eurocurrencies are not limited to Europe and as such it must not be confused with the Euro; indeed it is possible to have a Euroeuro (Euros deposited in the banks outside the Euro zone). The use of this idiosyncratic term arose from the fact that

Eurocurrency markets first developed in Europe during the 1950s when the former Soviet Union asked London banks to hold US dollar denominated deposits in the fear that deposits in US banks run the risk of being frozen or seized for political reasons.

The Eurocurrency market[24], in broad sense, is an offshore financial market for the trading of Eurocurrencies, such as Eurodollar, Euroyen.

Today, Eurocurrency markets are well-developed, sophisticated markets where the traded instruments are denominated in many currencies. These instruments include Eurodeposits, Eurocredit, Euronotes, Euroequity and etc. Therefore, now some authors would like to use a shorter term with broader sense — Euromarket[25] — to replace the term Eurocurrency market. No matter it is called Euromarket or Eurocurrency market, it is very active in the present world for the reason that they avoid domestic interest rate regulations, reserve requirements and other barriers to the free flow of international capital.

9.5.2　The Origins of Eurocurrency Market　欧洲货币市场的起源

The earliest Eurocurrency is Eurodollar, those US dollars deposited outside the US, especially in Europe.

Long before World War II it was not rare for banks outside the US to accept deposits denominated in US dollars. The volume of such deposits, however, was small and the market for them had little economic significance. During the 1950s things began to change. Since Russia and its allied countries had to deal in hard currency for their international trade transactions, the central banks of these countries ended up holding USD balances. Initially these balances were held in New York. But as the cold war tensions increased, these countries transferred these balances to banks in London and other European financial centers.

Reading Material

Eurobanks: More Competitive Rates

Eurobanks are those banks providing financing service in Eurocurrecies. Every bank could be a Eurobank when it has Eruodeposits.

The unregulated framework allows Eurobanks to be more competitive than domestic regulated banks. In general, due to competition and the unregulated nature of Eurobanking, the domestic deposit rate is lower than LIBID and the domestic lending rate is higher than the LIBOR.

While the cold war may have initiated the Eurocurrency market, there were other factors that stimulated its development. Historically, the pound sterling played a key role in world trade. A great deal of trade was settled in GBP. Two events helped to boost the USD as the prevailing currency for international trade. The first is the sterling crisis in the UK in the mid-1950s. In 1957, the UK imposed controls on non-resident GBP borrowing and lending by UK banks. These institutions then turned to the USD to finance international trade. Secondly, in 1958, West European countries in preparation for the creation of the EEC (now, EU) allowed their banks to trade freely in USD to finance trade.

On the other hand, the US government, unknowingly, gave a very important stimulus to the growth of the Eurocurrency market with several regulations. During the 1960s the US government imposed several measures to control international capital flows. These measures were aimed to improve the US balance of payments, which was in a big deficit.

(1) In 1963, the US government imposed an Interest Equalization Tax (IET) on foreign securities held by US investor. The government's idea was to equalize the after-tax interest rate paid by US and foreign borrowers, and, thus, discourage US residents to buy foreign securities (thus reducing capital outflows). The tax forced non-US corporations to pay a higher interest rate in order to attract US investors. Therefore, non-US corporations started to look into the Eurocurrency market to borrow USD.

(2) Since the IET did not reduce significantly capital outflows, the US Federal Reserve imposed another financial regulation in 1965, the Foreign Credit Restraint Program (FCRP). The FCRP restricted the amount of credit US banks could extend to foreign borrowers. Foreign subsidiaries of US multinational corporations were considered "foreign", under the FCRP. The government's idea behind the FCRP was also to reduce capital outflows. The FCRP started as a "voluntary" program but was changed to a mandatory program in 1968. Again, foreign borrowers and US subsidiaries were forced to go somewhere else to borrow USD.

(3) In 1968, the government passed the Foreign Investment Program, which limited the amount of domestic USD that US corporations could use to finance foreign investments. Therefore, many US corporations turn to Eurocurrency market for financing.

In addition, for a long time, the US Federal Reserve regulated the interest rates that US banks could pay on term deposit. This regulation was called Regulation Q. The tight money years of 1968 and 1969 made money market rates to rise above the rates banks where allowed to pay under Regulation Q. Regulation Q, widened the interest differential between a USD deposit in the US and a USD deposit abroad.

All these restrictions brought the major financial institutions to European financial centers like London, Zurich, and Luxembourg. This development had some spillover effects on financial centers in other parts of the world such as Tokyo, Hong Kong, Singapore, Bahamas, and Bahrain.

Several European governments also imposed capital controls during this period, which triggered the creation of the non-USD segments of the Eurocurrency market. For example, during the 1970s, the Bundesbank required foreigners with DEM accounts to place a fraction of their funds in non-interest-bearing accounts. This regulation gave an incentive to foreigners to make DEM deposits outside Germany, and, then, the Euro-DEM was born.

The regulations and restrictions that gave birth to Eurocurrency markets have all disappeared since then. However, Eurocurrency markets have continued to grow. Today, Eurocurrency markets are free from regulations, exempt from national taxes and reserve requirements. These conditions allow international banks to take advantage of the lower cost of funds. Then, they can lend the funds to borrowers at lower rates than those can be obtained in domestic markets.

9.5.3　The Major Instruments Traded in Eurocurrency Market
欧洲货币市场的主要交易工具

1. Eurodeposits

When Eurocurrency markets started to emerge, a typical Eurodeposit involved a time deposit, that is, a non-negotiable, registered instrument with a fixed maturity. When investing in a Eurocurrency time deposit, the investor commits funds for a certain period of time, at a specified rate. At maturity the investor receives the principal plus the interest. Later, Eurodeposits included more flexible instruments and the most popular instrument is the certificate of deposit (CD), which is negotiable and is often a bearer instrument.

Reading Material

A Eurodollar Deposit Transaction

Suppose IBM has USD 1 million in excess cash available for a week. IBM decides to invest this USD 1 million in a 7-day deposit. Bank of New York pays 5.25% for a 7-day domestic deposit. Banco Santander Central Hispano (BSCH) has a bid rate of 5.50% for a 7-day Eurodollar time deposit. IBM certainly will choose to deposits the money with BSCH because of its higher rate.

This transaction will involve the following steps.

(1) BSCH must have a USD bank account with a US bank, say, with Citibank.

(2) IBM deposits USD 1 million with Citibank for credit to the account of BSCH.

(3) BSCH withdraws the funds from its account at Citibank.

(4) In 7 days, BSCH will transfer USD 1 million plus accrued interest through its account at Citibank to the account designated by IBM.

Note that if Bank of New York had received the deposit, they should have set aside a part of the deposit as reserve, as required by the US Federal Reserve. BSCH is free to loan the Eurodeposit to anyone, without any reserve requirement. This is sure to lower the costs of BSCH.

The majority of the Eurodeposits have a very short-term duration, for example, one or seven days, or one, three, or six months. For long-term CDs (up to ten years), there is a fixed coupon or floating-rate coupon. For CDs with floating-rate coupons, the life of the CD is divided into sub-periods of usually six months. The interest earned over such period is fixed at the beginning of the period, the reset date. This interest rate is based on the prevailing market interest rate at the time. This market rate is the LIBOR which is determined by the supply of and demand for Eurocurrencies in the London inter-bank market.

Although the majority of Eurodeposits are in the form of time deposits, CDs play a significant role in the Eurocurrency market because of a liquid secondary market. Banks, regularly, buy and sell their own CDs in the secondary market to insure investor of the liquidity of the secondary market, and therefore, making the CDs more attractive. The CD rates shown in newspapers are usually the secondary market rates. Most CDs issued in London are denominated in USD.

In general, Eurodeposits will be effective two business days after the contract is in effect, and mature, for example, 30 days later. On maturity, payment is usually made by a transfer in the currency's home country (i.e., Japan for Euroyen). The minimum period for delivery of funds is usually two working days, which is the usual settlement period in the foreign exchange market.

2. Eurocredit

Eurocredit refers to a loan whose denominated currency is not the lending bank's national currency. For example, a US bank lends a corporation 100 million Russian rubles. Eurocredit facilitates the flow of international capital between countries and the financing of investments at home and abroad.

The short-term Eurocredit are generally conducted between banks and their operations are similar to the normal inter-bank markets. The benchmark interest rate is the LIBOR.

The long-term Eurocredit are largely borrowed by the multinational corporations from bank groups, and known as bank group loans[26]. The amount of such a loan usually exceeds 100 million dollars. A floating interest rate and various charges are often required. The operation of a bank group loan is much more complicated than that of a general loan and may involve almost twenty or even more banks. One principal bank acts as the leading bank and takes the chief responsibility while the other banks are managing banks or participating banks[27]. There is also an agent bank, which is usually the leading bank itself, to perform and supervise the whole progress of the lending. A credit contract overloaded with details is necessary to be made between the borrower and the lending bank group. Moreover, the amounts of some bank group loans are so great that the guarantees by relative governments may be required.

The medium Eurocredit with moderate amounts are usually lent by one bank and called bilateral loan[28], or sole bank loan. Generally speaking, such medium Eurocredit are with more loose conditions and lower interests and charges, compared to bank group loans.

3. Euronotes

Euronotes[29] means the short- dated notes issued by parties other than banks in a currency other than the local currency of the country where the market located in. It is another type of financing tools for corporations in Eurocurrency markets. Some authors prefer to call them Eurocommercial papers while there are other authors argue that Euronotes are not identical with Eurocommercial papers in issuing and trading operations.

An agreement between the issuer and banks is required for Euronotes. Then the Euronotes are underwritten by the banks (constituting a bank group) with the agreed interest rate (referring to the LIBOR). They are issued and underwritten in a revolving way in a long period (usually 10 years). Thereby, the issuer can obtain long term financing through issuing short-dated notes. In fact, this is a note issue facility (NIF)[30] provided by banks.

In contrast, those Euronotes without the NIF may be called Eurocommercial papers more commonly.

4. Eurobonds

Eurobond is a bond issued in a currency other than the currency of the country or market in which it is issued.

Usually, a Eurobond is issued by an international syndicate and categorized according to the currency in which it is denominated. A Eurodollar bond that is denominated in US dollars and issued in Europe by a Japanese company would be an example of a Eurobond. The Japanese company in this example could issue the Eurodollar bond in any country other than the US. So a Eurobond may have nothing to do with Europe (supposing the bond is issued in Singapore in the above example).

Eurobonds are attractive financing tools for governments and corporations as they give issuers the flexibility to choose the country in which to offer their bond according to the country's regulatory constraints. They may also denominate their Eurobond in their preferred currency. Eurobonds are attractive to investors as they have small par values and high liquidity.

9.5.4 Offshore Financial Center 离岸金融中心

As mentioned earlier, offshore financial centers (OFCs) are the financial markets providing offshore finance. Offshore finance[31] is, at its simplest, the provision of financial services by banks and other agents to non-residents.

Eurocurrency financing has very close relations with offshore finance. All offshore finance can be considered as Eurocurrency financing. However, strictly speaking, not all Eurocurrency financing are offshore finance. For instance, a French bank lends Eurodollars to French companies.

OFCs range from centers such as Hong Kong and Singapore, with well-developed financial markets and infrastructure, where a considerable amount of value is added to transactions undertaken for non-residents and which are called functional centers[32], to centers with smaller populations, such as Bermuda, British Virgin Islands, Cayman Islands, where value added is limited to the provision of professional infrastructure and which are called paper centers[33], and well known as "tax havens". In some very small centers, where the financial institutions have little or no physical presence, the value added may be limited to the booking of the transaction. Corporations choose to register in these centers for the purpose of tax avoidance.

But in all centers specific transactions may be more or less of an "offshore" type. That is in all jurisdictions it is possible to find transactions where only the "booking" has taken place in the OFC, while at the same time business involving much more value added may also take place.

Group Discussion

1. Compare the major types of international financial markets.
2. Discuss the relations between international exchange/money/capital markets.
3. Discuss the difference between Eurocurrency markets and offshore markets
4. Say something about the future development of international financial markets.

NOTES

1　offshore financial center (OFC)　离岸金融中心
2　offshore financial market　离岸金融市场
3　onshore financial market　在岸金融市场
4　ISO　国际标准化组织（全称为"International Standard Organization"）
5　foreign exchange rate　外汇汇率
6　exchange rate　汇率
7　direct quotation　直接标价法（或用"giving quotation"，即"应付标价法"）；indirect quotation 间接标价法（或用"receiving quotation"，即"应收标价法"）
8　basic exchange rate　基准汇率；cross exchange rate　套算汇率
9　CNY　人民币货币代码；HKD　港币货币代码
10　nominal exchange rate　名义汇率；real exchange rate　实际汇率
11　spot exchange rate　即期汇率；forward exchange rate　远期汇率
12　official exchange rate　官方汇率；market exchange rate　市场汇率
13　fixed exchange rate　固定汇率（制）

14 floating exchange rate 浮动汇率（制）

15 Quantum fund 量子基金

16 BIS 国际清算银行（全称为"Bank for International Settlement"）

17 LIBOR（London Inter-Bank Offered Rate） 伦敦银行同业拆放利率

18 LIBID（London Inter-bank Bid Rate） 伦敦银行同业拆入利率

19 LIMEAN（London Inter-bank Mean Rate） 伦敦银行同业平均利率

20 Euronext 欧洲证券交易所

21 HKEX 香港交易所

22 Hang Seng 香港恒生指数

23 Nikkei 日本日经指数

24 Eurocurrency market 欧洲货币市场（即从事境外货币资金业务的市场）

25 Euromarket 欧洲（货币）市场（有时与"Eurocurrency market"通用，有时也用来表示欧洲共同市场，即"European Common Market（ECM）"）

26 bank group loan 银团贷款（亦称为"syndicate loan"，即"辛迪加贷款"）

27 leading bank 牵头银行；managing bank 经理银行；participating bank 参与银行

28 bilateral loan 双边贷款

29 Euronote 欧洲票据（一种欧洲货币市场工具，也可指欧元纸钞）

30 note issue facility（NIF） 票据发行便利

31 offshore finance 离岸金融业务

32 functional center 功能型中心

33 paper center 记账型中心

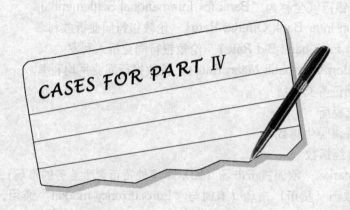

CASES FOR PART Ⅳ

China's Forex Reserves Are Biggest Globally
中国外汇储备全球第一

China surpassed Japan as the biggest holder of foreign currency reserves according to data at the end of February, 2006, as the country's trade surplus keeps growing and foreign investments continue to rise.

China's foreign reserves, topped US $ 853. 6 billion at the end of February, Premier Wen Jiabao said in a speech in Australia which was posted on the central government's Website. Japan's foreign exchange reserves totalled US $ 850. 06 billion at the end of February, down US $ 1. 61 billion from a month earlier, and it posted its first decline in four months, Japan's Ministry of Finance said on March 7.

Meanwhile, a record trade surplus and a flood of foreign investment has boosted China's foreign currency holdings. The nation's foreign currency reserves soared 34 percent in 2005 to a record US $ 818. 9 billion, the second biggest after Japan then while China's global trade surplus last year soared 217. 4 percent to US $ 101. 9 billion.

"China's booming foreign reserves can help boost economic stability with ample capital for foreign debt payment," Yi Xianrong, a researcher at the Chinese Academy of Social Sciences, said.

"A bulging foreign debt and small foreign reserves were blamed for causing the Asian financial crisis in late 1990s," Yi said. "China's strong forex reserves showed its capacity to ward off such crisis. "

China's foreign debt jumped 13. 56 percent to US $ 281. 05 billion at the end of 2005, the State Administration of Foreign Exchange (SAFE) stated in March. Yi also noted that wisdom is required in investing the reserves prudently, and turning to multiple investment channels is a wise move to seek higher returns and maintain stability. Wei Benhua, vice head of SAFE, said China is studying plans to expand its forex reserves' investment portfolio.

China now stockpiles its foreign currency in US Treasury bonds and other assets. Some economists advised that China should diversify its forex reserves portfolio.

Experts say that burgeoning foreign exchange reserves reflect China's growing strength, but warn that a high level of foreign exchange reserves also has a downside.

The country's hefty foreign exchange reserves make its fast economic development more risky, said Fan Gang, a member of the monetary policy committee under the People's Bank of China.

He said that the economy is showing signs of cooling down, with overheating being reined in as a result of macro-control measures. However, mounting foreign exchange reserves and excessive trade surpluses will create risks for the healthy growth of the economy.

He said that massive capital inflows from overseas are not seeking to speculate on the RMB, as many people believe, but instead eyeing business opportunities created by the booming economy.

The very modest RMB fluctuation band gives speculators little room to rake in profits. China's buoyant economic prospects are what investors really value, he said.

Zhong Wei, professor with the finance research center of Beijing Teachers' University, said hefty foreign exchange reserves require a brand-new management system in China.

Zhong suggested that China fix foreign exchange reserves at a level of no more than 800 billion US dollars and allocate the rest to useful purposes.

Zhong said the surplus reserves could be used to purchase strategic materials for China's economic development, to upgrade technologies in state-owned enterprises and to reform the state-owned financial sector. The extra foreign exchange reserves could also be used to introduce talented people from overseas and to boost the nation's social security fund, Zhong said.

The State Administration of Foreign Exchange, which has paid close attention to the increase in foreign exchange reserves, says maintaining a balance between international income and expenses is one of the major tasks for China's economic and social development.

The administration is considering taking measures to slow down the increase in foreign exchange reserves.

The management of foreign exchange reserves will be improved so that they can be used as effectively as possible, according to the administration.

London as an International Capital Market
作为国际资本市场的伦敦

I understand that this is an occasion for questions and discussion. I shall be brief, or relatively brief, and I will attempt to set out some of the main issues which are or should be of interest for international bankers working in London.

The first point to make is that London has been the most international of the world's capital market centers. The UK has benefited enormously from being neutral between foreign and British ownership of financial institutions working in Britain: we treat all banks, or brokers, or insurance companies, on a comparable basis, irrespective of the nationality of their shareholders or of their management team. I think it is fair to say that Britain has been more open to inward investment by foreign banks and foreign financial institutions than any other European country.

I am confident that policy will continue, despite the arguments sometimes advanced by some British financial institutions that, in a world of increasing consolidation, we should be more cautious in accepting foreign ownership, or should guard more jealously those remaining British institutions. I believe strongly that Britain will do best — and competitive British banks will do best — from establishing a marketplace which remains open; where the emphasis is on efficiency, good order and high standards; and where nationality of ownership or of management remains an irrelevance.

What is clearly not irrelevant is that there should be means of maintaining the high standards we expect of banks and other financial institutions. It is worth considering whether there are particular regulatory issues when dealing with foreign banks or foreign financial institutions which do not arise with British owned ones. I think it is clear that there are some issues which are worth discussion.

First, there is the need for us in the FSA (Financial Service Authority) as the regulatory organization in London to have a counterparty in the overseas institution here in London with whom we can do business. You know that one of the guiding principles of FSA is that we look to the senior management of those whom we regulate to take responsibility for their firms. It is their responsibility to act prudently and honestly, to set up and maintain controls which work, and to manage the risks which are inescapable in financial institutions. This responsibility must lie with the senior management of the company in the first instance: it is not something which principally lies with compliance functions or with internal audit — though, of course, both these can and should play useful supporting roles. So we need, for each financial institution operating in London, a clear means of communicating with the firm's senior management — which, in turn, means that we need the firm's London management to have the necessary clout within the firm. In a world of matrix management, where global product heads co-exist with those with geographical responsibilities, this clout is not self-evident. So you must expect us to be interested in you, in London, having a clear and respected voice back to Tokyo, or New York, or Frankfort, or any other head office.

Second, there are clearly regulatory issues which arise from all cross-border banking, and which revolve round the correct relationship between home and host regulator. This general problem comes in many guises. For large groups operating substantially in London and New York and other capital market centers there is a need for full consultation and exchange of views between the regulatory authorities in the countries — something which I think works well between the major regulatory organizations. The FSA talks repeatedly with the New York Fed, and the Japanese FSA; for major groups like UBS or Credit Suisse based in Switzerland we hold tripartite meetings of American, British and Swiss Banking authorities. In other instances, we can find an imbalance between the expertise of a small home country regulator on the one hand, and the different issues which arise in a much larger and more sophisticated market such as the London market on the other. Here again, I think that these problems have been dealt with quite successfully, with the fallback position of reverting to a subsidiary rather than a branch status used where necessary. But both instances represent complications on the regulatory template.

Third, there are regulatory complexities which come from different national systems of regulation: notably the difference between those countries like the UK, Germany or Japan in which regulation of (almost) all financial services falls under one regulator, and those countries where the responsibility is divided between several or even many regulators. For certain firms there has historically been no means of establishing a group view as well as a view of individual entities — something which the EU requirement for consolidated supervision will change. Last, there are some particular regulatory issues which arise for exchanges, where we need to make sure that different countries' requirements are properly identified and dealt with.

I list these various types of international regulatory complexity not to claim that they are insoluble — indeed, experience shows that with hard work and goodwill they are soluble, and indeed have been solved. Nor do I list them as an excuse for protectionism: one of the dangers against which we should guard is the argument that regulation requires national solutions, or national ownership or management. As I said, the UK has greatly benefited from having an open policy towards foreign financial services companies. It is important that we retain this policy. But we will do best if we recognize that there are special features which require additional work, and put in the additional effort.

With that background, let me turn to the wider issues of what we expect of international banks, and what they should expect of the FSA. You should expect us to work hard to promote wholesale markets which are efficient, orderly and clean. That is an objective which no-one argues against as a principle: it is necessary if London is to remain a competitive capital market centre that we should be efficient; it is in everybody's interests that markets are not disorderly; and it is clearly right that markets should be clean — that there is a set of rules, observed in practice as well as set out in rule books, which establish fair behavior and prevent improper preference being given to one category of market participant or market user over others. The objective, as I say, is unexceptionable. What is more debatable is the cost of achieving this objective: how much effort, how much cost, is justified in any particular case? And how does the cumulative cost of individual measures affect efficiency and competitiveness? These are questions which we at the FSA live with all the time. This is as you would expect from an organization which has a statutory duty, the requirement to act proportionately and efficiently, and which subjects all its proposals to cost benefit analysis. And — even were we not committed ourselves by law and by conviction to this principle — I am confident that the practitioners who pay the FSA's costs, and other commentators too, would make sure that this principle was repeatedly brought to our attention.

I take further encouragement from the results of a survey carried out last year by the Centre for the Study of Financial Innovation on behalf of the City Corporation. They asked 350 institutions — more than half of them under non-British ownership — for their views on the relative attractions of London, New York, Frankfort and Paris as major international financial centers.

Overall, London came a close second to New York in terms of international financial centre competitiveness. When asked to compare the different regulatory environments in the four centers, respondents put London on top of the list by a big margin. My own conversations with international bankers make clear to me that the threat to London as a major capital market centre arises more from the state of our transport systems than it does from the state of regulation. London also did well going forward; it was expected to have the most positive regulatory environment in five years' time, from the point of view of running a financial services business.

Is Low Volatility Making Global Financial Markets Too Complacent about Risks?
低波动率是否让全球金融市场得意忘形而忽视风险?

Financial market volatility across a broad range of assets has continued to decline to remarkably low levels and risk spreads are historically tight. A number of structural reasons have been advanced to explain this persistently low level of asset market volatility. One is that inflation risk is less of a concern, partly because emerging markets, in particular China and India, can help meet growing global demand for both goods and services despite narrowing capacity constraints in developed countries. Other explanations appeal to a shallower credit cycle due to improved macro-economic policies, including the credibility attached to central banks. In addition, the wider dispersion of risks in the financial system, facilitated by financial innovations and deepening markets for credit derivatives, may also have contributed to lower volatility.

However, cyclical components are also likely to be important in explaining the current low volatility. Despite the increase in uncertainty normally associated with this stage of the business cycle, volatility appears low. Three key factors are abundant global liquidity, still-low corporate leverage, and a high risk appetite. These factors could reverse in the future.

With respect to liquidity conditions, low real interest rates encourage investors to borrow in order to amplify the returns on their investments. As long as markets remain calm and liquid, this is a successful strategy, and market participants may be inclined to keep increasing leverage. Even as short-term nominal rates have risen in the United States and elsewhere (although real rates remain at or below long term trend levels), funds have been available from economies where nominal rates remain low, notably Japan and Switzerland. The resulting opportunity to borrow cheaply and invest in higher-return assets provides an incentive for investors to engage in cross-border carry trades.

Carry trades have typically targeted high yielding assets in both mature market economies—the United States, Australia, New Zealand, and the euro area—as well as emerging economies, including Brazil, Hungary, South Africa, Turkey, and some Asian economies. While there has been a secular interest by Japanese retail investors in overseas investment given low domestic returns, purchases by Japanese retail investors of bonds denominated in New Zealand dollars have increased in recent years to around $2 billion per month, spurred by an interest spread of around

700 basis points. One measure of the shift toward carry trade strategies is that institutional investors (so-called "real money") have positioned themselves strongly in favor of carry trades over the past six months—funding in Japanese yen and Swiss francs and investing in high-yielding assets in other currencies—to an extreme percentile position (assessed over 1994–2007).

The scale of yen-funded carry trades can be glimpsed by the level of "other" investment outflows from Japan, which include lending and derivatives flows from Japanese banks to non-residents. This component of the nation's balance of payments has become the major source of outflows in 2006, amounting to about $170 billion. The last time there were such bank and derivatives outflows was in 1997, in advance of the Asian financial crisis, the collapse of Long-Term Capital Management, and a sudden appreciation of the yen. While still a small proportion of foreign exchange trading, further evidence of the rising popularity of carry trades can be found in the speculative positions of traders of currency futures on the Chicago Mercantile Exchange, where short yen and Swiss franc positions reached record levels in January.

A second cyclical factor currently depressing volatility is the low degree of leverage among non-financial corporations. Low corporate leverage has the effect of dampening credit market volatility, as debt service costs are small and the threat of default is remote. Default rates have so far remained low, but easy financing conditions may have, in part, suppressed default rates, encouraging some to take on added exposures in credit risk. Pressure is building from private equity buyouts and the leverage cycle is beginning to turn. The US high-yield defaults tend to rise a year or so after the willingness to lend has turned back up as it did in 2005.

Third, strong risk appetite may also work to perpetuate low volatility. Hedge funds and other investors have been actively engaged in "selling volatility," which is the practice of selling options, collecting the option premium in the (so far largely justified) expectation that market moves will not be large enough for the option to finish in the money. Such strategies are also apparent in the willingness of investors to sell protection against default through credit default swaps (most notably in leveraged form through instruments such as constant proportion debt obligations). A further manifestation of increased risk appetite leading to low volatility is illustrated by the behavior of the price of options that are deeply out of the money, and used to insure against extreme outcomes. This suggests that "tail risk" is relatively cheap, at least with respect to the historical average difference between the implied volatilities of deeply-out-of-the-money and at-the-money options. Examples abound from other asset classes: what they have in common is the apparent confidence of investors that extreme events will not occur. High risk appetite is apparent in the increased demand for leveraged loans and an acceleration in the search for yield in riskier assets, including local-currency-denominated emerging markets instruments and the rise in exposure to market risk or leverage by hedge funds.

The cyclical factors contributing to the low volatility environment—abundant low-cost liquidity, low leverage in the corporate sector, and high risk appetite—may reverse. Overall liquidity may be expected to diminish with the eventual removal of monetary accommodation by the Bank of Japan and the European Central Bank. The leverage cycle has turned, and with it, default rates should rise. High risk appetite may reflect an underestimate of economic risks and an overestimate of liquidity in higher-risk and more leveraged investments. Financial markets may well adjust smoothly in the transition from the current state of low volatility to one in which volatility returns to historically more normal levels.

However, there is a risk that the adjustment will be less smooth. A volatility shock—perhaps caused by a downward shift in growth expectations or by renewed inflation pressures—could precipitate sharp portfolio adjustments and a disorderly unwinding of positions. The consequences of such a shock would be amplified by the rise in leveraged investment positions, the increased use of complex derivative instruments that remain untested in more volatile market conditions, rising portfolio exposure to illiquid instruments, and the prevalence of crowded trades.

Furthermore, rising correlations in returns across asset classes have meant that the volatility of the overall market basket has not declined as much as the volatility of its component parts— indeed, by some measures it has increased. Insofar as markets have become overly complacent, they may not yet have priced in this covariance risk, which could lead to the further amplification of any volatility shock. For instance, the recent market sell-off in late February 2007 illustrated how seemingly minor, unrelated developments across markets quickly led to the unwinding of risk positions across a wide range of financial assets.

A volatility shock could lead to the rapid unwinding of carry trades. To the extent that such unwinding involves a reduction in yen funding, a sharp yen appreciation would be possible, particularly in light of global imbalances. While in some cases a relief from appreciation pressures would be welcome in target-currency countries, rapidly depreciating exchange rates could fan inflation, or force higher interest rates that could destabilize financial markets. The impact of such a volatility shock would have a significant effect on emerging markets. The impact on EM (Emerging Markets) sovereign spreads of changes in equity implied volatility, a proxy for risk appetite.

A disruptive unwinding of yen carry trades occurred in October 1998. From October 6–9, the US dollar fell by almost 15 percent against the yen because of a large-scale unwinding of the yen carry trade, amplified by complex options and various hedging strategies. While the effects on the real sector were minimal, the unwinding of short yen positions by hedge funds and large financial institutions led to a rapid drying up of liquidity in key markets. This resulted in highly disruptive market conditions for a short period.

However, the current situation seems less worrisome than the run-up to the 1998 episode for a number of reasons. First, a gradual narrowing of interest rate differentials is the central scenario for monetary policy in the relevant countries. Second, the long side of the carry trade appears to be spread across a number of currencies, while in 1998 it was narrowly concentrated on the US dollar. Third, global macro hedge funds are now less dominant market players, and hedge funds in general have shown flexibility in unwinding their positions, thanks to better risk management techniques. Fourth, the investor base in Japan is more diversified, with retail investors adding stability to the financial landscape. Finally, financial markets are in general deeper than a decade ago and better able to absorb asset price volatility.

PART V

Financial Regulation and Control
金融调控

Chapter 10

Financial Regulation and Control

金融调控

Learning Objectives

☑ To learn the important instruments of monetary policy
☑ To understand the intermediate objectives and transmission mechanism of monetary policy
☑ To learn the methods of domestic financial regulation and supervision
☑ To know about the international financial regulatory cooperation
☑ To understand about the relationship between finance and economic development and know about the important theories about it

Opening Vignette

Financial Regulation and Control in Developing Countries: The Case of Turkey

The type of prudential regulation and control commonly used in developing economies aims directly to control of financial aggregates, such as liquidity expansion and credit growth, namely capital requirements with risk categories used in developed countries. The results achieved in the recent decades have clearly indicated, contrary to policy intentions, the very limited usefulness of those policies in helping those countries to contain the risks involved with more liberalized financial systems; especially in episodes of sudden reversal of capital flows.

In the case of Turkey, the new liberal economic policy began to be implemented in January 1980, which aimed at integration with world markets by establishing a free market economy. As a reflection of this policy, the 1980s witnessed continuous legal, structural and institutional changes and developments in the Turkish banking sector. During these years, Turkey experienced two very severe financial crises: one in early 1994 and the other one in early 2001. In mid-1994, Turkey adopted an IMF based stand-by agreement, and managed to calm the severe economic crises. However, macro-economic instability continued until the late 1990s. In December 1999, Turkey signed a three-year standby agreement with IMF. This program had failed due mainly to a major banking sector crisis in early 2001. Then Turkey started another stabilization program backed by IMF which is still being implemented in Turkey now. With this new program, an extensive streamlining plan on the restructuring of banking sector was started and announced to the public in May 2001.

Maintaining financial stability in global banking and financial markets continues to be an important objective of regulators, bankers, and other market participants, particularly because of the negative impact that financial instability has on economies as a whole. The Turkish economy was reformed and became more outward looking with the structural adjustment program launched in the 1980's. The main objectives of this program can be summarized as: (1) minimizing state intervention; (2) establishing a free market economy; (3) integrating the economy with the global economic system.

The Turkish experience testifies that traditional prudential regulatory policies used in developed countries have had limited effectiveness in controlling the adverse impacts of capital account volatility on financial systems in developing countries. The main reason for this disappointing result is that, by not taking into account the particular characteristics of financial markets in developing countries, these regulations cannot effectively control excessive risk taking by financial institutions.

In general, important features that distinguish financial markets in developing countries from those in developed countries are the predominance of assets with short maturity and high volatility as well as the large concentration of financial and real assets. These features significantly decrease the effectiveness of traditional prudential regulatory instruments.

Therefore, the developing countries ought to employ specific financial regulatory regimes according to their specific economic conditions.

Warm-up Questions

1. What ideas do you have about financial regulation and control?
2. Why is financial regulation and control necessary to developing countries?
3. Why should developing countries employ specific financial regulatory regimes?

10.1 Monetary Policy
货币政策

10.1.1 The Objectives of Monetary Policy 货币政策的目标

For most countries, the following four principal objectives of economic policy would apply.

（1）Full employment.

（2）Stable Prices.

（3）Economic growth.

（4）Balance of payments equilibrium.

In carrying out its economic policy, the government uses two principal means — fiscal policy and monetary policy. Fiscal policy is concerned with taxation, subsidies and government spending. In contrast, monetary policy is concerned with interest rates, the money supply and bank lending.

In general, monetary policy is defined as the actions of a central bank or other monetary authority that determine the size and rate of growth of the money supply, which in turn affects interest rates. As a type of economic policy, monetary policy has the same ultimate objectives to those of economic policy which has been mentioned above. Moreover, achieving financial stability is an extra and important objective of monetary policy because it has significant impact on the financial system.

10.1.2　The Instruments of Monetary Policy　货币政策工具

The instruments of monetary policy refer to the tools available to monetary authorities to carry out the monetary policy. There are two major types of monetary policy instruments: general monetary policy instrument[1] and optional monetary policy instrument[2].

1. General monetary policy instruments

General monetary policy instruments are those tools most commonly used by central banks and other monetary authorities.

1）Required deposit reserve ratio

Required deposit reserve ratio[3] is the percentage of deposits that commercial banks must hold as non-operational and non-interest-bearing deposits on their accounts with the central bank. The reserve requirement affects monetary and financial conditions. For example, a reduction in the reserve ratio decreases the amount of reserves that banks must hold and therefore banks can make more loans. The larger volume of loans creates money and stimulates the economy. Raising the reserve ratio has the opposite effect. Although the required reserve ratio is a potentially powerful tool, the central banks seldom change these requirements in the conduct of monetary policy. In general, reserve requirements are used cautiously to regulate banks to provide security and stability in the banking system.

2）Rediscounting

Through the rediscounting[4], the central bank acts as a safety valve in relieving financial market pressures. By rediscounting the notes hold by commercial banks or lending funds against acceptable collateral, the central bank provides essential liquidity to the banks, while helping to assure the basic stability of money markets and the banking system.

Today, commercial banks still borrow from the central banks. However, the term rediscount is simply an expression for loans provided by the central bank that are repaid with interest at maturity and secured by pledged collateral. The rediscount rate is the interest rate charged to commercial banks on loans from the central bank's credit facility.

Changes in the rediscount rate affect credit conditions and therefore the economy. An increase in the rate, for example, makes it more costly for commercial banks to borrow from the central bank. The higher cost discourages the banks from using the rediscount privilege. It may force banks to screen their customers' loan applications more carefully and slow the growth of their loan portfolios. Apart from these direct impacts, changes in the rediscount rate can affect expectations in financial markets. If, for example, the market interprets an increase in the rate as the beginning of a sustained program to tighten credit, lenders will cut back commitments, waiting for more attractive rates. Potential borrowers will try to borrow before the expected higher rates materialize. These actions by lenders and borrowers will produce the expected tight credit.

3) Open market operation

Open market operations[5] are the purchase or sale of government securities by the central bank. Each purchase or sale of securities directly affects the volume of reserves in the banking system, and therefore the whole economy. Purchases of government securities increase reserves and ease credit while sales decrease reserves and tighten credit. With a purchase of securities, the central bank pays for the purchase by crediting the reserve account of the selling commercial bank. The central bank can then loan out the reserves and increase the supply of money. Conversely, sales of securities reduce reserves and tighten credit because the central bank charges the reserve account of the buying bank, decreasing the reserves available for loans.

Open market operations are either "dynamic" or "defensive". Dynamic operations are those taken to increase or decrease the volume of reserves to ease or tighten credit. Defensive operations are those taken to offset effects of other factors influencing reserves.

Open market operations are the most useful and operable tools of central banks. However, it will have best effect in those countries with powerful central banks and mature security markets.

2. Optional monetary policy instruments

Besides the general instruments, the central bank may, when necessary, choose to use some optional tools to carry out monetary policy. It may raise the base interest rates or other measures to control the consumer credit, the credit supply in security and real estate markets in order to stabilize the prices of consumer goods and regulate the security and real estate markets. It may also provide some favorable interest rates to ease the credit supply in those fundamental industries to support their development. Occasionally, the central bank may require the importers to deposit a guarantee fund in advance to depress the import to improve the balance of international payments.

The credit control measures taken by the central bank could be categorized into two groups: direct and indirect credit control. The direct credit control measures commonly include interest rate limitations, credit rationing[6], requirements of the liquidity ratios[7] on financial institutions and direct intervene. The indirect credit control generally means that the central bank regulates the financial markets and institutions through moral suasion[8] and window guidance[9].

10.1.3   The Transmission Mechanism of Monetary Policy
货币政策的传导机制

The transmission mechanism of monetary policy[10] is the process through which monetary policy decisions affect the economy in general and the price level in particular. The transmission mechanism is characterized by long, variable and uncertain time lags. Thus it is difficult to predict the precise effect of monetary policy actions on the economy and price level.

Figure 10 – 1 provides a schematic illustration of the transmission of monetary policy.

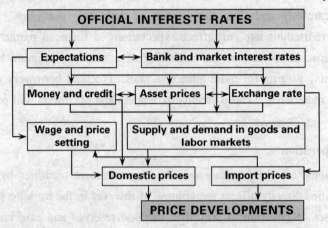

Figure 10 – 1   The transmission mechanism of monetary policy

First, official interest rate decisions affect market interest rates to varying degrees. At the same time, policy actions and announcements affect expectations about the future course of the economy. Expectations of future official interest-rate changes affect medium and long-term interest rates. In particular, longer-term interest rates depend in part on market expectations about the future course of short-term rates.

Second, the impact on financing conditions in the economy and on market expectations triggered by monetary policy actions may lead to adjustments in asset prices (e.g. stock market prices) and the exchange rate. Changes in the exchange rate can affect inflation directly. Changes in interest rates affect saving and investment decisions of households and firms. For example, everything else being equal, higher interest rates make it less attractive to take out loans for financing consumption or investment. In addition, consumption and investment are also affected by movements in asset prices. For example, as equity prices rise, share-owning households become wealthier and may choose to increase their consumption. Conversely, when equity prices fall, households may reduce consumption. All these changes have effects on the supply of credit to varying degrees. For example, higher interest rates increase the risk of borrowers being unable to pay back their loans. Banks may cut back on the amount of funds they lend to households and firms. This may also reduce the consumption and investment by households and firms respectively.

Third, asset prices can also have impact on aggregate demand via the value of collateral that allows borrowers to get more loans and/or to reduce the risk premium demanded by lenders/banks. Changes in consumption and investment will change the level of domestic demand for goods and services relative to domestic supply. When demand exceeds supply, upward price pressure is likely to occur. In addition, changes in aggregate demand may translate into tighter or looser conditions in labor and intermediate product markets. This in turn can affect wage and price-setting in the respective market.

Fourth, exchange rate movements have a direct effect, though often delayed, on the domestic prices of imported goods and services, and an indirect effect on the prices of those goods and services that compete with imports or use imported inputs, and hence on the overall price level.

10.1.4   The Intermediate Objectives of Monetary Policy
货币政策的中介指标

In order to achieve the ultimate objectives of monetary policy, the central bank can only take direct actions on some particular intermediate targets and thereby affect the ultimate objectives indirectly through the transmission mechanism. The major intermediate targets (objectives) of monetary policy[11] are examined as follows:

1. The growth in money supply

It is a vital feature of monetarist theory that the link between the money supply and prices, incomes and expenditure is reasonably predictable and stable. Thus the velocity of circulation must remain fairly stable so that money income and money expenditure are directly determined by changes in the money supply. If this is not, then attempts to control inflation will be made more difficult.

2. The interest rate levels

It is generally accepted that there is a connection between interest rate and business investment and consumption expenditure, though the link is not predictable and stable. Moreover, there is likely to be a time lag before interest rate changes affect expenditure levels.

Some governments use high interest rates as a means of monetary control, contending that:

(1) this will discourage consumer borrowing;

(2) those with existing mortgages and other loans will have less to spend on other things;

(3) the position of the local currency will be strengthened so reducing the chance of cost-push inflation from imports;

(4) foreign investors will be attracted into buying the domestic currency denominated securities, with the capital inflows into the countries, helping to finance a balance of payments current account deficit.

In conclusion, it can be said that the monetary authorities are able to influence interest rates more effectively than they can influence other policy targets.

3. The growth in the volume of credit

Higher bank lending is likely to result in higher bank deposits and thus an increase in the money supply. Furthermore, the consequence of an increase in bank lending is likely to be a rise level of expenditure in the economy. Therefore the government might decide to restrict the power to grant credit. However, to be at all effective and to avoid discrimination the control would need to be over all financial institutions and all means of lending money. Even then, money could come into the country from "offshore" institutions (no longer subject to exchange control).

4. The exchange rate

When the domestic currency is high relative to other leading currencies — notably the US dollar, the Euro — it makes business difficult for the exporters of the country, but eases inflation in the short-term by making imports cheaper. However, this is bad for the balance of payments, and in the long run has adverse effects on money growth and inflation.

China Might Possibly Further Raise Interest Rate

China's central bank governor Zhou Xiaochuan said that inflation figures might further climb in the near future, in that case, the possibility was not excluded for China to further raise the interest rate. He predicted that economic growth might slow down during the second quarter of this year. He made the statement while attending an annual forum of the Bank for International Settlements held recently in Brussels, Belgium.

The CPI figures for last May were within the range of what he expected. "We have adjusted the interest rate. However, inflation rate might climb a bit higher now," he said.

China will allow Renminbi to exchange freely. However, this will be a gradual process. China will make the exchange rate policy based on its own understanding and such process will be gradual and controllable, and with China taking the initiative, Zhou said.

He said that he was paying close attention of the development of mainland stock market, but he was not sure whether bubbles had existed in Chinese stock market.

10.1.5 The Coordination of Monetary and Fiscal Policy
货币政策与财政政策的协调配合

As the two principal means of economic policy, monetary policy and fiscal policy have the same goals of full employment, stable prices, economic growth and balance of payments equilibrium.

However, their effects are not identical and each has some particular limitations and negative impacts. For example, governments always face the dilemma that the high interest rates resulted from a tight monetary policy help to control inflation, but through retarding export growth make it more difficult to eliminate a deficit on the balance of payments; whilst any major lowering of the exchange rates (to stimulate exports and discourage imports) would raise the rate of domestic inflation. Such dilemma of monetary policy has to be relieved by fiscal policy.

The international experience also told us that it would be better to the economy if the fiscal and monetary authority cooperate and consult each other while making policy decisions. In the UK, there was the coexistence of high inflation and higher unemployment in 1970s and 1980s which was the direct result of non-cooperation between monetary and fiscal authorities. Tight monetary policies were used to cure the inflation with rising fiscal deficits and prices. This resulted in a non-cooperative solution mentioned above. After the independence in the Bank of England, there is more cooperation between fiscal and monetary authorities with a pleasant result of low inflation, higher employment and lower interest rates.

In a word, it is absolutely necessary for the governments to coordinate monetary policy and fiscal policy to manage the economy effectively and efficiently so as to secure the upward and healthy economic development.

10. 2   Financial Supervision
金融监管

10. 2. 1   A Brief Introduction to Financial Supervision   金融监管简介

Financial supervision[12] is a form of supervision or regulation (and another compound term "financial regulation & supervision" may be used more commonly), which subjects financial institutions to certain requirements, restrictions and guidelines, aiming to take precautions against financial risks, maintain the stability and security of the financial system and promote the fair competition in financial business. This may be handled by either a government or nongovernment organization.

The specific aims of financial regulation and supervision are usually:

(1) to minimize financial loss of depositors in banks or policy holders of insurance companies;

(2) to enforce applicable laws;

(3) to prosecute cases of market misconduct;

(4) to license providers of financial services;

(5) to protect clients, and investigate complaints.

10. 2. 2   Financial Risks and Financial Crisis   金融风险与金融危机

1. Financial risks

Financial risks, in broad sense, refer to all the risks which have adverse effects on the stability and security of the financial system in a country.

Theoretically, financial risks could be divided into the inside and outside risks.

Inside financial risks include the institutional risks which are endogenous inside particular financial institutions (such as fiscal risks, operational risks, technological risks, legal risks, credit risks, strategic risks, etc.), market risks which caused by the unexpected changes in financial markets (such as counterpart risks, trading risks, the risks of bank run, the risks of overvalued assets, etc.), and the risks on financial infrastructure (such as the risks of the settling and clearing system, the frangibility of financial infrastructure, the risks of bank run caused by the credit crunch and the domino effects).

In contrast, the outside financial risks refer to the outside risks detrimental to the financial system, such as the fluctuation of the economic environment, the failures of economic policy, political turbulences and natural calamities, and the international financial crises.

2. Financial crisis

There is not a widely accepted definition of the financial crisis. Some authors consider it the same as a currency crisis which occurs when the value of a currency changes quickly, undermining its ability to serve as a medium for exchange or a store of value. Other authors particularly defined a financial crisis as a disruption to financial markets in which adverse selection and moral hazard problems become much worse, so that financial markets are unable to efficiently channel funds to those who have the most productive investment opportunities. As a result, a financial crisis can drive the economy away from an equilibrium with high output in which financial markets perform well to one in which output declines sharply.

No matter what the financial crisis is defined as, it is absolutely undoubted that financial risks may lead to a financial crisis. Therefore, financial regulation and control are of vital importance to keep away the financial crisis.

The 1997–1998 Asian Financial Crisis may be the bitterest experience of some Asian countries and regions in the last ten years. The crisis had significant macro-level effects, including sharp reductions in values of currencies, stock markets, and other asset prices of several Asian countries. Many businesses collapsed, and as a consequence, millions of people fell below the poverty line. Indonesia, South Korea and Thailand were the countries most affected by the crisis.

The crisis also led to political upheaval, most notably in Indonesia and Thailand. There was a general rise in anti-Western sentiment, with George Soros and the IMF in particular singled out as targets of criticisms. Islamic and separatist movements intensified in Indonesia as the central authority weakened.

More long-term consequences include reversal of the relative gains made in the boom years just preceding the crisis. For example, as reported, the per capita income in Thailand declined from $8,800 to $8,300 between 1997 and 2005; in Indonesia it declined from $4,600 to $3,700; in Malaysia it declined from $11,100 to $10,400. Over the same period, world per capita income rose from $6,500 to $9,300. The economy of Indonesia was still smaller in 2005 than it had been in 1997, suggesting an impact on that country similar to the Great Depression. Within East Asia, the bulk of investment and a significant amount of economic weight shifted from Japan and ASEAN to China.

The crisis has been intensively analyzed by economists for its breadth, speed, and dynamism; it affected dozens of countries, had a direct impact on the livelihood of millions, happened within the course of a mere few months, and at each stage of the crisis leading economists, in particular the international institutions, seemed a step behind.

After the Asian crisis, international investors were reluctant to lend to developing countries, leading to economic slowdowns in developing countries in many parts of the world. The powerful negative shock also sharply reduced the price of oil, which reached a low of $8/barrel towards the end of 1998, causing a financial pinch in OPEC nations and other oil exporters. Such sharply reduced oil revenue in turn contributed to the Russian financial crisis in 1998, which in turn caused Long-Term Capital Management[13] in the US to collapse, after losing $4.6 billion in 4 months. A wider collapse in the US financial market was avoided when Mr. Greenspan and the Federal Reserve Bank of New York organized a $3.625 billion bail-out.

The crisis in general was part of a global backlash against the Washington Consensus and institutions such as the IMF and World Bank, which simultaneously became unpopular in developed countries following the rise of the anti-globalization movement in 1999. Four major rounds of world trade talks since the crisis, in Seattle, Doha, Cancun, and Hong Kong, have failed to reach a significant agreement as developing countries have become more assertive, and nations are increasingly turning toward regional or bilateral FTAs (Free Trade Agreements) as an alternative to global integration. Many nations learned from the crisis, and quickly built up huge foreign exchange reserves as a hedge against attacks, including Japan, China, South Korea.

10.2.3　Domestic Financial Regulation and Supervision　国内金融监管

1. Bank regulation & supervision

Bank regulation and supervision take the fundamental part of financial regulation and supervision because the financial system in a country is based on the banking system.

The general objectives of bank regulation and supervision are promoting the safety and soundness of the banking industry to maintain public confidence in the banking industry; encouraging fair competition in the banking industry to improve its competitiveness.

The specific objectives are protecting the interests of depositors and consumers through prudential supervision; boosting market confidence by prudential supervision; increasing public knowledge about modern financial products, services and the related risks through education and information disclosure; and maintaining financial stability by reducing banking related crimes.

The necessary regulation and supervision on banks include reserve requirement, capital adequacy requirement, activities and affiliates requirements, the criterion of entry into banking, external auditing requirements, internal management/organizational requirements, liquidity and diversification requirements, depositor (savings) protection schemes, information disclosure requirements, the rules of problem institutions' exit, etc.

In general, every country has a bank regulation authority designated by the governments. In China, the China Banking Regulatory Commission (CBRC) is responsible for bank regulation and supervision. Its main functions are to:

(1) formulate supervisory rules and regulations governing the banking institutions;

(2) authorize the establishment, changes, termination and business scope of the banking institutions;

(3) conduct on-site examination and off-site surveillance of the banking institutions, and take enforcement actions against rule-breaking behaviors;

(4) conduct fit-and-proper tests on the senior managerial personnel of the banking institutions;

(5) compile and publish statistics and reports of the overall banking industry in accordance with relevant regulations;

(6) provide proposals on the resolution of problem deposit-taking institutions in consultation with relevant regulatory authorities;

(7) take responsibility for the administration of the supervisory boards of the major state-owned banking institutions; and other functions delegated by the state council.

The supervisory and regulatory standards of the CBRC are:

(1) promoting the financial stability as well as the financial innovation;

(2) improving the competitiveness of the Chinese banking industry in the global financial market;

(3) formulating appropriate supervisory and regulatory requirements to remove all unnecessary restrictions;

(4) encouraging fair competition and preventing disorderly competition;

(5) defining clear and rigorous accountability systems for both supervisor and supervised institutions;

(6) allocating supervisory resources in an efficient and cost-effective manner.

The current supervisory focuses of the CBRC are conducting consolidated supervision to assess, monitor and mitigate the overall risks of each banking institution as a legal entity; staying focused on risk-based supervision and improvement of supervisory process and methods; urging banks to put in place and maintain a system of internal controls and enhancing supervisory transparency in line with international standards and practices.

2. Non-bank regulation & supervision

Non-bank regulation and supervision also play important roles in the financial regulation and are necessary to keep the security of the financial system.

The regulation and supervision on non-bank financial institutions are similar to bank regulation and supervision, including market access rules, activities and affiliates requirements, solvency adequacy requirements, external auditing requirements, internal management requirements, information disclosure requirements, the rules of problem institutions' exit.

In China, the China Insurance Regulatory Commission (CIRC)[14] and the China Securities Regulatory Commission (CSRC)[15] are respectively responsible for the regulation and supervision of insurance and securities business.

10.2.4 International Financial Regulation and Supervision 国际金融监管

1. The financial regulation & supervision in developing countries

Most developing countries have adopted or are in the process of adopting prudential regulations that can increase the stability of financial systems. Prudential regulations and the supervision of banks are important tools to alleviate adverse selection and moral hazard in the banking business. The increased integration of financial markets requires standardized methods to promote international financial stability. Capital adequacy requirements have been among the most debated regulations.

However, further effort is needed to reduce moral hazard practices and to identify and make provision for risks. In the same spirit, many countries have adopted international auditing and disclosure standards that enhance private monitoring and increase the efficiency of prudential regulations and supervision. Yet, some countries lag behind in implementing important disclosure measures and should be encouraged to promote a transparent and more efficient financial system.

2. Basel Agreements

Basel Agreement is an accord developed during a 1975 meeting in Basel, Switzerland, of central bankers of the industrialized nations setting forth guidelines for the supervision of banks. Included are guidelines for minimum capital requirements. The agreement was reached by the Committee on Banking Regulations and Supervisory Practices[16] (also known as the Cooke Committee after its chairman, Peter Cooke and now called Basel Committee), meeting under the auspices of The Bank for International Settlements (BIS).

In 2004, preceded by several revisions in the previous years, the Basel Committee on Banking Supervision published a new framework agreement, most commonly called the Basel II[17], which aims to make the international financial system safer by having the riskiness of banks' loan portfolios to be reflected in the capital charges they need to set aside against unexpected losses. The agreement sets out the details for adopting more risk-sensitive minimum capital requirements for banking organizations.

The Basel II has been employed by most countries around the world, especially those developed nations which have large international banks operating globally.

China is making efforts to prepare for the implementation of the Basel II by domestic banks. In the CBRC's Guidelines for the Implementation of the New Basel Capital Accord by the Chinese Banking

Industry that is about to be publicized, it is specifically stipulated that:

(1) the large commercial banks having overseas operational entities and substantive international business are required to implement the New Basel Capital Accord, while the small-and medium-sized commercial banks can choose to implement the new accord on a volunteer basis.

(2) the commercial banks are requested to calculate capital requirements for credit risk with the Internal Rating Based Approach[18], while being recommended and encouraged to practice the Advanced IRB Approach[19].

(3) the large commercial banks should implement the new accord from the end of 2010, and if could not meet the minimum requirements set by the CBRC, they would be granted 3 years of graceful period after approval.

Pushing forward the implementation of the Basel II by the large domestic banks is of great significance under the backdrop of the progressive banking reform and opened up financial market.

Firstly, the implementation of the Basel II is propitious to improving the communication and interaction between the banks and their supervisor. As what is emphasized in the new accord on flexible regulation, is consentaneous with the CBRC's "principle-oriented" supervisory thinking.

Secondly, it could promote the rational and elaborate banking management, make sure that adequate loan provisions and regulatory capital are in place, and push the transformation of the profit-making models and the pattern of business growth.

Thirdly, the implementation goes with the rapid development of the domestic financial market, and will be supportive to the domestic financial innovations.

Fourthly, the implementation acts in conjunction with the internationalization strategies of the domestic large commercial banks, as practicing the IRB approach is fundamental to sharpening the banks' competitive edge in the global financial market.

Nevertheless, the Basel II is, after all, oriented from western practices of banking risk management, in this regard, the domestic banks should actually have the recognition that the new accord has its own limitations. Every bank is required to implement the new accord on the basis of Chinese realities, and the bank's own complexions.

Reading Material

Translations May Hold up Basel II in EU

Delays in translating complex new legislation on bank capital into the 20 official EU members' languages may slow down EU adoption of the key rules, Internal Market Commissioner Charlie McCreevy indicated on Monday.

"There is definitely an issue about translation. The European Parliament is very concerned. This is something I am aware of, but hopefully it will not hold up things unduly," McCreevy told a financial conference in Paris.

The new bank capital legislation needs the endorsement of both finance ministers and the European Parliament to become law across the 25-nation bloc.

The European Commission has suggested translating the legislation into French and English only to speed up the process, but the Parliament insisted on translation into all official EU languages.

EU finance ministers are due on Tuesday to give their backing to the rules, enshrined in the Capital Adequacy Directive, but there is concern that delays due to translation may postpone the formal adoption till the end of 2006.

The planned rules are the EU's version of the global Basel II accord on bank capital unveiled earlier this year, designed to improve the safety of the global financial system. EU banks and investment firms are expected to start implementing the simpler aspects of the new capital adequacy rule at the end of 2006, while the more complex part of the plan would be in use from the end of 2007.

10.3　Finance and Economic Development
金融与经济发展

10.3.1　The Relationship between Finance and Economic Development
金融与经济发展的关系

It is undoubted that finance plays a very important role in economic development of a country. Generally speaking, finance services facilitate and promote the economic development through the integrated settling and clearing system and provide easy measures for the corporations and authorities to monitor the cash flows. The basic function of finance is to finance the various corporations and thereby the economic development. The efficiency of resources allocation and economic development could be improved by the operations of financial institutions. Moreover, the output of the financial business would directly contribute to the economic growth.

Traditionally, economic growth depends on the accumulation of input factors in the production process and technical progress. Finance has been linked primarily with the first of these sources of growth, regarding capital as an important input factor and its accumulation as a condition for sustainable economic growth. Furthermore, finance contributes to the realization of technical progress to the extent that technical advances need to be embedded in the capital stock to influence production. In particular, in periods of rapid technical progress, an efficiently structured financial sector appears to be required in order to facilitate embedding technical advances in capital formation and allowing countries to benefit from this development in terms of higher rates of economic growth.

Growth theory assumes that the interest rate plays the main role in equilibrating an economy's savings and investment. According to the neo-classical economics, the optimal growth path is equal to the real interest rate. For a long time, the design of the financial sector was thought to be of no major importance for economic decision making because in the presence of perfect markets, the financial sector produces nothing but a veil on the true determinants of economic developments. Today's realistic understanding of market imperfections has allowed this view to be put aside, although the exact transmission channels from finance to economic activity and in particular any estimate of their quantitative impact are still subject to considerable uncertainty.

In the presence of imperfect markets, the relation between investors/borrowers and savers/lenders is characterized by problems caused by conflicting interests. Such problems exist as regards hidden action and hidden information of the borrower, who is perceived to be better informed than the lender and to be able to influence the return of an investment. Coping with these problems would need a comprehensive contract between lender and borrower covering all eventualities and ensuring the compatibility of individual incentives.

The value of the financial sector consists in reducing the special transaction costs that emanate from the asymmetric information in the relation between investor/borrower and saver/lender. Financial contracts are often designed to ensure incentive compatibility between both, for instance in the choice of equity versus debt contracts, by allowing rights to monitor, or by differentiating the investment projects in stages which can be easily monitored. Furthermore, corporate statutes and public law express rules to ensure investor protection and therewith reducing the informational imbalance between borrower and lender. In principle, it is the role of the financial system to provide optimally designed contracts with the comparative advantage of financial intermediaries consisting in the implementation and enforcement of these contracts.

This micro-economic explanation differs somewhat from the traditional approach, which views financial intermediaries as being a bridge between the differences in interests between borrowers and lenders concerning the size of a financial investment, its maturity and risk. While households usually have a preference for short-term investment at low risk and are typically endowed with small amounts, enterprises have divergent preferences and need large sums to finance capital accumulation. Financial institutions and especially banks use economies of scale to transform households' savings into corporate debts.

The approach linking financial institutions with asymmetric information and agency costs gives the financial system a more prominent role in accomplishing an efficient allocation of capital. Financial institutions accumulate special knowledge in evaluating and monitoring investment projects, they have comparative advantage in evaluating risks and designing financial contracts. In particular, banks may gain information advantages from lasting relations with customers by learning from past experience, and realize economies of scale from offering payment services. Thereby, an upgrading in the efficiency of the financial system may lead to a higher level of GDP, which is accompanied, at least temporarily, by higher rates of economic growth.

Nevertheless, at the same time, there are some financial downside risks which have adverse effects on economic development and are required continued vigilance. Such downside risks mainly include imbalance of international payments, financial bubbles caused by the credit inflation, excessive fictitious capital and the over-speculations in financial markets.

10.3.2 The Two Theories of Finance 金融二论

The theory of financial repression[20] initiated by Ronald McKinnon and the theory of financial deepening[21] put forward by Edward Shaw in 1970's are the theoretical sources of financial liberalization.

The target of financial liberalization is financial deepening. Financial repression means that government controls finance rigorously. Interest ceiling and reserve requirements are the main measures that government takes.

Financial repression gives rise to low real interest rate, insufficient saving and investment, as well as slow economic growth. Financial liberalization means that government removes all sorts of interventions on financial markets. It involves the liberalization of interest rate, capital flow, exchange rate, banking business, and financial markets, etc. Its core rests upon interest rate liberalization.

The theories believe that negative real interest rate may reduce the attraction of financial institutions towards savings and consequently, the supply of credit may decrease. This may limit productive investment and barricade economic growth. Due to the short supply of credit, non-price allocation of investiture resources could occur. On the contrary, the positive interest rate is beneficiary for the increase of saving and investment and finally facilitates the growth of national economy. Unfortunately, few developing countries succeeded in implementing interest rate liberalization and some of them even suffered financial crises.

Relationship between Interest Rate Liberalization and Financial Crisis

Interest rate liberalization doesn't necessarily bring about financial crisis. Nevertheless, if the relevant reforms have not been taken, interest rate liberalization may cause financial crisis.

When we carry out interest rate liberalization, much attention should be attached to the following points.

(1) Interest rate liberalization should be implemented gradually.

(2) Before interest rate liberalization is carried out, the macro-economy should be stabilized and the financial supervision should be improved.

(3) Financial restraint is an optimal choice when pushing interest rate liberalization. Financial restraint means government keeps interest rate positive but lower than equilibrium level. In this way, government creates rent opportunities for financial sectors so that they are motivated to supervise enterprises and to overcome information asymmetry.

10.3.3 The Financial Liberation in Developing Countries
发展中国家的金融自由化

Many developing countries, especially the Latin American countries, carried out both domestic and external financial liberation in the belief of the two theories of finance mentioned above. However, they experienced several financial crises in the 1990s during the process of financial liberation.

Despite the crises in Latin America, developing countries should still maintain an active attitude towards financial liberalization and globalization. Financial liberalization is neither a panacea nor a devil.

However, the developing countries must learn lessons from the Latin American financial crises. It should be recognized that financial liberalization and capital account opening are necessary, but they should be carried out in a gradual and prudential way.

Group Discussion

1. Explain the general monetary policy instruments.
2. Describe the transmission mechanism and intermediate objectives of monetary policy.

3. Tell the objectives and principles of Chinese bank regulation and supervision.
4. Discuss the financial liberalization in developing countries.
5. Tell your opinions on the prevention of financial crises in China.

 NOTES ▶▶▶

1 general monetary policy instrument　一般性货币政策工具

2 optional monetary policy instrument　选择性货币政策工具

3 required deposit reserve ratio　法定存款准备金率

4 rediscounting　再贴现

5 open market operation　公开市场业务

6 credit rationing　信用配给，信贷配额

7 liquidity ratio　流动性比率

8 moral suasion　道义劝告

9 window guidance　窗口指导

10 transmission mechanism of monetary policy　货币政策的传导机制

11 intermediate targets (objectives) of monetary policy　货币政策的中介指标

12 financial supervision　金融监管（更多用"financial regulation and supervision"）

13 Long-Term Capital Management　长线资本管理公司（美国对冲基金公司，于1998年被收购）

14 China Insurance Regulatory Commission (CIRC)　中国保险监督管理委员会

15 China Securities Regulatory Commission (CSRC)　中国证券监督管理委员会

16 Committee on Banking Regulations and Supervisory Practices　银行规例与监管事务委员会（后更名为"Basel Committee on Banking Supervision"，即"巴塞尔银行监管委员会"，简称"巴塞尔委员会"，即"Basel Committee"）

17 Basel II　新巴塞尔协议（即"New Basel Capital Accord"，全称为"International Convergence of Capital Measurement and Capital Standards"）

18 Internal Rating Based Approach　内部评级法

19 Advanced IRB Approach　高级内部评级法

20 the theory of financial repression　金融抑制论

21 the theory of financial deepening　金融深化论

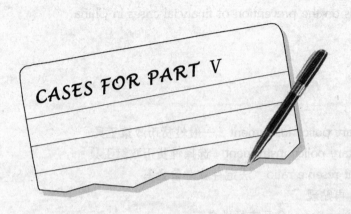

Monetary Policy Gears to Economic Development
货币政策推动经济发展

The People's Bank of China recently raised its one-year deposit by 27 percentage points and the one-year lending rate by 18 basis points. And it announced at the same time it would again raise the rate of deposit reserve ratio by 50 basis points on June 5. Moreover, it enlarged the fluctuation area of the RMB-US dollar peg by 0.5 percentage points, either on positive or negative, from May 21. The joint use of these tools — interest rate, deposit reserve ratio and exchange rate (or three joint moves) — has indeed been rare in the course of China's macro-economic regulation. On this topic, a People's Daily reporter had an exclusive interview with Yu Yongding, director of the Institute of World Economics and Politics under the Chinese Academy of Social Sciences. The questions and answers of the interview are as follows:

Q: How do you look at the effect of the current macro-economic regulation and control?

Yu: The signal transmitted by the "three joint moves" of the central bank is lucid and totally correct. Their role of publicity is bigger than their essential role though the intensity of each move is not so big. The direction of the central bank's policies in recent months show that China's monetary policy is still heading for the direction of inclined tightness this year and the exchange rate is moving toward the direction of increasing its market role. So the policies and measures that can and should be used include the monetary policy, financial policy, management of transborder capital flow, financial supervision and control, the development and reform of the capital market, and the ownership reform of the state-owned enterprises.

Q: While the achievements of China's economic development have captured global attention and instability represents the prominent problem, then in what aspects is it manifested?

Yu: The outstanding problem of Chinese economy is instability and disequilibrium. At present, its outstanding problem is the rapid rise of stock prices. The increase range of Chinese stocks has been more doubled in less than two years since September 2005. Stock index recently rised from 3,000 points to 4,000 points. And millions of ordinary people poured saving deposits into stock market. Once stock bubble bursts, it would mean an immeasurable blow to economic and social stability.

On the other hand, China's trade surplus continues to enlarge. If such a situation cannot improve, the trade frictions between China and the United States, between China and European Union and between China and other nations will possibly further intensify, and will give rise to a negative impact on the Chinese trade and economic growth. Consequently, it is essential for China to increase its flexibility with RMB exchange rate.

With a trend to rise since the last quarter of 2006, China's inflation rate has topped a three-percent level, a level China should not exceed, generally speaking.

Furthermore, the fixed asset investment rate is too fast and, so far, there has been no obvious marked improvement with high energy consumption and grave environment pollution, which could have a trend to possibly worsen in some aspects.

Q: What are the causes for the stock market bubble and accumulated risks?

Yu: Assets bubble and the disequilibrium of balance of international payment further deteriorates, the rate of the fixed asset investment is still on rise excessively and inflation has surfaced. These problems, however, are interrelated, in spite of different causes for their occurrence. The direct cause for the current bubble and accumulate risks with Chinese stock markets is a question of excess fluidity.

First of all, the increase rate of China's currency has for long surpassed that of GDP, and the country's ratio between M2 and GDP was more tan 160 percent, the highest in the world. Veteran economists have often referred the ratio between M2 and GDP to "a tiger in cage". In the past, inflation was anticipated to stay at a low level, so "the tiger" has been confined "to the cage" for a dozen years and more. To date, with the soaring of stock prices, residents have begun pouring their saving deposits into stock market.

Second, due to the China's ever-increasing trade surplus and capital surplus, the central bank, in a bid to maintain the stability of the RMB exchange rate, has to meddle in the foreign exchange market by buying US dollars and releasing RMB yuan and thus resulted in new excessive fluidity.

Despite repeated interest increases, the interest rate in name has been kept at a very low level, and the rise of inflation rate has in fact obliged the interest rate in essence to further drop. With a lack of new, heated consumption growth areas or other channels of investment, large amounts of capital flow into stock market and real estate market, so the skyrocketing of share prices is hardly avoidable.

Moreover, the drastic rise of China's assets prices (first real estate and then stock shares) has become a vital, essential factor for the inflow of speculating capital from overseas in recent years.

Q: What do you think where the advantages of the "three joint moves" taken by the central bank lie?

Yu: The "three joint moves" the central bank has introduced indicate its resolve to safeguard economic stability and balanced growth. It is the duty of the central bank to contain the further increase of excess fluidity and absorb the existing excess fluidity. Therefore, the policy tools to this end include an increase of the reserve fund ratio, the issue of more bank bills, and an increase in both interest rate and exchange rate. If only a single tool is exploited or used, it might bring about an excessive lash to a certain economic entity.

The costs for China's macro-economic regulation should be shared rationally by various social strata, trades and enterprises of different industries. Besides, as the problems we face are interrelated, so it is necessary to resort to all kinds of methods simultaneously.

Another hallmark in the central bank's regulation lies in differentiating the increase range for the interests of both saving deposits and loans. The excessive-low deposit interest is a major reason for the transfer of people's saving deposits into the stock market, and the raising of saving deposit interest could possibly ease the pressures on stock market, whereas a lesser increase of loan interest has mainly taken the interests of economic entities into account. Of course, this would impose more pressures upon banks with their effort to improve their management.

Monetary policy alone cannot curb the assets bubble effectively. So I deem that the government will also resort to its fiscal policy and other related measures to help maintain economic stability.

How Risky Is Financial Liberalization in the Developing Countries?
发展中国家进行金融自由化有多危险?

Something has changed in the world of financial crises. While crises could occur anywhere in the world, they now seem circumscribed to developing countries. While contagion used to spread crises among the large financial centers, it now affects developing countries on a regional basis, sometimes even mysteriously on a worldwide basis. While crises could unmistakably be linked to serious macro-economic policy mismanagement, now they hit countries with no serious imbalances.

These changes carry profound implications. They challenge the wave of capital liberalization observed over the last decade. They affect the way developing countries carry out policy, including at the deeper, structural level. They require new thinking among the international financial institutions and in particular those of their most directly affected shareholders, the developed countries. They also affect banks and financial institutions which have moved significant parts of their activity to emerging markets.

Since the heydays of Reagan-Thatcher activism, developing countries have been encouraged to establish financial markets and integrate themselves into world markets. The reasoning behind the push is based on a straightforward implication of first economic principles: financial markets allow the proper allocation of savings to productive investment, be it at the national or international level. Financial repression discourages savings and/or encourages capital flight. Borrowing on non-market terms often results in investment spending of poor quality, since borrowers are not selected on the merit of their projects but on questionable criteria, which include particular connections with financial institutions and governments, sheer political power, or graft. Insulated financial markets prevent access to cheaper resources and are often characterized by poor competence borne out of lack of adequate competition and supervision.

All these arguments are uncontroversial theoretically. But it is by no means obvious that first economic principles apply to the real world, especially to emerging market economies, as forcefully noted by Diaz-Alejandro (1985). These principles are developed for simple cases and based on exacting assumptions regarding the economic structure and the political environment. Some assumptions may be acceptable for some countries, but not for others. The presumed efficiency of financial markets is predicated on the existence of many intermediaries with the ability to collect and process all relevant information.

It also assumes that goods markets function properly. If any of these conditions is violated, the benefits of operating large and integrated financial markets can be called in doubt. It is well-known that, owing to a serious problem of asymmetric information, financial markets tend to behave erratically at times. The first best response to asymmetric information is regulation and supervision. This is indeed the direction taken in the developed countries where, after several decades not free of crises, a corps of savvy and honest administrators contrive to keep the information asymmetry problem manageable. This should also be the goal pursued by the developing countries, but it takes time to reach the stage where financial markets can be freed and integrated.

What can be done, in the meantime? Two approaches have been proposed and implemented.

The first one aims at a gradual process of liberalization, starting with domestic financial markets and moving cautiously on to external integration. The premise is that financial markets can only be built up gradually and that they must have achieved enough resilience to meet the risks associated with the next step before it is taken — which is matter of decades, not of months or years. This was the approach adopted in post-war Europe, where capital account liberalization was not completed until the end of the 1980s. The second approach aims at a rapid, *erga omnes*, liberalization. The premise is that financial repression serves powerful private and political interests apt at thwarting serious reforms, and that only a "kick in the anthill" will unleash liberalization. This approach, which has been added to the "Washington consensus", has been applied in a number of transition countries. Viewed from the angle of macro-economic stability, both approaches have occasionally been followed by deep currency crises — for example, the EMS crisis of 1992/1993 and the South-East Asian crisis of 1997/1998. In each case, special factors have been advanced to explain the crisis seen as one of its kind, implicitly denying that the path to free markets is inherently dangerous.

The 1990s have been years of activism. The developed countries and most international financial organizations have been urging the developing countries to undertake rapid and comprehensive domestic and external financial liberalization. The crises that followed have now instilled a healthy dose of caution.

It is being increasingly recognized that financial markets suffer from occasional failures. Promoting proper governance, both economic and political, makes good sense in theory but it is easy to underestimate the difficulty of challenging entrenched interests and of reshaping the political status quo. A silver lining of the recent crises is that the liberalization activism of the 1990s is now *passé*.

At the same time, financial liberalization may be desirable, if only because it increases competition and reduces monopoly powers, and not just in the financial markets. But liberalization is a risky step, one on which our knowledge remains rudimentary. It concerns the exchange markets but also many other aspects, including welfare and growth performance. Many countries, in Europe and also in Asia, have been able to grow fast over decades while retaining heavy-handed financial restraints. This alone shows that there is no urgency to undertake financial liberalization, even though that step should be clearly be taken somewhere down the road. And when it is taken, it should be approached as a delicate step calling for cautious policy reactions.

Glossary
专业词汇表

A

accruals basis　权责发生制

active balance　活动余额

active capital　流动资本

Advanced IRB Approach　高级内部评级法

aggressive growth fund　积极成长型基金

Agricultural Development Bank of China（ADBC）　中国农业发展银行

American option　美式期权

annual percentage rate（APR）　年收益率

annual percentage yield（APY）　年收益

anti-money-laundering　反洗钱

asked price　卖价

assuming reinsurance 分入保险

automatic adjustment 自主性调节

B

bailout　最后贷款人，拯救银行

balance of current account（current account balance）　经常账户差额

balance of international payments　国际收支，国际收支平衡（表）

balance of payments（BOP）　国际收支，国际收支平衡表

balance of payments disequilibrium　国际收支不平衡

balance of payments equilibrium（BPE）　国际收支平衡

balance of payments surplus（deficit）　国际收支盈余（赤字），国际收支顺差（逆差）

balance of trade（trade balance）　贸易差额

balanced fund　平衡基金

bank bill　银行汇票

bank bill　纸币，钞票

Bank for International Settlements（BIS）　国际清算银行

bank group loan　银团贷款

bank note　纸币，钞票

Bank of Communications　交通银行

bank run　银行挤兑

banker's bill　银行汇票

bankers' acceptance（BA）　银行承兑汇票

Basel Committee on Banking Supervision　巴塞尔（银行监管）委员会

Basel II（New Basel Capital Accord）　新巴塞尔协议

basic exchange rate　基准汇率

benchmark interest rate　基准利率

bid price　买价

Big Board　纽约证券交易所（行情牌）

bilateral loan　双边贷款

bills of exchange　汇票

Bretton Woods System　布雷顿森林体系

broad money　广义货币

Bulge Bracket　华尔街投资银行领导集团

C

call option　看涨期权，买权

captive insurance companies　附属保险公司

carry trade　套利交易

cashier's check　银行支票

ceding reinsurance　分出保险

central bank　中央银行

certificate of deposit（CD）　存款单

China Banking Regulatory Commission（CBRC）　中国银行业监督管理委员会

China CITIC Bank　中信银行

China Development Bank（CDB）　国家开发银行

China Insurance Regulatory Commission（CIRC）　中国保险监督管理委员会

China International Capital Corporation（CICC）　中国国际金融公司

China International Trust and Investment Corporation（CITIC）　中国国际信托投资公司

China Leasing Company Ltd.　中国租赁有限公司

China Securities Regulatory Commission（CSRC）　中国证券监督管理委员会

clearing house　票据交换所

closed-end fund　封闭式基金

closed-end management investment company　封闭式管理投资公司

CNY　人民币货币代码

commercial bank　商业银行

commercial credit　商业信贷

commercial note/bill　商业票据

commercial paper　商业票据

Committee on Banking Regulations and Supervisory Practices　银行规例与监管事务委员会

common share　普通股

common stock　普通股

community bank　地区银行

community development bank　地区开发银行，地区发展银行

compound interest　复利

Consols　统一公债（由英国政府 1751 年开始发行的长期债券）

consumer credit　消费信贷

corporate trust services　法人信托业务

coupon bonds　附息债

credit card　信用卡

credit rationing　信用配给，信贷配额

credit sale　赊销，先售后付交易

credit union（credit cooperative）　信用合作社，合会，信用合作机构，信贷联盟

cross exchange rate　套算汇率

current account deficit　经常账户赤字（逆差）

current account surplus　经常账户盈余（顺差）

current deposit　活期存款

current return　现行收益率

current yield　现行收益率

D

deflation　通货紧缩

demand deposit　活期存款

demand draft　即期汇票

derivative financial instrument　衍生金融工具

direct quotation　直接标价法

dividend　股息

domestic currency　本币

double-entry bookkeeping　复式记账

Dow Jones Industrial Average（DJIA）　道·琼斯工业平均指数

E

equity stock　普通股

estate administration　遗产管理

Eurocurrency market　欧洲货币市场

Euromarket　欧洲（货币）市场

Euronext　欧洲证券交易所

Euronote　欧洲票据，欧元纸钞

European Common Market（ECM）　欧洲共同市场

European option　欧式期权

exchange rate　汇率

Exchange Stabilization Fund　外汇平准基金

Export-Import Bank of China（China Exim Bank）　中国进出口银行

F

face value　面值

Federal Reserve System（Fed）　美国联邦储备系统

fiat money　不兑现纸币

finance company　金融公司

financial（regulation and）supervision　金融监管

financial leasing company　融资租赁公司

fixed deposit　定期存款

fixed exchange rate　固定汇率（制）

fixed interest rate　固定利率

floating capital　流动资本

floating exchange rate　浮动汇率（制）

floating interest rate　浮动利率

floor trading market　场内市场

fluid capital　流动资本

foreign direct investment（FDI）　外国直接投资

foreign exchange buffer policy　外汇缓冲政策

foreign exchange control　外汇管制

foreign exchange rate　外汇汇率

forward exchange rate　远期汇率

functional center　功能型中心

fundamental analysis　基本面分析

future value　终值

G

general interest rate　一般利率

general monetary policy instrument　一般性货币政策工具

general stock　普通股

gilt-edge security　金边证券

giving quotation　应付标价法

gold standard　金本位

Gold Standard　国际金本位制度

H

Hang Seng　香港恒生指数
hedge fund　对冲基金
hire purchase（hp）　分期付款购买
HKD　港币货币代码
HKEX　香港交易所
home currency　本币

I

I.O.U.s　借据，欠条
idle balance　闲置余额
imbalance of payments　国际收支不平衡
indirect quotation　间接标价法
industry & commercial loans　工商企业贷款
inflation　通货膨胀
initial public offering（IPO）　首次公开募股（发行）
installment credit　分期还款信贷
intermediate targets（objectives）of monetary policy　货币政策的中介指标
Internal Rating Based Approach　内部评级法
International Standard Organization（ISO）　国际标准化组织

L

leading bank　牵头银行
legal tender　法定货币
liability insurance　责任保险
liquid capital　流动资本
liquidity preference　流动性偏好
liquidity ratio　流动性比率
Lloyd's of London　伦敦劳埃德海上保险协会，伦敦劳埃德商船协会
local currency　本币
London Inter-bank Bid Rate（LIBID）　伦敦银行同业拆入利率
London Inter-bank Mean Rate（LIMEAN）　伦敦银行同业平均利率
London Inter-Bank Offered Rate（LIBOR）　伦敦银行同业拆放利率
long-term interest rate　长期利率

M

managing bank　经理银行
market exchange rate　市场汇率
market interest rate　市场利率
money demand　货币需求
money flow　货币流量
money stock　货币存量
money supply　货币供给
Moody's　穆迪投资服务公司
moral suasion　道义劝告
mortgage　抵押，抵押贷款
mutual fund　共同基金

N

narrow money　狭义货币
near money　近似货币
Nikkei　日本日经指数
nominal exchange rate　名义汇率
nominal interest rate　名义利率
nominal yield　名义收益率
non-bank financial institution　非银行金融机构
note issue facility（NIF）　票据发行便利

O

offered price　卖价
official exchange rates　官方汇率
official interest rate　官方利率
offshore finance　离岸金融业务
offshore financial center（OFC）　离岸金融中心
offshore financial market　离岸金融市场
onshore financial market　在岸金融市场
open market operation　公开市场业务
open-end fund　开放式基金
open-end management investment company　开放式管理投资公司
operating capital　流动资本
optional monetary policy instrument　选择性货币政策工具
ordinary stock/share　普通股

original financial instrument　原生金融工具
overall balance of payments　国际收支总差额
over-the-counter（OTC）　场外市场，店头市场

P

paper center　记账型中心
paper currency　纸币，钞票
paper money　纸币，钞票
paper note　纸币，钞票
par（face）value　面值
participating bank　参与银行
pawnbroking　典当
peppercorn rent　徒有其名的租金
policy adjustment　政策性调节
preference stock　优先股
preferred share　优先股
preferred stock　优先股
premium bonds　溢价债券，（英）政府有奖债券
present value　现值
primary dealer　一级交易商
primary financial instrument　原生金融工具
promissory notes　本票，期票
public interest rate　公定利率
put option　看跌期权，卖权

Q

Quantum fund　量子基金
quasi-money　准货币

R

real estate loans　不动产贷款
real exchange rate　实际汇率
real interest rate　实际利率
receiving quotation　应收标价法
rediscounting　再贴现
reinsurance company　再保险公司，分保公司
repo（repurchase agreement）　回购协议
representative money　可兑现纸币

repurchase agreement（repo）　回购协议
required deposit reserve ratio　法定存款准备金率
reserve position　储备头寸，准备金头寸
reverse repo　逆回购（协议）
risk premium　风险升水，风险补偿
risk-free rate of interest　无风险利率

S

S&P 500　标准普尔 500 股票指数
sale on open account　赊销
second mortgage（remortgage）　二次抵押，再抵押
secured loan　担保贷款
securities company　证券公司
short-term interest rate　短期利率
sight draft　即期汇票
simple interest　单利
smart card　智能卡
special drawing rights（SDRS）　特别提款权
spot exchange rates　即期汇率
Standard & Poor's　标准普尔公司
State Administration of Foreign Exchange（SAFE）　国家外汇管理局
store value card　储值卡
syndicate loan　辛迪加贷款

T

technical analysis　技术分析
teller's check　出纳支票
term deposit　定期存款
term repo　定期回购（协议）
theory of financial deepening　金融深化论
theory of financial repression　金融抑制论
time deposit　定期存款
time draft　远期汇票
trade bill　商业汇票
trade control　贸易管制
trader's draft　商业汇票
transmission mechanism of monetary policy　货币政策的传导机制
treasury bill（T-bill）　国库券
treasury department　财政部

trust and investment corporation　信托投资公司
trust company　信托公司

U

UITs（unit investment trusts）　单位投资信托基金
unsecured loan　无担保贷款
usance draft　远期汇票

V

venture capital firms　风险投资公司

W

window guidance　窗口指导
working capital　流动资本

Y

yield-to-maturity　到期收益率

References
参考文献

[1] 李健. 金融学. 北京：中央广播电视大学出版社，2004.

[2] 姚长辉. 货币银行学. 北京：北京大学出版社，2005.

[3] 戴国强. 货币金融学. 上海：上海财经大学出版社，2006.

[4] 孙桂芳. 金融学概论. 北京：中国金融出版社，2003.

[5] 黄达. 货币银行学. 北京：中国人民大学出版社，2000.

[6] 刘文国. 金融英语. 上海：复旦大学出版社，2006.

[7] 李丽. 金融英语. 北京：对外经济贸易大学，2007.

[8] Banking certificate economics. Hong Kong：Hong Kong Institute of Bankers（HKIB），1996.

[9] KOOL C. Essays on money, banking, and regulation：essays in honour of C. J. Oort. Boston：Kluwer Academic Publishers, 1996.

[10] RITTER L S. Principles of money, banking, and financial markets. Reading, Massachusetts：Addison-Wesley, 2000.

[11] CECCHETTI S G. Money, banking, and financial markets. 北京：北京大学出版社，2006.

[12] MISHKIN F S. The economics of money, banking, and financial markets. Boston：Pearson/Addison Wesley, 2007.

[13] 郑毅刚. 金融英语案例精选. 北京：中国水利水电出版社，2006.